GUITAR LESSON GOLDMINE

AUDIO ACCESS INCLUDED

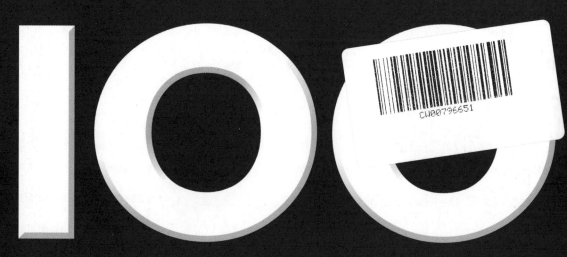

100 ACOUSTIC LESSONS

BY CHAD JOHNSON MICHAEL MUELLER

To access audio visit:
www.halleonard.com/mylibrary

Enter Code
7842-6484-2342-2443

ISBN 978-1-4234-9882-7

HAL•LEONARD®
CORPORATION

7777 W. BLUEMOUND RD. P.O. BOX 13819 MILWAUKEE, WI 53213

Visit Hal Leonard Online at
www.halleonard.com

CONTENTS

Lessons 1–50 by Chad Johnson

Lessons 51–100 by Michael Mueller

LESSON #1: BRUSHING UP ON COWBOY CHORDS

When most players learn guitar, open "cowboy" chords often are the first subject taught. They're useful, relatively easy, and sound great. However, I've seen many players throughout the years that, although otherwise accomplished on the instrument, have neglected these and/or have trouble getting them to sound clear and professional. I think the reason is that, after learning these chords, players are eager to move on to more "complex" aspects of guitar. However, a beginner's version of an acceptable-sounding chord differs from that of a seasoned pro. When playing cowboy chords, some players allow a few poor techniques, or "crutches," slip through the cracks. This lesson aims to fix any vestige of that beginner period by brushing up on those cowboy chords.

One String at a Time

Let's start by determining where any problems may exist. The easiest way to do this is to work through the following chords, playing them two ways: First, strum them, and then play them one string at a time, from low to high.

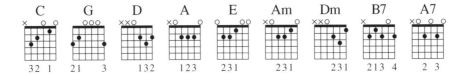

When strumming the chords, fret them quickly and strum them immediately—the way you would in a song. You must be able to switch between them effortlessly and efficiently.

When playing the chords one string at a time, listen extremely carefully and be critical of any shortcomings. Now is the time to fix them for good, undoing any engrained bad habits.

Generally, any shortcomings will fall into one of two categories:

1. A note (or notes) is not ringing out clearly;
2. An unintentional open string is sounding.

The former is common in many chords, including A, A7, B7, D, Dm, E, and G.
The latter is mostly common in A, Am, B7, C, D, and Dm.

Fixing the Glitches

After identifying the problem, it's time to fix the glitch. Usually, only a slight adjustment is necessary to correct the issue. Muscle memory is a powerful thing, and when we learn something the wrong way, it will stick with us five, ten, 15, or even 20 years later if we don't do anything differently.

Adjusting Finger Placement

If some notes aren't ringing clearly, it's because one of your fretting fingers is not doing its job properly—it's most likely either touching an adjacent string, which won't allow that string's note to sound clearly, or it's misplaced in the fret area (i.e., it's too far forward or too far back), which will produce a dull or buzzing note.

Strum each individual string of the chord, from low to high, find the problem finger, and adjust its position. It's a simple fix, but it's amazing how many players will go years without addressing this simple problem. I had played for well over ten years before I realized that my Dm chord wasn't as clean as my other cowboy chords!

Using the Thumb to Keep the Lower Strings Quiet

Your classical guitar teacher may cringe at that suggestion, but if you're having problems with the low-E string ringing out when you strum a C, D, Dm, or A chord, you can easily fix it by allowing the tip of your fret-hand thumb to reach over the neck and lightly touch it. That approach will enable you to strum away with abandon without having to worry about maintaining the uncanny amount of precision it would take to strum only the top five strings every time.

Discovering existent problem areas should only take a few minutes, and reprograming years of bad habits should only take a few days or weeks. Cleaning up all the messy areas that you've neglected for so long is well worth the time, as you'll feel much more confident in the end. Enjoy!

THE BASICS OF CHORD STRUMMING

Studies show that acoustic guitarists spend 84.7% of their time strumming chords. OK, I made up that statistic, but I bet it's not too far off. And for some people, it's much higher. Suffice it to say, a solid command of strumming technique is absolutely essential for the acoustic guitarist. Strumming is the most common accompaniment method for singer/songwriters and it sounds great as an extra layered part in a full-band recording as well. So let's take a look at the basics of chord strumming.

FIRST THING'S FIRST

Before we get to strumming, you need to make sure that you're fretting all your chords cleanly. All the notes that you want to sound should be clear as a bell, and conversely, unwanted strings should not be ringing out. If your chords aren't clean, even great strumming technique will sound terrible!

The Basic Technique

When strumming, most people use a combination of wrist and forearm motion, with most of it coming from the wrist. It's rare to see players strum only with their forearm, keeping their wrist rigid. Try to hold the pick as if you were holding a bird—firmly enough to keep it there, but not enough to crush it.

Rule #1: Downstrokes on Downbeats

The first thing you want to drill into your brain is that you should pair downstrokes with downbeats. That is, as your foot taps down to the floor on the beat, your hand should be strumming down through the strings, toward the floor. This concept is really essential and will pay dividends when you get to more complicated strum patterns.

Let's try a few simple examples that contain only quarter-note strums (i.e., one downstroke on each beat).

TRACK 1
0:00 **EXAMPLE 1**

TRACK 1
0:19 **EXAMPLE 2**

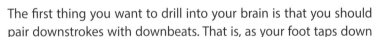

Play through these examples until you're able to stay in tempo throughout—that includes through the chord changes as well! Plowing through the strums of one chord at one tempo and then stalling for several beats while you re-finger the next chord really does you no good. Start off as slowly as necessary in order to transition from chord to chord in tempo.

Adding 8th Notes

When we add 8th notes to moderate or faster tempos, we usually bring upstrokes into play for the strums in between the beat. 8th notes, counted "1-and, 2-and, 3-and, 4-and," use downstrokes for all the numbers (the downbeats), and upstrokes for all the "ands" (the upbeats, or offbeats). Try to keep a relaxed and steady pick motion as you play through the following examples.

Follow the symbols for downstrokes (⊓) and upstrokes (∨), which are notated below the staff; they'll help you pair downstrokes with downbeats.

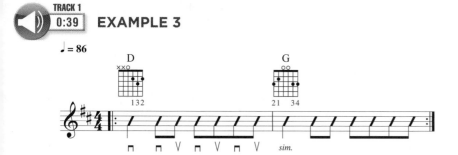

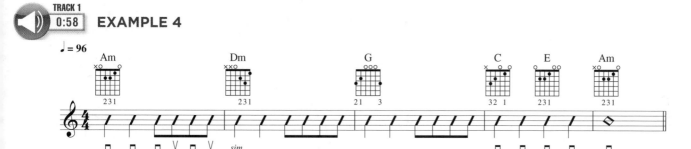

Adding Accents

In these final examples, we're going to add accents to a few spots to help make the strum patterns come alive a bit. To add an accent, simply strum a bit harder. In these examples, we're going to add accents to beats 2 and 4, collectively known as the backbeat. This approach is a simple yet effective way to make the music groove nicely.

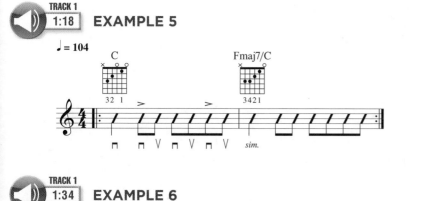

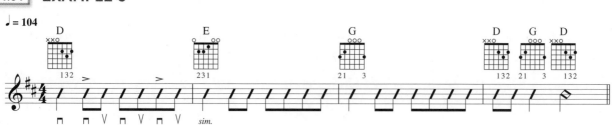

If you follow the guidelines in this lesson, you'll be well on your way to developing a solid strumming foundation upon which you can easily build. Remember: downstrokes with downbeats! Happy strumming!

CHANGING CHORDS SMOOTHLY WITH THE "OPEN-STRING CHEAT"

Chances are, if you're a singer/songwriter or you play acoustic guitar in a band, you'll be strumming a lot of open chords as accompaniment. While a band can help to cover up some less-than-graceful chord transitions, they are much more conspicuous when you're the sole accompanist. Although this may seem like a minor detail, smooth chord changes can make a huge difference. Many times, graceful transitions are what set apart a truly professional-sounding performance from a mediocre one. In this lesson, we'll explore how to change chords smoothly with the "open-string cheat."

It's Not Really Cheating—It's Just Efficient

If a song is played at a moderate tempo or faster, you can "cheat" a bit by lifting your fret hand off the fretboard on the last 8th note of the measure, giving you extra time to plant your fingers cleanly for the next chord. If you lightly strum, with an upstroke, only the top few strings after lifting your fingers, the momentum is maintained and the effect of the open strings is negligible to the ear. In fact, the effect is one of a smooth transition, with a solid, new chord on the downbeat. Try it with the following progressions.

TRACK 2
0:00 **EXAMPLE 1**

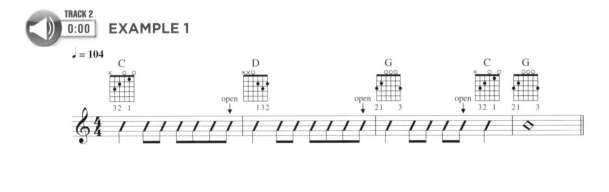

TRACK 2
0:17 **EXAMPLE 2**

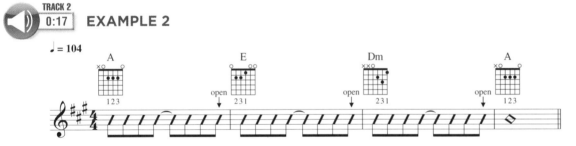

For best results, remember these key points:

▶ Try to catch just the top few open strings on the upstrokes;

▶ Try to strum the open strings lightly;

▶ And, most importantly (and the sole reason for using this technique), use the extra time to get each new chord planted cleanly.

The open-string cheat can be used equally as well for barre chords. As in the previous examples, try to keep the open strings nice and quiet. Notice that, in Example 4, the low open-E string (beat 2, measure 4) is picked just before the syncopated, final E chord is strummed.

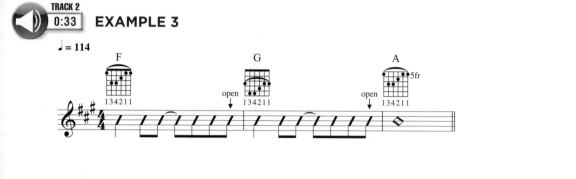

TRACK 2
0:33 **EXAMPLE 3**

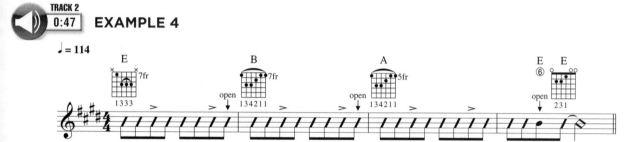

TRACK 2
0:47 **EXAMPLE 4**

The Intentional Cheat

If you're so inclined, you can make the open-string cheat more deliberate and noticeable as part of a rhythmic style. Kurt Cobain did this a good bit, as did several other grunge bands. The idea is not to be discreet about it at all. Instead, strum those open strings (all of them if you'd like!) loud and proud while you change strings to add weight and grit to the riff.

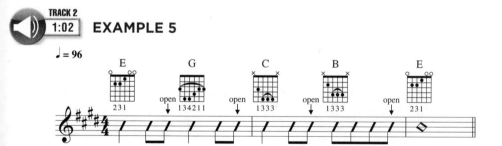

TRACK 2
1:02 **EXAMPLE 5**

Eventually, you'll become so adept at this trick that you'll do it without having to give it any thought. Whether you're playing with a full band or you're the only accompaniment, the open-string cheat is nearly imperceptible (i.e., you'll have to listen really closely to hear it). So go on… cheat a little.

LESSON #4: SCRATCH RHYTHMS

If you're a chord strummer who's looking for ways to add more dimensions to your playing, then it's time to check out scratch rhythms. Though scratch rhythms are common to electric guitar, they sound great on acoustic and have been used to liven up countless classic acoustic tracks, including those from Boston, Guns N' Roses, David Bowie, and many others. It's time to scratch the surface of scratch rhythms.

Let's Get Scratching

What do we mean by "scratch rhythm," anyway? Basically, the term refers to the use of dead notes (i.e., notes that have been muted by the fret hand and strummed) to produce a scratchy, rhythmic effect.

To create the basic sound, follow these steps:

1. Fret an A major barre chord in fifth position;
2. Release the pressure in your fret hand but don't lift your hands off the strings (your fingers should be touching the strings but the strings shouldn't be touching the fretboard);
3. Strum the strings.

You should hear a muted, "dead" sound.

TRACK 3
`0:00` **EXERCISE 1**

That's the basic idea. Now the task is to include this sound amongst chords that are strummed normally to create a more complex sound.

8th-Note Examples

Let's begin with a couple of examples that incorporate scratch rhythms into 8th-note strum patterns. Your fingers can remain in contact with the strings throughout the whole example. You simply apply full pressure when you want the chord to sound and release pressure a bit when you want the scratch-rhythm sound.

TRACK 3
`0:09` **EXAMPLE 1**

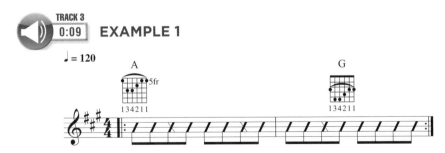

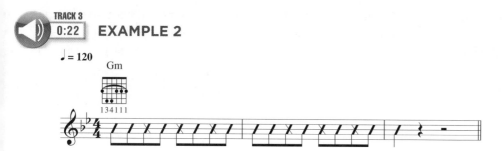

TRACK 3 `0:22` **EXAMPLE 2**

16th-Note Examples

Scratch rhythms sound great with 16th notes as well. You can use them in a more straightforward fashion or syncopate them to get a bit of a funky sound.

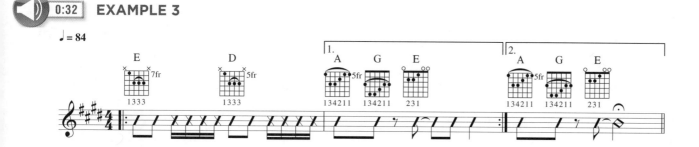

TRACK 3 `0:32` **EXAMPLE 3**

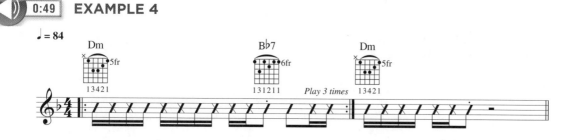

TRACK 3 `0:49` **EXAMPLE 4**

Note that scratch rhythms are most commonly used when playing barre chords, as opposed to open chords. The reason? You're already barring the strings, so it's just a matter of releasing the pressure and deadening the strings. With open chords, you're not set up the same way, so it's a good bit trickier.

LESSON #5: STRUMMING 16TH NOTES

When you move from strumming 8th notes to strumming 16th notes, it doesn't need to be nearly as complicated as some players make it. Sure, twice as many notes may be involved, but if you follow the basic guidelines in this lesson, you'll be able to navigate even the most syncopated strum pattern with little effort. So get your pick ready and let's start strumming 16th notes!

What Is a 16th Note?

A single measure can contain as many as eight 8th notes, whereas 16 16th notes can occupy a full measure. Makes sense, right? We count 8th notes as "1-and, 2-and, 3-and, 4-and." The numbers are the downbeats, and the "ands" are the upbeats. When we strum this type of pattern, we normally pair downstrokes (⊓) with downbeats, and upstrokes (∨) with upbeats.

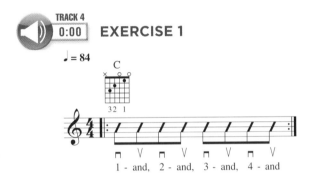

When we add 16th notes, we count them as "1-e-&-a, 2-e-&-a, 3-e-&-a, 4-e-&-a" (the "a" is pronounced as "uh"). To strum 16th notes, we simply strum twice as fast as when strumming 8th notes.

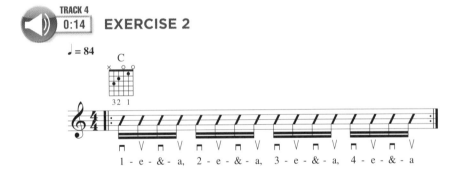

Turn on the Autopilot

This is very important: To easily strum any 16th-note pattern, without getting your pick hand jumbled up, you need to turn on the autopilot. Here's the rule:

When you're strumming a pattern that contains 16th notes, every 8th note should be articulated with a downstroke of your pick hand.

In other words, it's basically the same concept as strumming 8th notes, but twice as fast. However, since the tempo of 16th note-based songs is generally slower than the tempo of 8th note-based songs, we typically won't be strumming twice as fast. Nonetheless, the concept is still valid: If you're playing a 16th note-based pattern, keep your pick hand moving downward on every 8th note.

To state it another way: You'll pick all *numbers* and "*&s*" with a downstroke, and every "*e*" and "*a*" with an upstroke.

Examples

Let's look at some basic examples that employ 16th notes. Be sure to follow the pick directions below the music staff. Your pick hand should be moving steadily in beat (i.e., down on every 8th note).

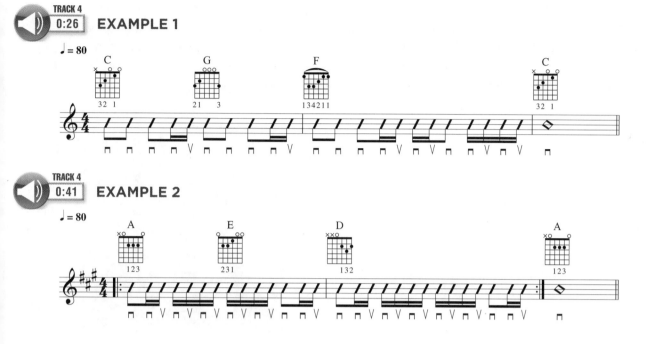

Adding Syncopation

Here's where the autopilot will really come into play. When we syncopate a rhythm, we stress a weak beat. In this case, we'll be stressing either the "e" or the "a." If you keep your pick hand moving downward for each 8th note, this won't be a problem—you'll never have to think about pick directions again. Instead, you'll simply use a "ghost stroke," if necessary (i.e., you'll move your pick hand, but won't contact the strings). In the following examples, ghost strokes are indicated via picking directions that are enclosed by parentheses.

I've also included a "wrong" way to strum the examples, indicated via parenthetical picking directions. These directions are common among beginners. Please do yourself a favor and don't fall into this trap! Follow the correct picking directions!

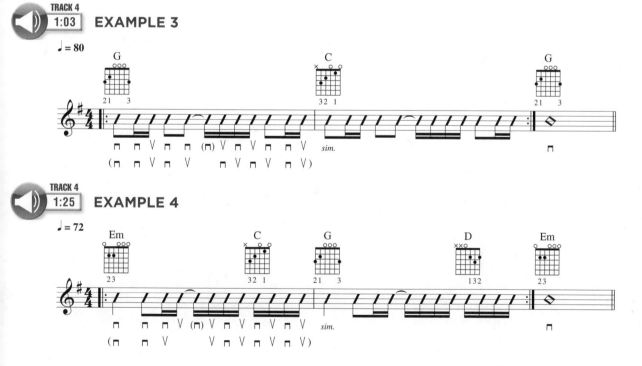

If you remember this basic axiom, you'll develop a solid strumming technique that will enable you to handle, with little difficulty, any 16th-note pattern thrown your way. And, because your pick hand will always be moving with the beat, you'll produce a more solid groove.

LESSON #6: PALM MUTING

The acoustic guitar is often used as an accompaniment instrument for singer/songwriters, and for good reason—it's portable, creates a full-bodied sound, and is capable of handling various styles of music extremely well. It makes sense then, to arm oneself with all the expressive devices that the instrument has to offer. If you've developed a good, basic strumming technique and you're looking for ways to liven things up a bit, give palm muting a try.

How It Works

When we palm mute a string, we muffle its sound by making contact with it near the bridge with our palm. The further you make contact away from the bridge, the more muffled the sound. Depending on the circumstance, players employ various amounts of muting, but in most cases the notes are still discernible.

Let's listen to the way open strings sound when muted. In the following example, you'll first hear the strings unmuted and then palm muting will be applied.

 TRACK 5 0:00 **EXAMPLE 1**

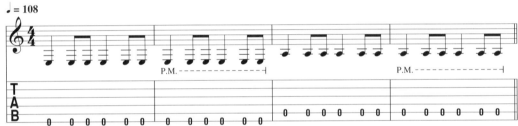

How to Use It

When applied to strummed chords, palm muting can create some really interesting dynamics. The palm-muted notes are almost swallowed, while the unmuted notes become more accented. This technique is used all the time for intimate, smoky grooves such as these:

 TRACK 5 0:15 **EXAMPLE 2**

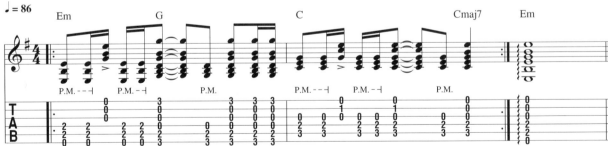

TRACK 5
0:35 **EXAMPLE 3**

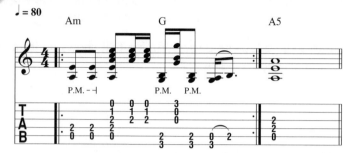

You also can apply a constant palm mute to get an extremely mellow sound.

TRACK 5
0:51 **EXAMPLE 4**

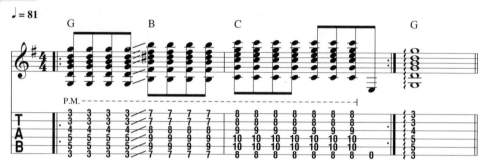

Or you can dig in with the constant palm mute to get a more intense effect.

TRACK 5
1:12 **EXAMPLE 5**

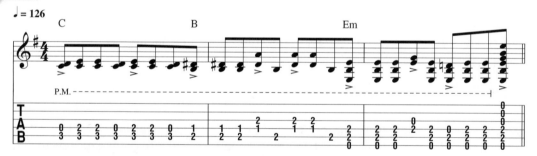

And, finally, palm muting also is useful for single notes, as you can create a nice feel by palm muting a melody on top of another instrument. The following is a reggae-type example in this vein that features an overdubbed electric guitar.

TRACK 5
1:22 **EXAMPLE 6**

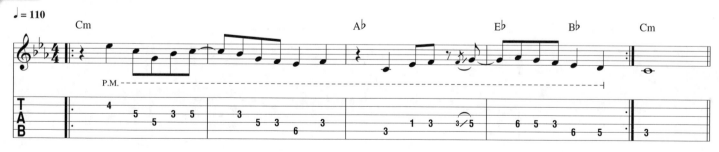

Experiment with this technique and try to spot it in the songs of your favorite artists. Palm muting is an expressive tool that should be exploited. Have fun with it!

LESSON #7: MELODIC STRUMMING

If you listen to classic guitar songs, you'll often hear something in the track that stands out from the norm—a great melodic hook, some unique chords, or perhaps a unique instrument altogether. Often, it's these touches that turn an already great song into an unforgettable classic. For example, try to envision "Norwegian Wood" without hearing that trademark sitar.

In this spirit of decorating a track to make it memorable, I'd like to share a favorite device of mine that shows up in many songs, melodic strumming—a combination of strumming chords and playing melodies.

The Basic Idea

Melodic strumming involves simultaneously strumming a chord and interweaving a melody. The melody is typically fingered by embellishing the chord over which the melody is sounding, although there are exceptions. A classic example of this idea can be heard in several Beatles songs, including the aforementioned "Norwegian Wood" and George Harrison's "Here Comes the Sun."

Let's use a D chord to examine the basic idea. We're going to be playing straight 8th notes, but for the first four notes, we're going to be targeting this melody on top: F#–E–D–E. Consequently, we won't be strumming through all four strings of the chord for every strum.

EXERCISE 1

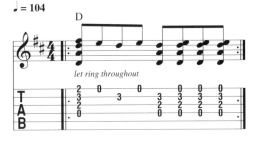

It takes a bit of practice to get the coordination down, but eventually it'll feel more and more natural.

Examples

Now let's take a look at some longer examples that apply melodic strumming to several chords. Keep in mind that the notation in these examples is a bit of an estimation of what's actually played. The most important goal is to get the melody to ring out clearly—the other notes below (or sometimes above) the melody aren't as critical. This first example is in the key of G and repeats the same melody over G, D, and C chords.

EXAMPLE 1

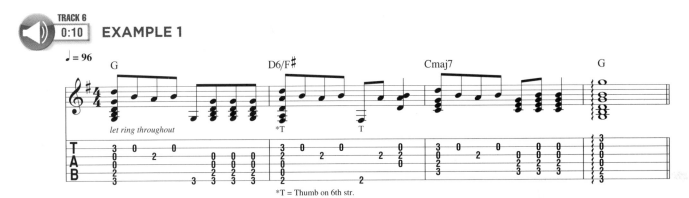

Here's a similar example, this time in the key of A:

EXAMPLE 2

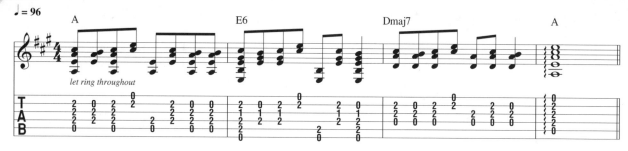

In this 6/8 example in the key of C, the melody is placed in the lower register. Although it's neither the lowest nor the highest note, the articulation (grace-note slurs) helps to draw the ear to it.

EXAMPLE 3

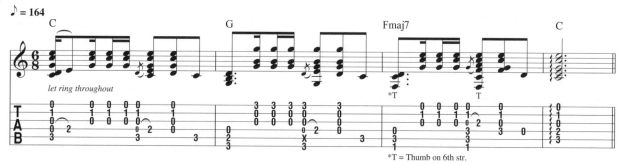

In this final E minor example, the melody begins in the lower register, but slowly migrates to the upper register as it moves through the chords.

EXAMPLE 4

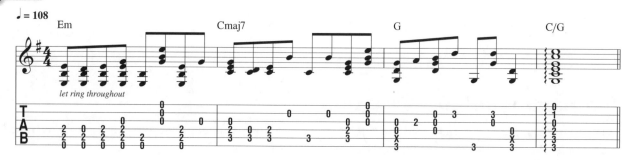

The next time you find yourself strumming along on some chords, think about giving the melodic strumming idea a try. You can mimic a vocal melody from the song or just create a melody from scratch. Either way, it's a lot of fun and a great way to add some more depth to a track.

COUNTRY AND BLUEGRASS STRUMMING PATTERNS

Country music always has featured some stellar guitar playing, and that's not just in the lead department. The rhythm parts of country guitarists are often interesting as well, and sometimes quite challenging, considering the tempo of some bluegrass music. In this lesson, we'll examine some of the elements that make country and bluegrass strumming patterns so appealing.

The "Boom-Chucka" Sound

One of the most ubiquitous elements of country and bluegrass rhythm is the "boom-chucka" sound. Basically, this name is derived from the technique that is used to create the sound. The "boom" represents a bass note that is played on beats 1 or 3; the "chucka" represents two 8th-note chord strums that follow the booms on beats 2 and 4. Typically, the chord strums involve just the top few strings of the chord.

Using a C chord, here's what the basic idea looks like:

 TRACK 7 0:00 **EXERCISE 1**

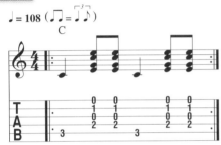

Developing the necessary coordination to accurately alternate single bass notes and chord strums takes some time, but with practice, it'll come. You will see variations on this boom-chucka pattern, depending on the tempo and feel of a particular song.

Adding the Alternating Bass Variation

To make this pattern more interesting, the bass note usually alternates between the root and the 5th. Let's take a look at that C chord again, adding the alternating bass-note element. We'll be playing a C bass note on beat 1 and a low-G bass note on beat 3.

 TRACK 7 0:10 **EXERCISE 2**

Adding the Hammered-3rd Variation

Another possibility for dressing up the pattern is to use the hammered-3rd idea. On beat 1, we still play the root as the bass note. On beat 3, however, we'll hammer from the C chord's 2nd to its 3rd. Here it is:

 TRACK 7 0:18 **EXERCISE 3**

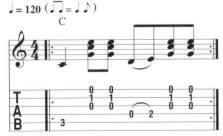

Typically, this device is used on only C, G, and F chords, because those three chords allow the hammer-on to the 3rd to occur from an open string.

Examples

Now let's look at some examples in various keys and tempos. Depending on the example, we'll be mixing and matching the variations. This first example moves through the I, V, and IV chords in the key of C.

EXAMPLE 1

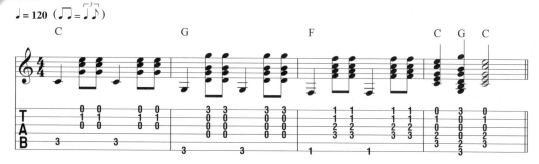

Below is a similar idea, this time in the key of D. The example moves through a I–IV–V7 progression and includes the alternating root/5th bass line.

EXAMPLE 2

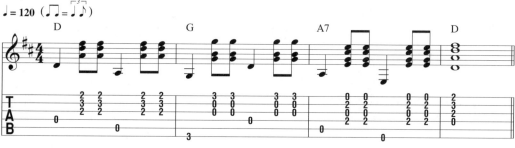

Let's finish up with an up-tempo bluegrass example in the key of C. Considering how fast it could be played, this example is fairly tame, but it'll still require some practice if you're not used to this type of thing.

EXAMPLE 3

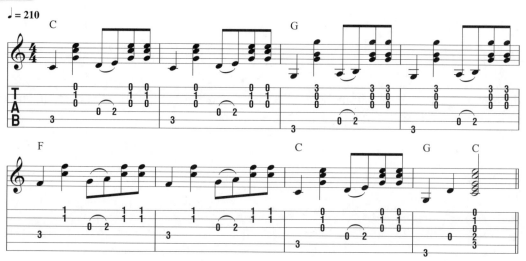

This style of rhythm guitar is an awful lot of fun to play and it really helps to create a full-bodied accompaniment as well. When played at the breakneck speeds that bluegrass is known to reach, these rhythms are truly impressive to hear, but that precision can only come from a properly engrained technique, so start off slowly and make sure it's clean. Enjoy!

LESSON #9: ADDING BASS LINES TO CONNECT CHORDS

If you've listened to much country or bluegrass music, you've no doubt heard some interesting and impressive rhythm playing. Country rhythm parts are rarely sterile; instead, they contain all kinds of unique elements that sound easy to play in the hands of seasoned pros. However, that's not always the case—especially in the context of a super-fast bluegrass tune. One device that these players love is adding bass lines to connect chords, the focus of this lesson.

Never a Dull Moment

This approach takes some thought and practice before it becomes second nature. What you're going to do is play a typical "boom-chucka" pattern on one chord for a bit and then, right before you get to the next chord, you're going to walk the bass notes up (or down) to the root of the new chord.

Below is how the basic idea would sound while moving from a C chord to an F chord. In this exercise, we'll play only the bass notes; we won't worry about strumming the chords at all.

TRACK 8
0:00   EXERCISE 1

And here's that same idea, with some strumming filled in on top:

TRACK 8
0:12   EXERCISE 2

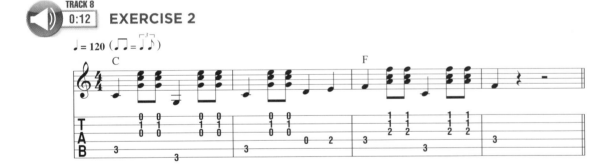

Depending on how far away the root of the new chord is from the original chord, you may have to start the bass run one beat earlier or later, which will become second nature with experience and trial and error.

Examples

Let's take a look at various examples that work in several different keys and tempos. This first example works the I, IV, and V chords in the key of C.

TRACK 8
0:23 **EXAMPLE 1**

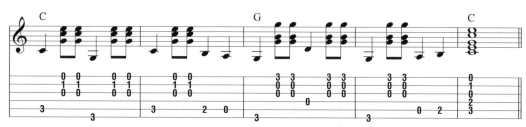

Here's a similar idea, this time in the key of A. For the C♯ bass note on beat 3 of measure 2, I use my pinky so that I'm able to sustain the D chord for just a bit longer and avoid an unmusical gap.

TRACK 8
0:46 **EXAMPLE 2**

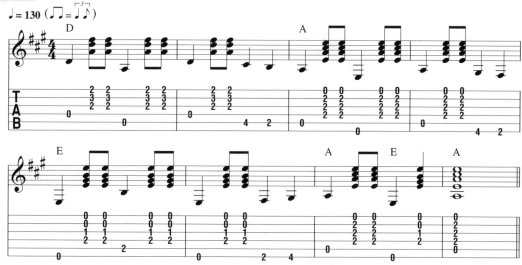

This next example is in the key of G and demonstrates that you don't always have to run straight up the scale to connect chords. Sometimes, the bass lines can just form a nice melody, as demonstrated here with the transition to (and from) the D chord.

TRACK 8
1:06 **EXAMPLE 3**

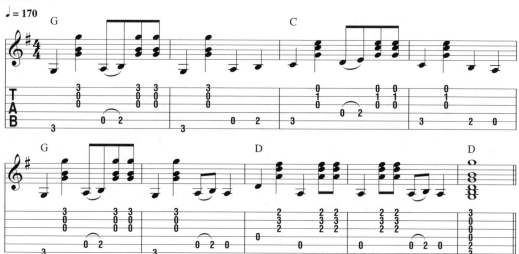

LESSON #10: "SUS" CHORDS

In addition to typical major and minor triads, plenty of other chords can be used to add more dimensions to your songs. One of the most common chordal choices is the "sus" chord, which sounds great on acoustic guitar and has fueled the riffs of many classics by the Who ("Pinball Wizard," "Behind Blue Eyes"), the Beatles ("Ticket to Ride"), and countless others. So let's check out what these sus chords are all about.

The Theory

"Sus" is short for "suspended." Cool name—but what does it mean? Well, if you look at a typical C major triad, for instance, you'll find that it's built from three different notes: a root, 3rd, and 5th.

In a sus chord, however, the 3rd is not present—it's replaced by either the 2nd or the 4th. In the key of C, the 2nd is D, and the 4th is F. When the chord is spelled root–2nd–5th, we call it a "sus2"; when it's spelled root–4th–5th, we call it a "sus4."

Common Guitar Voicings

Let's look at some common voicings for these sus chords in both open and moveable forms.

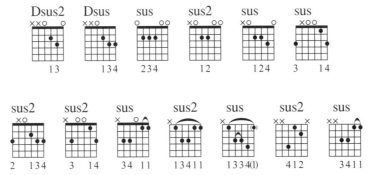

Examples

Now let's check out how these sus chords sound in a few chord riffs. Here's a typical application in the key of D:

EXAMPLE 1

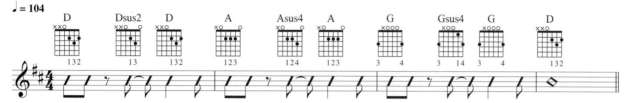

In this example in the key of E, we use several different sus chords to maintain a common A note on the third string throughout the progression.

EXAMPLE 2

Sus chords are often played along the fretboard to create an ethereal, mysterious sound, as demonstrated here:

EXAMPLE 3

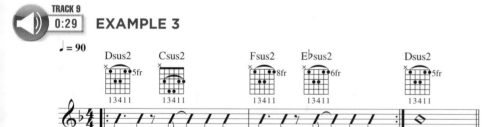

Finally, here's a fingerstyle example in the key of G:

EXAMPLE 4

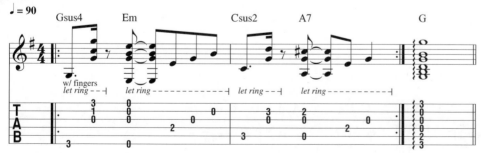

As you can hear, these chords can create a great vibe that sounds expansive, open, and sometimes a bit mysterious. Experiment with them and be sure to listen for them in riffs from your favorite players. Have fun!

LESSON #11: USING OPEN STRINGS TO CREATE COLORFUL CHORD VOICINGS

As an instrument, the guitar has many advantages and disadvantages. Because any given note can be played at several different locations on the neck, sight reading is more difficult on a guitar than on a piano. However, transposing keys is easier on a guitar because we can just slide our hand position up or down the neck—we don't have to worry about different configurations of white and black keys.

Another advantage of the guitar is the ability to combine fretted notes and open strings in unique ways to get different sounds. Of course, we do this all the time with open chords. However, in this lesson, we won't be playing in open position; instead, we'll be looking at ways that we can use open strings to create colorful chord voicings.

The Basic Idea

Using open strings to create colorful chord voicings is a really simple concept. To get started, we're going to play an open chord—one of the five big ones: C, A, G, E, or D—then slide the fretted notes up to different spots on the neck while still including the open strings in the chord.

Let's start with a C-chord shape. Here are some of the few different chords we can get with this idea:

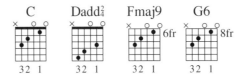

Now let's try an A-chord shape:

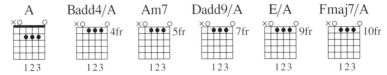

Here's what we can do with the D-chord shape:

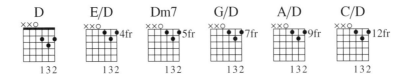

And let's check out some possibilities with the E-chord shape:

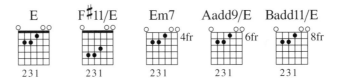

The G-chord shape is probably the least popular voicing with respect to this idea, but you can still get a few nice sounds out of it:

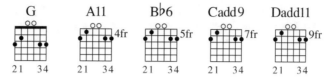

Examples

Let's hear how some of these chords sound in a few examples. This first example incorporates the E form for a lush-sounding progression in the key of E.

TRACK 10
0:00 **EXAMPLE 1**

Here's one that uses the C form in similar fashion:

TRACK 10
0:19 **EXAMPLE 2**

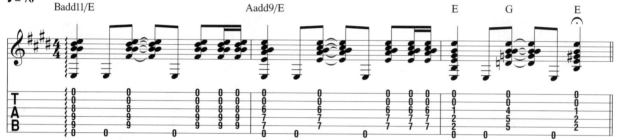

In this final example, we're working out of the A shape.

TRACK 10
0:33 **EXAMPLE 3**

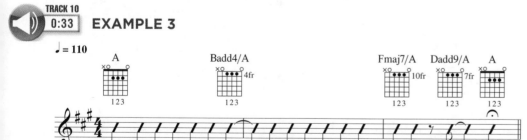

This concept is something with which you can experiment for a long time without getting bored. And remember—you don't have to limit yourself to typical open-chord shapes played higher up the fretboard. Instead, you can experiment with other less-common shapes as well. Enjoy the discoveries!

LESSON #12: THE BENEFITS OF USING A CAPO

As guitarists, we have a great need to be able to play a song in any key—especially if you sing as well. While barre chords can help out in this regard, sometimes they get uncomfortable for an extended period of time. Besides, some songs just don't sound right without a signature guitar part that can only be played effectively in open position. The capo to the rescue! Once you know what can be done with this handy little device, the capo can become your best friend. Fortunately, this lesson is all about the benefits of using a capo.

Which One to Use?

Several variations of the capo are available on the market. The "quick change" type is easy to maneuver and certainly lives up to its name. However, quick-change capos don't allow you to adjust the pressure of the clamp, and many times they clamp harder than necessary, which pulls the strings sharp. The "original" capo, most notably made by Shubb, costs a bit more and can't be changed quite as quickly (it still doesn't take long, though), but it's more precise, tuning-wise, because you can adjust the pressure of the clamp.

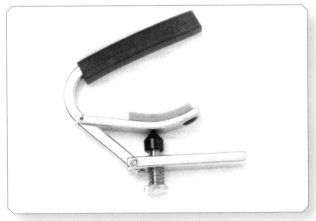

SHUBB "ORIGINAL" CAPO

KYSER "QUICK CHANGE" CAPO

Avoiding Barre Chords

When using a capo, you should avoid barre chords. Let's say, hypothetically, that your keyboardist brings a song to the band that's in the key of B♭. The chords are B♭, F, Gm, and E♭:

TRACK 11
0:00 **EXAMPLE 1**

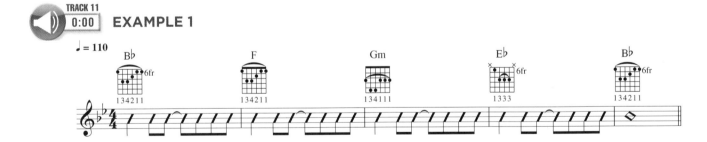

That's just not fun to play over and over again on a guitar. But what if you could play the same song with G, D, Em, and C chords? If you place a capo on the 3rd fret, you can do just that!

TRACK 11 `0:17` **EXAMPLE 2**

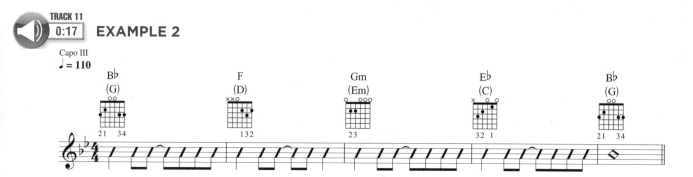

Adjusting the Key for Vocal Range

Another use for the capo is adjusting the key for vocal range. Let's say, hypothetically, that you're going to accompany a singer for a song in your sister's wedding. You've learned it note for note with the recording, the rehearsals with the singer have gone great, and you're ready to roll. On the big day, however, when you show up you learn that the original singer is sick and another one is filling in for her. And this singer is a soprano—not an alto, like the other one. She asks if you can do the song in A, instead of E. After panicking for a second, you reach for your capo, place it on fret 5, and say, "Whenever you're ready."

TRACK 11 `0:33` **EXAMPLE 3**

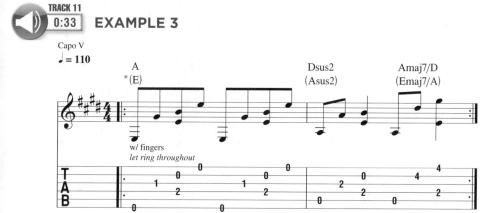

*Symbols in parentheses represent chord names respective to capoed guitar.
Symbols above reflect actual sounding chords. Capoed fret is "0" in tab.

Otherwise Unplayable Voicings

Still another use for the capo is to play something that's otherwise unplayable. Let's say, hypothetically, that you're working in the studio on one of your masterpieces and you want to lay down a nice, arpeggiated guitar part. The song is in Gm and the melody that you hear in your head for the first chord is G–A–Bb–D. Try as you may, you just can't figure out how to make it happen. However, if you place a capo on fret 3, it becomes relatively easy.

TRACK 11 `0:48` **EXAMPLE 4**

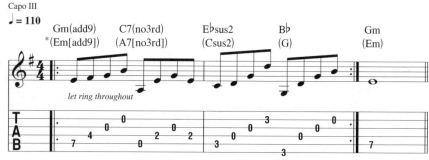

*Symbols in parentheses represent chord names respective to capoed guitar.
Symbols above reflect actual sounding chords. Capoed fret is "0" in tab.

Once you discover how useful the capo really is, you'll never want to travel without one again. Keep one in your guitar case so you're always prepared!

Many players, for one reason or another, never try their hand at fingerstyle playing, and that's a shame. Fingerstyle really is not any more difficult than playing with a plectrum and can open up a whole new world of possibilities on the guitar. Perhaps players shy away from fingerstyle because, after using a pick for so long, fingerstyle can almost feel like starting over. Keep in mind, however, that you're only starting from scratch with one hand—your fret hand won't have anything new to learn! So if this sounds like you, then it's time to stop procrastinating. Put down that pick and let's talk about the basics of fingerstyle.

BEFORE YOU BEGIN

Some players prefer to use a thumbpick and/or finger picks for this style. If either of those suit you, feel free to use them—everything in this lesson remains the same. If you decide to use bare fingers, it should be noted that most players will grow their nails out slightly, using them to pluck the strings, as it results in a more brilliant tone.

Hand Position

The fingers of your plucking hand are labeled as follows:

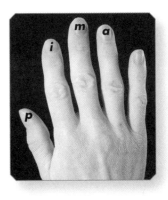

p = thumb $\quad$ i = index $\quad$ m = middle $\quad$ a = ring
(Typically, the pinky is not used.)

The thumb usually handles the bass strings, while the fingers typically pluck the treble strings. The thumb is positioned more forward along the strings than the other three fingers (see photo).

Arpeggios

OK, it's time to get your feet wet. An arpeggio is simply the notes of a chord played separately—as in a melody—instead of simultaneously. Arpeggios are one of the most commonly used devices in fingerstyle playing.

Let's check out some basic examples. Make sure each note sounds clearly and that the volume remains consistent throughout.

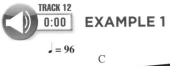

TRACK 12
0:00 **EXAMPLE 1**

Now let's reverse the order in which the top three strings are plucked.

 TRACK 12 `0:12` **EXAMPLE 2**

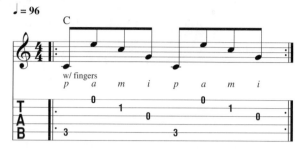

Below are a couple of variations in which the thumb is moved to a different string. Be sure to follow the pick-hand fingerings, which are notated between the notation and tab staves.

 TRACK 12 `0:23` **EXAMPLE 3**

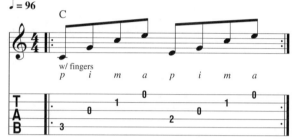

 TRACK 12 `0:35` **EXAMPLE 4**

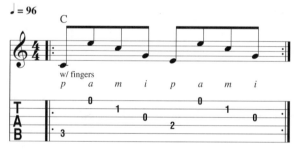

To close out the lesson, let's play our first chord progression with the fingerstyle technique. Again, be sure to follow the fingerings, as we'll be shifting down one string group for the G chord. For the final C chord, brush the strings with your thumb.

 TRACK 12 `0:46` **EXAMPLE 5**

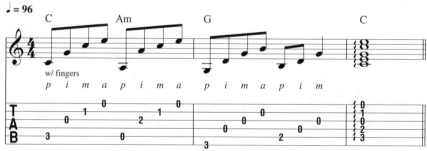

Though we've only scratched the surface, you've taken your first step into a whole new world of guitar playing. Fingerstyle is an incredibly rewarding style that is full of challenges and capable of astounding results. Enjoy the journey!

LESSON #14: BLOCK-CHORD STYLE

In the world of fingerstyle guitar, numerous approaches can be taken to create guitar parts for songs. One of my particular favorites is the block-chord style, which enables us to get a unique sound that's impossible with the pick alone, and when combined with a few other techniques, it can create a full and exciting texture that sounds greater than the sum of its parts. So put away the pick and let's talk about the block-chord style.

The Basic Idea

In the block-chord style, we're going to pluck the notes of a chord simultaneously with our fingers, much like a pianist pounds out a chord. (That's just an expression—the block-chord style can be used for delicate playing, as well!) Since the thumb and index, middle, and ring fingers are typically used in fingerstyle, we can play four notes at a time with this method. (Of course, if you really need a fifth note, you could add the pinky.)

To hear how the block-chord style sounds, let's take a look at a simple example.

TRACK 13 0:00 **EXAMPLE 1**

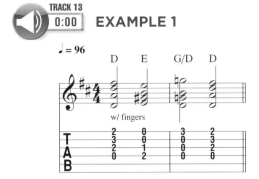

With a little syncopation, we can turn the previous example into a nice little riff.

TRACK 13 0:12 **EXAMPLE 2**

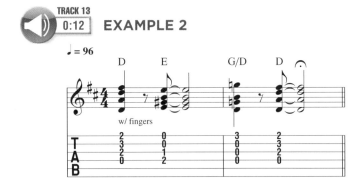

Of course, we can play chords on strings other than the top four.

TRACK 13 0:23 **EXAMPLE 3**

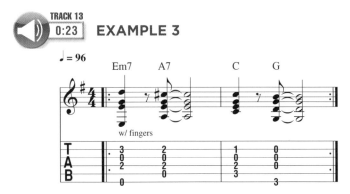

Dressing Things Up a Bit

This technique can be dressed up a few ways as well. Let's check them out.

BREAKING UP THE CHORDS AND BASS

If you listen to pianists, you'll often hear them play bass notes independently of the chords, and we can do that, too. The most common way is to anticipate a chord with the bass note played an 8th note earlier, as in this example:

EXAMPLE 4

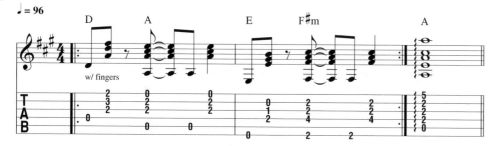

ADDING A PERCUSSIVE BACKBEAT

Another super-cool device is the percussive backbeat, which is accomplished by planting the pick-hand fingers (in preparation for the next chord) with great force, resulting in a percussive click. The percussive backbeat simulates the snare drum of a full-band context. When combined with the aforementioned method of splitting the chords and the bass, we can create some heavy grooves:

EXAMPLE 5

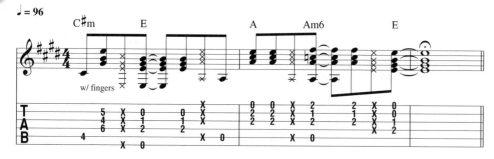

EXAMPLE 6

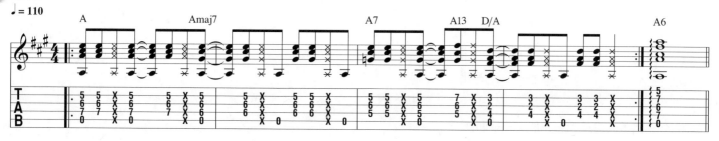

The more you work with this concept, the more you'll find new ways to use it. The block-chord style is a versatile tool that sounds equally good in a solo setting or a full band. Enjoy!

THE BASICS OF TRAVIS PICKING

The world of fingerstyle guitar is vast and expansive, but several key concepts have become must-know skills for any serious player. Undoubtedly, one of the most common concepts is Travis picking—a style of playing that has probably fueled the guitar arrangements of more fingerstyle songs than any other, and for good reason. Travis picking sounds great, is not terribly difficult to learn in its most basic form, and is incredibly versatile. So let's see what all the fuss is about by taking a look at the basics of Travis picking.

Break It Down

Named for country legend Merle Travis, the Travis-picking technique can be broken down into two basic elements:

1. Alternating bass notes on every beat (played by the thumb);
2. Notes played on the treble strings in between bass notes (played by the fingers).

These aren't hard-and-fast rules and you will find some exceptions, but anything that contains these elements most likely will qualify as "Travis picking." By the way, in this lesson, we'll use the standard pick-hand fingering notation:

p = thumb i = index m = middle a = ring

For starters, let's look at a C chord. The first thing that we're going to do is rock the thumb between string 5 and string 4 on the beats. It looks like this:

EXERCISE 1

Once you're comfortable with the bass notes and you can play them without much thought, add the fingers on strings 3 and 2 in between the bass notes.

EXERCISE 2

That's the basic idea. You're Travis pickin'!

Examples

Let's look at some examples that move through different chord progressions. In this first example, we're moving from C to G. Notice that our thumb will move between string 6 and string 4 on the G chord.

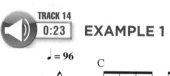

EXAMPLE 1

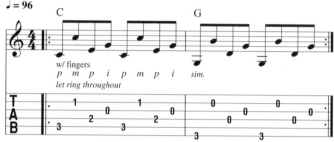

In this A minor example, we're switching the order of the fingers, so watch out. We also introduce a rhythmic variation at the end of measures 2 and 4, where we play a quarter note on beat 4, leaving out the last 8th note. This approach helps to make the chord transitions smooth; it avoids abruptly cutting off the last C (measure 2) and B (measure 4) notes.

EXAMPLE 2

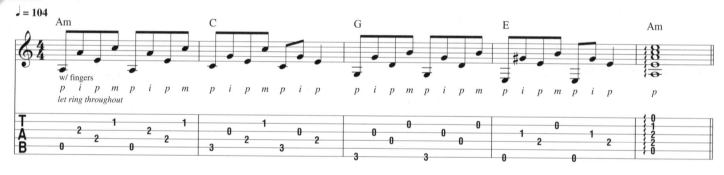

Here's a nice-sounding example in the key of E that maintains the same chord on top while changing bass notes:

EXAMPLE 3

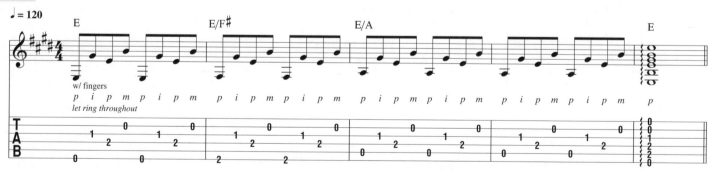

Countless variations on this basic technique exist but, armed with this knowledge, you've developed a good, solid foundation on which to build. To hear this technique in full flight, check out the man himself, Merle Travis, or "Mr. Guitar," Chet Atkins.

LESSON #16: ARPEGGIO PATTERN SAMPLER FOR FINGERSTYLE GUITAR

Arpeggios are one of the most commonly employed devices in fingerstyle guitar. However, after becoming adept at one or two patterns, many players don't bother to explore some of the more interesting ones, which is a bit of a shame because some really nice sounds can be discovered if you just take the time. With that in mind, in this lesson I've put together an arpeggio pattern sampler for fingerstyle guitar that contains a little of this, a little of that, and hopefully will whet your appetite for more.

Rolling Pattern

This first pattern is what I call a "rolling pattern" because it rolls up and down the strings as if through hills and valleys. This example is in the key of C, 6/8 meter, and uses a *p–i–m–a–m–i* pattern throughout (*p* = thumb, *i* = index, *m* = middle, and *a* = ring).

TRACK 15 `0:00` **EXAMPLE 1**

Rooftop Pattern

I call this next example a "rooftop pattern" because it reminds me of throwing a ball onto a roof and watching it roll back down. This is in the key of E and uses a *p–a–m–i* pattern throughout. It moves in diatonic 3rds along strings 4 and 3 against open-B and open-E strings on top.

TRACK 15 `0:20` **EXAMPLE 2**

Stairstep Pattern

The following pattern "stairsteps" its way through the strings. I use the pick-hand fingerings that are notated between the notation and tab staves because they make sense to me, but feel free to experiment.

EXAMPLE 3

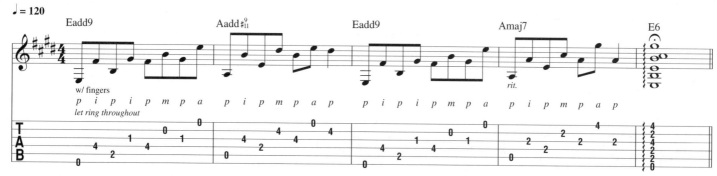

Fingertap Pattern

This final pattern reminds me of someone rhythmically tapping their fingers on a desk. (OK, so these names may make sense only to me—I'm fine with that.) This next example is in the key of C and alternates between C and A9 (no 3rd) chords with an interesting pattern in which the changing bass notes dovetail with the changing treble notes. A *p–i–m* pattern is used throughout.

EXAMPLE 4

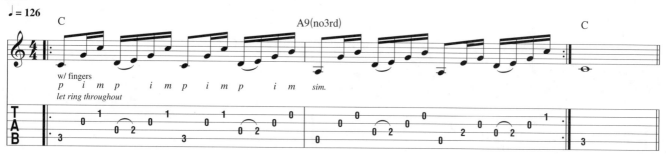

Well, that's it for the sampler. I hope you found some tasty morsels that… OK, I'm done with the food puns. Seriously though, experiment with these patterns to see what else you can come up with. Check out some Simon & Garfunkel or John Fahey to hear some beautiful examples of these patterns and more.

LESSON #17: SMOOTH CHORD TRANSITIONS WITH TRAVIS-PICKING TECHNIQUE

The Travis-picking technique is commonly used among fingerstyle players and can produce some beautiful results. However, once familiar with the basics of Travis picking, we often turn on the autopilot when using the technique and stop listening closely to what we're actually playing. Consequently, we don't realize that some chord transitions end up sounding a bit abrupt. Once we become aware of this, however, we can take steps to prevent it. In this lesson, I'll discuss some strategies that we can use to help achieve smooth chord transitions with the Travis-picking technique.

What Not to Do

So you'll know what to listen for, let's check out an example of a common Travis-picking mistake. The following example moves from C to G. Listen closely to the last note (C) in measure 1.

EXERCISE 1

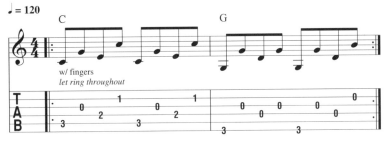

Hear how it gets clipped short? That's our culprit and that's the kind of thing that we'll attempt to avoid.

Common Tones

A great way to smoothly transition from one chord to another is to find common tones—if they exist—and try to use the same fingers to fret the notes in both chords. Common-tone fingerings are a simple matter in a progression like the C-to-Am change in the example below. Be sure not to lift your index finger when changing chords!

EXAMPLE 1

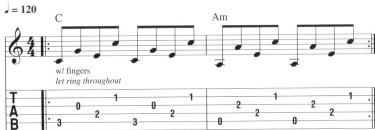

Other times, common tones are less obvious. Take a look at the progression in Example 2. The F♯ on string 1 is a common tone, but normally it's fretted with the middle finger for the D chord, whereas it would be fretted by the ring finger for the E9 chord. This progression is a good candidate for re-fingering. To implement the common-tone technique and achieve a smooth sound, fret the D chord with your middle, pinky, and ring fingers (low to high).

EXAMPLE 2

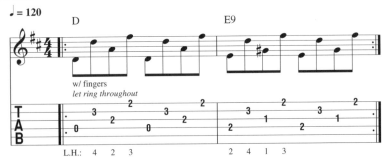

Partial Fretting

Since we're often striking only one or two notes at a time, we usually don't need to fret the entire chord on the downbeat. Many times, you'll need to fret only the bass note on beat 1, thereby leaving you extra time to fret the rest of the chord, which can cut down on unmusical gaps that occur when no common tones are present. Consequently, you are able to sustain the last treble note right up until the point where the new bass note is struck.

In the following example, if we barre all six strings throughout, we have until the second 8th note of the Gm chord to get our fingers into position for that chord. Consequently, we have time to make sure that the last E♭ note of the Cm chord is not cut off before the low G note in measure 2 is struck.

TRACK 16
0:41 **EXAMPLE 3**

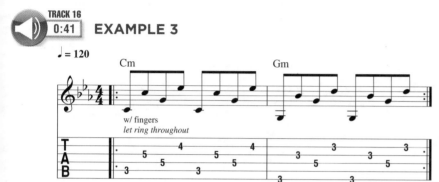

Omission

Sometimes, when you need to shift positions but have no common tone, your best bet to achieve a smooth transition is to omit the final 8th note of the measure before the chord change. This approach is not ideal, but it usually sounds smoother than the alternative. In the following examples, listen to the difference between the measures without the 8th-note omissions and the measures in which the final 8th note has been eliminated.

TRACK 16
0:54 **EXAMPLE 4**

Many times, simply becoming aware of this issue is enough to correct the problem. Our original C-to-G progression could be made much smoother simply by making sure that the last C note is sustained until the low G note is plucked. After all, that low G note is the only note that we need to fret for the G chord. Therefore, don't feel compelled to rush and, in turn, create a jerky transition. If you keep this idea in mind, you can transform a mediocre guitar track into one that really shines.

LESSON #18: INTERMEDIATE AND ADVANCED TRAVIS-PICKING CONCEPTS

Most fingerstyle players are familiar with some level of Travis picking; after all, it's probably the most widely used fingerpicking pattern in the world. Moreover, the variations on this style are nearly limitless and you can certainly take it further than the basic "Dust in the Wind" style pattern. In this lesson, we'll look at some advanced Travis-picking concepts and what we can do with them.

The Basic Pattern

Before we talk about dressing it up, let's look at what most people consider the basic Travis-picking pattern, shown below in a few variations on a C chord.

TRACK 17 0:00 **PATTERN 1**

Once you've got those down, let's look at where else we can take the pattern.

Adding the Third Finger

Though Merle Travis (the technique's namesake) used only the thumb and one finger, most players use the thumb and two (index and middle) fingers for their patterns. However, we can add another dimension to the pattern by occasionally bringing in the third (ring) finger. Check out how the following C–G6/B–Am pattern is given a fresh life by bringing in the ring finger for the open E string (*p* = thumb, *i* = index, *m* = middle, *a* = ring).

TRACK 17 0:28 **EXAMPLE 1**

Here's an example in the key of G that uses the ring finger (*a*) to create a melodic voice on top:

TRACK 17 0:44 **EXAMPLE 2**

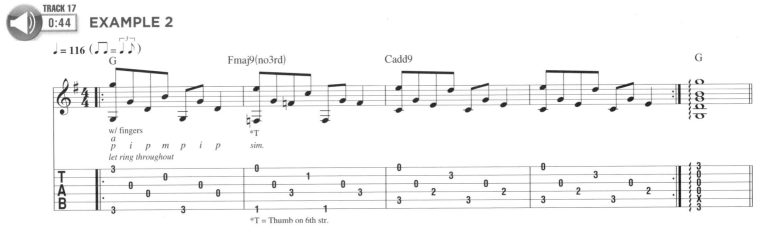

*T = Thumb on 6th str.

Adding the 5th in the Bass

When playing a C-type chord, A-type chord, E-type chord, or D-type chord, we can incorporate the 5th in the bass on beat 3 to add a bit of depth. On a C-, D-, or A-type chord, the 5th is located below the root. On an E-type chord, the 5th is above the root. Here's an example in the key of C that employs C-type (C), A-type (Am), and E-type (E and F) chords with this device:

EXAMPLE 3

This next example is in the key of D and uses a few other tricks to make the chord transitions smooth. First of all, the first D chord is fingered with your fret hand's middle, pinky, and ring fingers, low to high, so that there won't be an unmusical gap when moving to D7. Secondly, the final 8th notes in measures 2 and 4 are omitted to avoid the same gap. Also, take note of the picking pattern on the G chord; we keep the index (*i*) and middle (*m*) fingers on strings 2 and 1, respectively, so that we can add the alternating 5th (D) in the bass.

EXAMPLE 4

Adding Melodies on Top

We also can dress up our Travis picking by bringing out melody notes on top, which can be accomplished in various ways. The following example is in the key of D minor and moves between Dm and B♭ chords, with A–G–F (over Dm) and D–C–D (over B♭) melodies on top. Notice that, in order to preserve the melody on top, we occasionally break away from the normal picking patterns.

EXAMPLE 5

LESSON #19: ORNAMENTING FINGERSTYLE RIFFS WITH HAMMER-ONS AND PULL-OFFS

After you become adept at playing through progressions with various fingerstyle techniques, you may want to explore ways to dress up your chords a bit. A great way to do this is by slurring to, and from, notes. Slurs can add depth and complexity to your song without much additional difficulty, which is always a good thing! In this lesson, we'll talk about ornamenting fingerstyle riffs with hammer-ons and pull-offs.

Travis Picking

The following is a common Travis-picking trick, especially when used in conjunction with a "pinch," in which a bass note and treble note are struck simultaneously. When that occurs, you can hammer on, or pull off, to the target chord tone. Here's how the basic idea sounds in a simple riff in in the key of C:

TRACK 18
0:00   EXAMPLE 1

In the following A major example, we're repeating the same hammer-on (B to C#) over several chords to create a motif.

TRACK 18
0:15   EXAMPLE 2

Block-Chord Style

In the block-chord style, we attack all the notes at once, similar to the way a pianist does. When we add hammer-ons and/ or pull-offs to this style, we can create little sub-melodies that add depth to the riff. Following is a D major riff that creates an E–F#–E melody on top during the D and E chords, and then a C#–B–A melody in the middle register over the G and D chords.

EXAMPLE 3

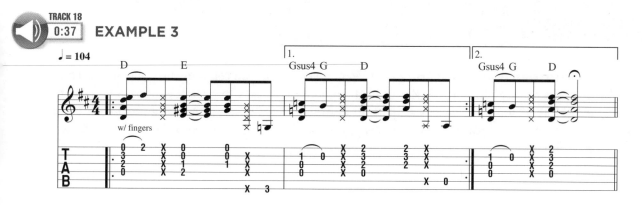

Here's a modal-mixing example in the key of E that repeats an E–F♯ motif on string 1 to generate some interesting harmonies:

EXAMPLE 4

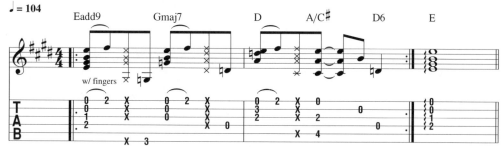

Arpeggios

The aforementioned ornaments sound great on arpeggio patterns as well. We can create little motifs that serve as hooks within the larger riff. Here's a pretty-sounding pattern in the key of A that repeats a C♯–B pull-off over several different chords:

EXAMPLE 5

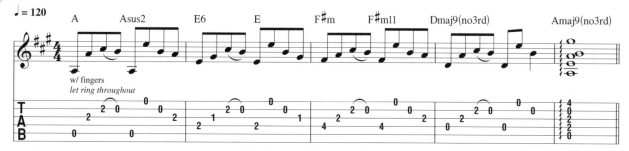

Finally, here's a classic hammer-pull move that's used in a lot of songs:

EXAMPLE 6

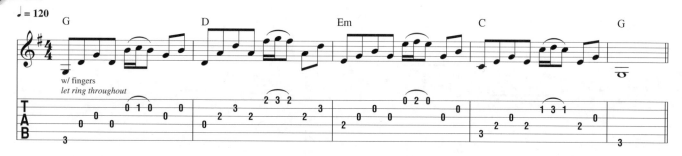

If you experiment a little with this idea, you'll find all kinds of ways to dress up your chord riffs. Hammer-on and pull-off ornamentation is a great, simple tool that can add a whole new dimension to a song.

LESSON #20: ORNAMENTING FINGERSTYLE RIFFS WITH MELODIC CONNECTIONS

After learning some basic fingerstyle techniques, you may want to explore ways that you can dress up your chords a bit and take your riffs to the next level. One listen to James Taylor or Paul Simon is all it takes to hear how good a fingerstyle riff can sound. A great way to do this is by adding melodies that lead from one chord to the next. These melodies can add a memorable (and singable) element to your playing, which is always a good thing! In this lesson, we'll discuss ornamenting fingerstyle riffs with melodic connections.

It's All About the Bling

Think of this idea as a good bit of "bling" or "ear candy" that provides the listener with something to grab onto when nothing else is really going on. Melodic connections are great for intros, outros, or as filler between vocal lines. Basically, what we'll do is briefly abandon an established pattern right before we reach a new chord—two beats is a common length, though it can certainly vary. To fill the space, we'll play a melody that leads smoothly to a chord tone of the new chord.

Here's the basic idea in an example that moves from C to G7:

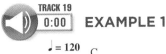

EXAMPLE 1

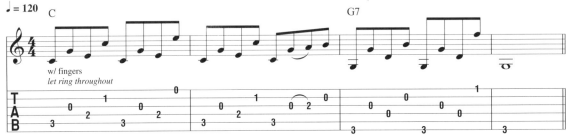

Sounds nice, huh? Sometimes, this melodic device needs only one or two notes to be effective.

EXAMPLE 2

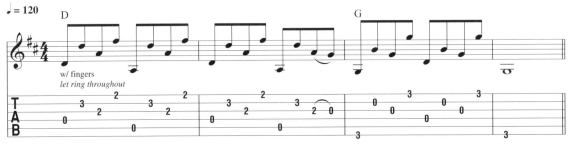

In this next example, we move back and forth between A and Cmaj7 chords via melodic lines that connect both chords.

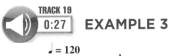

EXAMPLE 3

Double Stops Are Nice

Melodic connections sound great as double stops as well. The double stops can be used for parallel motion, as in the following banjo-esque example in the key of D, which employs harmonized 10th intervals.

TRACK 19
0:43 **EXAMPLE 4**

Or the double stops can use oblique motion, in which one note moves while the other remains stationary.

TRACK 19
0:57 **EXAMPLE 5**

Don't Forget About the Bass!

Melodic connections also are commonly used in the bass register. Check them out in the following C-to-Am example. With one smooth motion, the pick-hand thumb is dragged from the last G note of measure 2 to the open A string at the beginning of measure 3. Nevertheless, feel free to experiment with alternative picking patterns.

TRACK 19
1:10 **EXAMPLE 6**

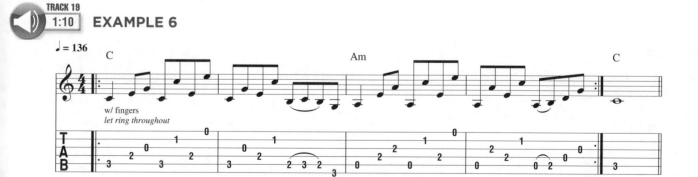

You can take this idea as far as you want to take it. The results can be quite impressive and memorable, and it can often set apart a stellar guitar part from a serviceable one. Enjoy coming up with your own ideas, and listen for these melodic connections in other songs, such as James Taylor's "Fire and Rain" and Eric Clapton's "Tears in Heaven." You'll hear it more often than you might think!

THE FUNDAMENTALS OF RIGHT-HAND INDEPENDENCE

If you're new to the fingerstyle technique, you'll find that it's full of challenges. Nonetheless, it's worth the effort, as the results can be truly impressive. One particular challenge that's extremely common, especially in the solo guitar genre, is having to play one rhythm with the thumb while playing another rhythm with the fingers. Sometimes, the different parts line up nicely and don't pose too much of a problem. At other times, though, you'll be required to play something that will feel like simultaneously rubbing your stomach and patting your head. When that happens, you'll be glad that you took the time to work on the fundamentals of right-hand independence.

DISCLAIMER

For the lefties out there, please don't be offended by the title of this lesson. When I say "right hand," I'm referring to the plucking hand. Besides the fact that the vast majority of players are right-handed, I simply thought "Right-Hand Independence" sounded better than "Plucking-Hand Independence."

The Basic Idea

Right-hand independence simply refers to the ability to play disparate rhythms with the thumb and fingers of your right hand. Developing this rhythmic separation is critical if you want to be able to tackle some of the more complicated fingerstyle problems that will come your way.

To begin, let's look at a basic example.

TRACK 20 0:00 **EXAMPLE 1**

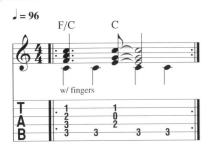

Most beginning fingerstyle players will feel compelled to restrike the bass note along with the chord on the "and" of beat 2. This inclination is what this concept is all about. You need to separate the role of bass and treble so that they're allowed to do what's asked of them, independent of one another.

Try to separate the parts and play them independently. Once you've got that down, put them back together. In example 1, the bass is the timekeeper (as is often the case) and is in charge of keeping the beat. Try to keep that in mind.

Examples

When you get the first example down, try the following ones, in which we'll be working through various rhythms in the treble against a steady, on-the-beat bass.

TRACK 20 0:12 **EXAMPLE 2**

EXAMPLE 3

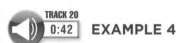

EXAMPLE 4

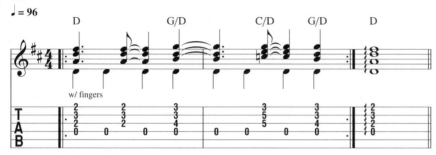

Adding Arpeggios

Thus far, all the examples have featured a single bass note against block chords on top. In the next two examples, we'll keep the steady bass note, but we'll arpeggiate the chords on top. This approach will require a bit of practice as well.

EXAMPLE 5

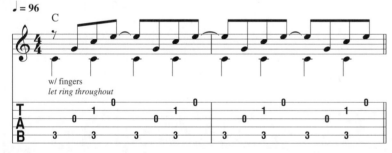

EXAMPLE 6

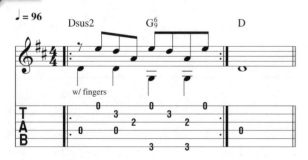

This skill will take some time to master, but once you do, it's very liberating, as it really can help you to simulate the sound of two instruments playing at once. To hear how awesome this can sound, check out anything by Chet Atkins.

LESSON #22: ADVANCED RIGHT-HAND INDEPENDENCE

As you develop your fingerstyle chops and begin to tackle more challenging pieces, the technical demands become greater in many areas. One demand, in particular, is right-hand independence, which is basically the ability to play disparate rhythms with your thumb and fingers. This lesson is aimed at players who have already dealt with this concept a bit, so we'll be exploring some more advanced right-hand independence studies.

Flipping Things on End

Since most players are somewhat used to holding down a steady beat with the thumb and playing various rhythms on top with the fingers, a great exercise involves flipping this idea. In other words, we'll keep a steady beat with chords atop a bass line that works independent rhythms. Separate the parts at first if necessary.

This first example, in the key of E minor, is relatively basic and features an Em chord played in straight quarter notes on top and a melody in the bass, which is played by the thumb.

TRACK 21
0:00 **EXAMPLE 1**

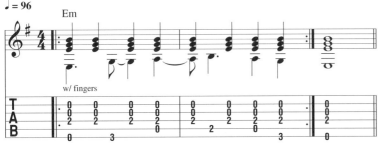

This next example, in the key of G major, is a bit more involved. We're in Drop D tuning for this one, so lower your sixth string from E to D. We've got a chord ostinato on top that involves a percussive "tick" sound on beat 2, articulated by forcefully planting your fingers onto the strings. You need to be careful so as to plant only your fingers and not your thumb, otherwise you'll interfere with the bass line. Another tricky spot is the beginning of measure 4, where you'll be simultaneously hammering a bass note and plucking a chord on top. This passage will probably feel a bit weird at first, but it's an example of what right-hand independence is all about!

TRACK 21
0:19 **EXAMPLE 2**

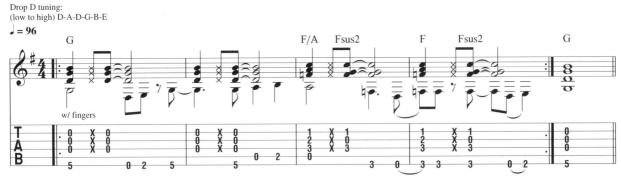

Three-Against-Four Feel

OK, let's get back to the bass keeping the pulse. (We're also back in standard tuning, by the way.) In the next examples, the fingers will play melodies or arpeggios in a three-against-four pattern while the thumb keeps time on the beat. This approach will take a bit of left-brain work until you get the basic feel for it.

TRACK 21
0:47
EXAMPLE 3

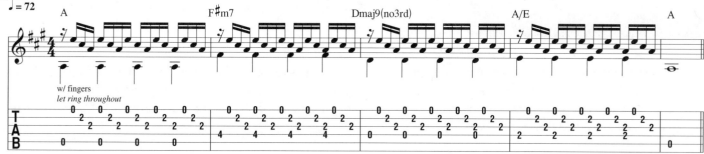

Although the following example doesn't employ groups of three notes, it still uses a three-against-four feel. The opening 16th note/8th note rhythmic grouping on top (C♯–E) is repeated over and over again as the double stops climb diatonically along strings 1 and 2, creating a lopsided, syncopated feel that takes three beats to cycle back around rhythmically. Meanwhile, the bass keeps steady quarter notes.

TRACK 21
1:12
EXAMPLE 4

Adding Slurs to the Melody

Now we're going to complicate things a bit more by adding some slurs to the melody. That's no big deal, right? We use slurs all the time. The normal practice is to pluck two notes simultaneously and then slur the top note to another. In these next two examples, however, we'll be picking the melody note independently and then picking the bass note as we execute the slur. If you've never used this technique, it can feel pretty awkward, so slow it way down if necessary. In this first example, the slur occurs on beat 4.

TRACK 21
1:29
EXAMPLE 5

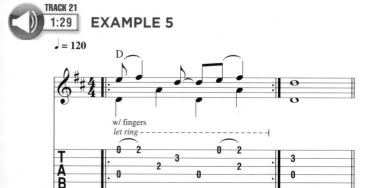

We'll finish up with a country-blues pattern in the key of E that you may have heard before. Again, the second slur on beat 4 is the one that may give you trouble.

TRACK 21
1:41
EXAMPLE 6

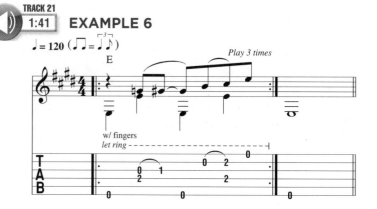

LESSON #23: THE "REAL" TRAVIS PICKING

Interestingly, one of the most ubiquitous techniques in the entire fingerstyle guitar genre is actually a bit of a misnomer. "Travis picking" generally is considered to consist of alternating bass notes and treble notes that are played by the fingers. However, if you listen to the man from which the name of this technique is derived—the legendary Merle Travis—you'll realize that he actually never played this way.

Less Polish, More Mute

Merle's technique was not nearly as polished-sounding as the technique of most players today. Below are a few notes on his technique that may come as a surprise to those who are familiar with only the modern form of Travis picking.

▶ He always played with a thumbpick;

▶ He almost always applied a thick palm mute to the lower strings;

▶ He consistently used his thumb to fret bass notes on string 6 (and sometimes string 5);

▶ He used only the index finger of his right (pick) hand (the other three fingers were firmly planted on the face of the guitar).

Obviously, you're free to use two fingers; it's just nice to know how Merle did it because his technique can provide some insight into the style.

The Meat and Potatoes: The "Boom-Chick" Pattern

Merle spent the majority of the time chunking out alternating notes with his thumbpick—a style that wasn't as precise as one of his famous disciples, Chet Atkins. Merle would roughly pluck strings 6 and 5 on beats 1 and 3, followed by strings 4 and 3 on beats 2 and 4—all palm muted.

TRACK 22 0:00 **EXAMPLE 1**

(Note: Keep in mind that, although the alternating bass will be simplified to single notes on the lowest string of the chord, they aren't necessarily played that precisely.)

Additionally, Merle would add treble notes, played in various rhythms.

TRACK 22 0:05 **EXAMPLE 2**

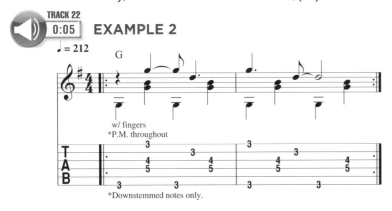

When you apply the aforementioned ideas to a full chord progression, you get that classic Merle Travis sound.

EXAMPLE 3

w/ fingers
*P.M. throughout

*Downstemmed notes only.

The "Boom-A-Chick-A" Pattern

Another pattern that Merle used quite a bit is what I like to call the "boom-a-chick-a" pattern, which is comprised of straight 8th notes. On a G chord, the basic pattern looks like this:

EXAMPLE 4

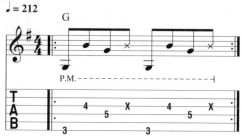

Merle liked to run that idea up or down the scale, sometimes incorporating passing diminished chords.

EXAMPLE 5

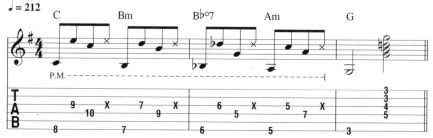

Banjo Rolls

Finally, another Merle classic is the banjo roll, which normally consisted of ascending three-note patterns. Merle would drag the thumbpick across the bottom two strings and use his index for the top note. You don't have to do it that way, though.

EXAMPLE 6

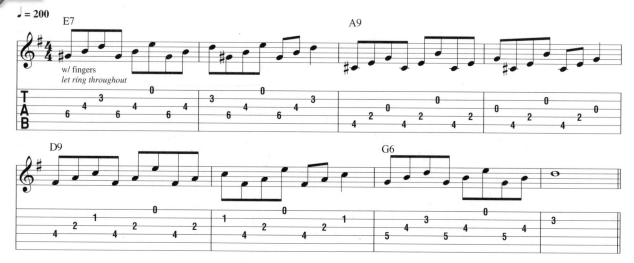

w/ fingers
let ring throughout

If you've avoided the fingerstyle technique but would like to achieve a similar sound without dropping your pick, it's time to check out hybrid picking. This technique allows you to seamlessly move from strumming to fingerstyle-like playing and it's something that you can employ equally well on an electric. So let's check out what hybrid picking is all about.

The Basic Idea

The term hybrid picking refers to the use of both the pick and the fingers of your picking hand. Generally speaking, the pick would handle the lower strings, while the fingers would pluck notes on the higher strings. With this technique, a good, basic starting position is to place your pick on string 5 or string 4 and your middle and ring fingers on strings 3 and 2, respectively.

This technique consists of two basic approaches: the block-chord style and the arpeggio style. In the block-chord style, all the notes are struck at once, similar to a piano.

EXERCISE 1

In the arpeggio style, the pick and fingers are used independently to play through the chord, one note at a time.

EXERCISE 2

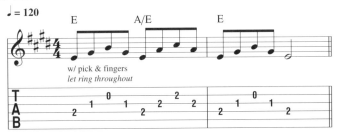

Exceptions to Every Rule

Exceptions do exist, however. For example, we can play in a block-chord style, but occasionally separate the bass and chord notes as in the following example.

EXERCISE 3

Or we can play in an arpeggio style but occasionally "pinch" a bass and treble note together.

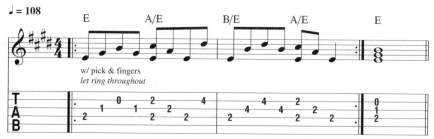

Examples

Now let's check out a few more practical examples to see what we can do with this technique. This first one is a bluesy lick in the key of E that uses the pick on string 4, while the fingers handle all the notes on top.

Next is an example of what the Travis-picking technique sounds like with hybrid picking. The pick alternates between strings 5 and 4 for the Bm and D/A chords and strings 6 and 4 for the Gmaj7 chord. The fingers handle the notes on strings 3–1.

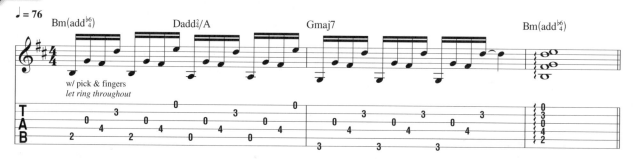

Our final example is a nice groove in in the key of G that's assisted by percussive backbeats, which are created by forcefully planting your pick hand onto the strings on beats 2 and 4. The pick jumps between strings 6 and 4 in this one, while the fingers remain on strings 3 and 2 throughout.

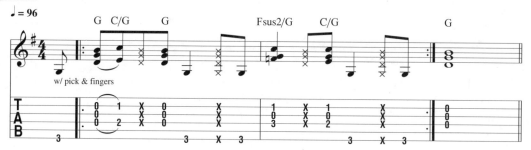

Have fun with this technique; it's extremely versatile and can add a whole new dimension to your playing. Country and jazz players use it extensively, as do a good deal of rock players. Happy pickin'!

LESSON #25: NATURAL HARMONICS

Harmonics have fascinated guitarists for generations, and it's no wonder—there's brilliance to their tone and their mechanics seem a bit magical. Although different types of harmonics exist, in this lesson we'll examine the most basic form: natural harmonics.

How They Work

Natural harmonics normally are the first type learned on the guitar, as they sound great and are easy to master. To play a natural harmonic, you touch the string (but don't push it down to the fretboard) at specific points called nodes, pluck the string, and then quickly remove your finger. You can touch the string at different locations to produce different pitches. The most important point to remember is that you should touch the string *directly over the fretwire*—not slightly behind it, as in normal fretting technique—for the clearest tone.

The 12th-fret natural harmonic is the lowest-pitched harmonic that you can produce on a given string (any other natural harmonic produced on that string will be higher in pitch). The science of natural harmonics is beyond the scope of this lesson, but the short story is that the available harmonic nodes on any string follow the harmonic series. A quick online search should shed some light on this subject.

FRET OF HARMONIC	PITCH PRODUCED
12	One octave higher
7	One octave plus a 5th higher
5	Two octaves higher
4	Two octaves plus a major 3rd higher

Examples

The following examples demonstrate what natural harmonics can do. This first example, a fingerstyle arrangement in the key of E minor, features haunting harmonics that are played at the 5th, 7th, and 12th frets on top of a monotonic quarter-note bass line.

EXAMPLE 1

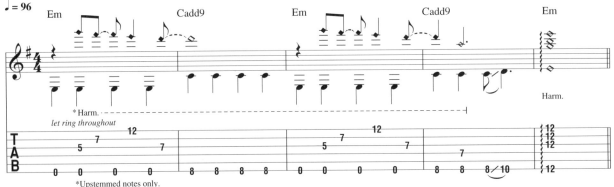

Below is a happy, little melody that uses 7th- and 12th-fret harmonics.

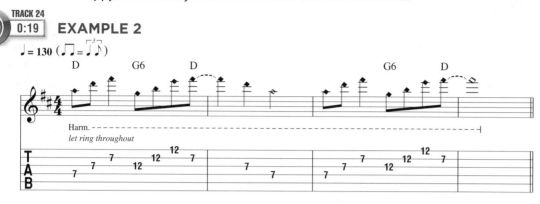

This next example is kind of funky and features some chunky low chords, which are contrasted by a surprise harmonic chord. To add another element, a little bass line is played under the harmonics on string 6.

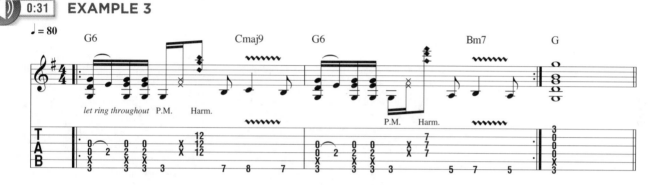

In this final example, I've tuned my low-E and A strings down a whole step to D and G, respectively. So the tuning is, low to high, D–G–D–G–B–E. The result is similar to Open G tuning, and this example would work in that tuning. But since I don't use string 1 at all, I didn't bother to tune it down. The chord progression is Travis-picked throughout, using 12th-fret harmonics on top and changing bass notes on the bottom. Notice that the bass notes are created by a mixture of fretted notes and harmonics.

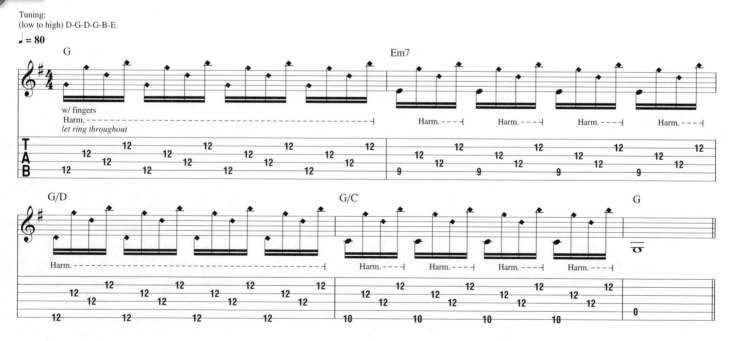

You can find harmonics gracing the riffs of countless classic recordings, including Yes' "Roundabout," the Rolling Stones' "Wild Horses," and the Black Crowes' "She Talks to Angels." Experiment with natural harmonics and have fun applying them to your own style.

LESSON #26: HARP HARMONICS

If you've ever listened to Chet Atkins in his early days, you know that he had a million tricks up his sleeve. One of the most ear-catching tricks was his use of artificial harmonics. An artificial harmonic is basically any harmonic that is not a natural harmonic. In other words, an artificial harmonic deals with a fretted note, thereby requiring the harmonic to be created "artificially." And perhaps the ultimate application of this technique is the harp harmonic, which is the subject of this lesson.

First Thing's First

Before you can play harp harmonics, you need to know how to play artificial harmonics. Although artificial harmonics can be played numerous ways, we'll focus on the way that they'll be used with the harp technique.

To perform an artificial harmonic, begin by fretting a note normally—preferably, around the 5th or 7th fret. Next, with your pick hand's index finger, lightly touch the string 12 frets higher than the fretted note. Remember, as with a natural harmonic, you want to touch the string directly over the metal fretwire. Finally, pluck the string with either the pick hand's ring finger or with the pick, which is held between the thumb and middle finger.

You should hear a chiming note that's one octave above the fretted pitch.

TRACK 25
0:00 **EXAMPLE 1**

PLUCKING WITH PICK

PLUCKING WITH FINGER

Now that you know how to perform artificial harmonics, let's get down to business.

The Basic Idea

To perform harp harmonics, you barre a fret and then skip strings with the plucking hand, alternating a normal, fretted note with an artificial harmonic. For example, you could pluck the fourth string normally and then play an artificial harmonic on the sixth string. Then you could pluck the third string normally, followed by an artificial harmonic on the fifth string, etc.

This technique typically is performed without a pick (or with a thumbpick). The artificial harmonic is produced by plucking with the thumb (while the index finger touches the harmonic spot, or "node"), and the higher strings are typically plucked with the ring finger.

Here's how the basic idea sounds with a barred 5th fret:

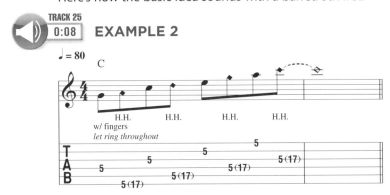

TRACK 25
0:08 **EXAMPLE 2**

You also can apply this technique to extended chords to create lush sounds. By adding a two-note, 7th-fret barre to our 5th-fret shape, we can create an Am13 sound.

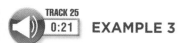

EXAMPLE 3

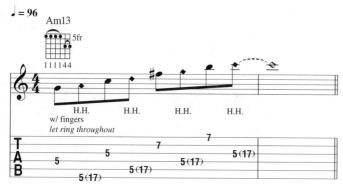

And below is a nice E13 chord. Here, I'm fretting both the fifth and sixth string with my middle finger.

EXAMPLE 4

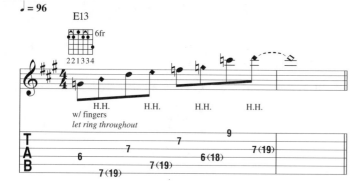

Adding Slurs

To take harp harmonics to another level, you can add hammer-ons and pull-offs to some of the normally picked notes to create connecting tones. Seven-note scales can be played this way. Here's a C major scale in fifth position:

EXAMPLE 5

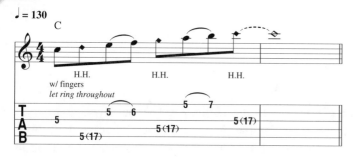

Or you can play short repetitive licks, like this B♭ dominant one:

EXAMPLE 6

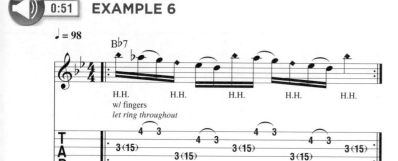

LESSON #27: SLAP HARMONICS

If you've ever heard the late, great acoustic virtuoso Michael Hedges, then you're probably familiar with the slap-harmonic technique. He had mastered it—along with just about every other acoustic technique—to the point of making it sound effortless. Slap harmonics offer a great sound that can really turn heads, and they look impressive too, which is always nice. So without further ado, let's talk about slap harmonics.

The Basic Idea

When we slap a harmonic, we're playing an artificial harmonic. An artificial harmonic is basically any harmonic that is not a natural harmonic. In other words, an artificial harmonic deals with a fretted note, thereby requiring the harmonic to be created "artificially." To hear how an artificial harmonic sounds as a single note, do the following:

1. Fret the C note on fret 5 of string 3 with your index finger.

2. Lay the other three fingers of your fret hand across the neck, lightly touching the strings. You should be touching all the strings, except for the one that you're fretting, so only the third string will ring out.

3. Now, quickly and forcefully slap the string directly above the fretwire of the 17th fret (12 frets above the fretted note) and quickly remove your finger, as if the string were a hot stove.

TRACK 26 0:00 **EXAMPLE 1**

You should hear a C note that's one octave above the one that you're fretting. To get the precision down, this technique may take a bit of practice. The fret hand should make the technique easier to perform though, by muting all but the string that you want to articulate.

Playing Melodies

Once you get the hang of slap harmonics, you can play entire melodies with this technique. The lower your fret hand is on the neck, the easier it will be to make the harmonics ring out. Conversely, slap harmonics are more difficult to perform on the higher strings. Try to be consistent with your fret-hand muting so that only one string rings out. This first example pecks out an A minor pentatonic melody.

TRACK 26 0:08 **EXAMPLE 2**

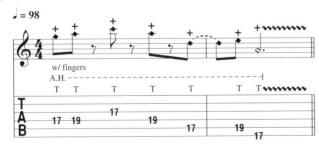

Here's a quirky line that moves from G7 to C:

TRACK 26 0:18 **EXAMPLE 3**

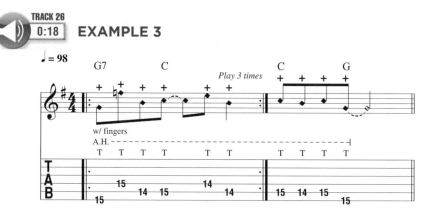

Playing Full Chords

This technique can also be used on full chords. Obviously, because we have only a straight finger with which to slap, we're unable to get every note of every chord to sound clearly. However, we can get pretty close on many chords.

TRACK 26 0:33 **EXAMPLE 4**

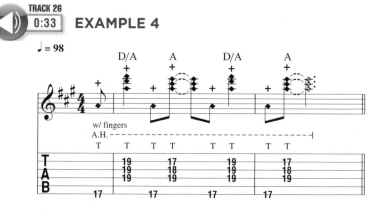

TRACK 26 0:42 **EXAMPLE 5**

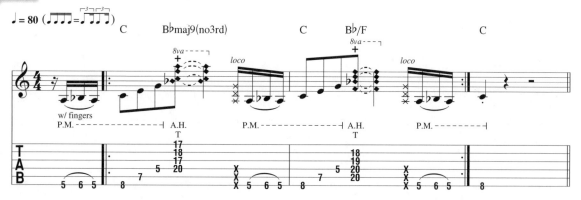

I would be remiss if I didn't mention that this technique is often used with alternate tunings in the fingerstyle world, which can create some truly awesome sounds. Slap harmonics are a lot of fun to play around with, so experiment. As mentioned earlier, Michael Hedges was "the man" when it came to this technique. To hear it mastered on electric guitar, check out Eric Johnson.

LESSON #28: STRING STOPPING

As you progress in your fingerstyle studies, you'll no doubt want to add new techniques to your arsenal to further increase your expressiveness and clarity. One such technique that should not be overlooked is string stopping. The first person I heard use this technique was the great acoustic virtuoso Michael Hedges and it really opened my eyes to a whole other world of attention to detail. If you've never tried it, string stopping may feel weird at first, but the results are well worth the effort. Once it's mastered, you'll gain much more control over your sound.

The Basic Idea

With string stopping, your pick-hand fingers will not only pluck the strings at the appropriate time, they will also stop them from ringing when needed. When performed properly, this technique really can add clarity to your melodies.

Let's look at a basic example that uses a C chord. First, we'll play the phrase without using the string-stopping technique. Be sure to follow the pick-hand fingerings, indicated between the notation and tab staves.

TRACK 27 0:00 **EXERCISE 1**

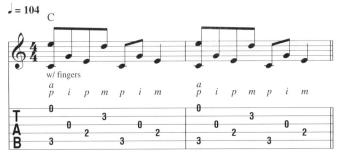

Now let's try it with string stopping. In the following phrase, we'll need to stop only one note—the open high-E string. As we play the D note on string 2 with the middle (*m*) finger, we'll simultaneously plant the ring (*a*) finger on string 1 to stop it from ringing. Listen to the difference string stopping makes. Stopped strings are indicated in the notation and tab staves as parenthetical "X" notes.

TRACK 27 0:10 **EXERCISE 2**

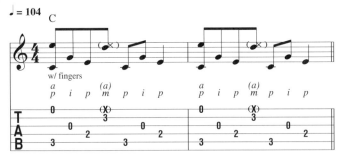

String stopping is not something that'll hit you over the head but, when it's not present, it's definitely something that you miss.

Examples

To really hear what you can do with string stopping, let's check out a few lengthier examples. The first one is in the key of A and uses the same concept as our previous exercise: the open E string as a melody note for each chord, stopped when a new melody note sounds on the B string.

EXAMPLE 1

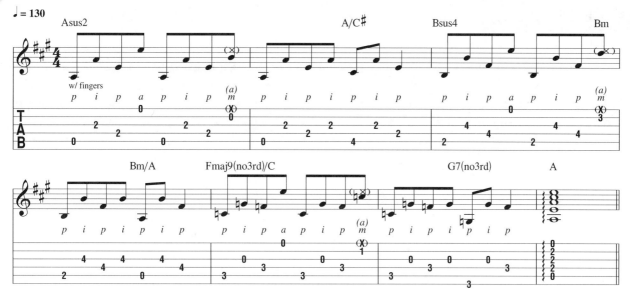

Below is a bit of a longer example in the key of G that shows just how much care can go into the melody when you're aware of the string-stopping concept. In several spots, you'll need to stop a string immediately following a melody note. Take this example slowly and closely observe the pick-hand fingerings.

EXAMPLE 2

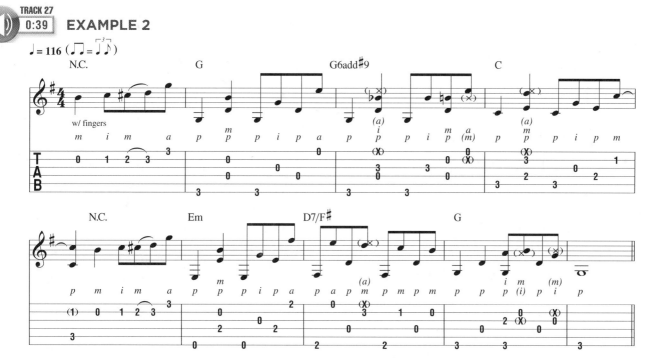

To the Extreme

You can take this idea to the extreme by using it on every note of an arpeggio pattern. Although this approach will take a good bit of practice, the result is ear-opening; it almost sounds computer-generated when done properly (but in a good way!). Take the example very slowly at first, synchronizing the stopping of each note with the beginning of the next one.

EXAMPLE 3

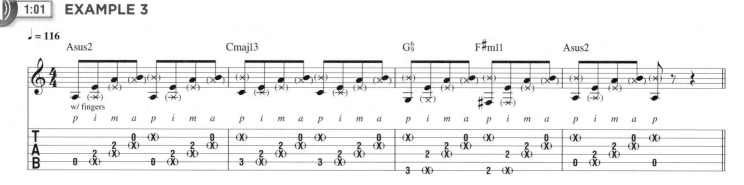

THE BASICS OF ALTERNATE TUNINGS

Alternate tunings have a rich and diverse history. The great bluesmen of the past made extensive use of numerous open tunings. Keith Richards and Jimmy Page carried the torch through the sixties and seventies, and solo acoustic virtuosos like Michael Hedges continued to explore their possibilities in the eighties and beyond. In that same spirit, let's explore the basics of alternate tunings and expand our horizons.

What Is an Alternate Tuning?

An alternate tuning is created when one or more strings are tuned to notes that differ from standard tuning (E–A–D–G–B–E). Obviously, the architecture of the fretboard changes when alternate tunings are introduced, which is the bad news. The good news is that you'll be able to access fresh new sounds that are inaccessible in standard tuning.

Drop D Tuning (D-A-D-G-B-E)

Drop D tuning, perhaps the most common alternate tuning, involves the retuning of only one note. In Drop D, the sixth string is tuned down a whole step, to D.

Drop D tuning is a great way to get started because, for the most part, your guitar fretboard doesn't change. Let's hear a couple examples of what you can do with this tuning.

TRACK 28 0:00 **EXAMPLE 1**

Here's why fingerstyle players like Drop D: those droning octave bass notes.

TRACK 28 0:13 **EXAMPLE 2**

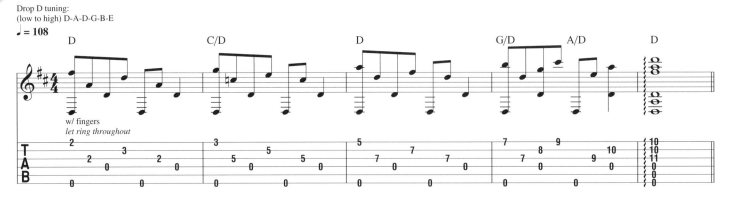

Double Drop D Tuning (D-A-D-G-B-D)

The next logical step from Drop D is Double Drop D, in which the high E string is also tuned down to D. Although the latter begins to complicate the fretboard a bit more, we can still play a good deal of familiar material.

In the following example, we're using the high open-D string to create a lush Dmaj9 (no 3rd) harmony—impossible in standard tuning.

TRACK 28 0:29 **EXAMPLE 3**

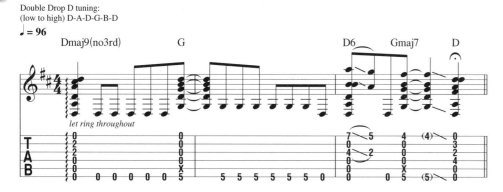

DADGAD Tuning (D-A-D-G-A-D)

The name of this tuning literally gives you the notes: D–A–D–G–A–D. From Double Drop D tuning, you only need to lower the second string down a whole step to A.

DADGAD is popular among fingerstylists but has also made numerous appearances in the rock world—notably in the Led Zeppelin classic "Kashmir." The presence of an interval of a 2nd between strings 3 and 2 really adds a lot of possibilities for unique sounds. For one, it makes a ringing F♯–G–A melody readily accessible, as seen in the following example.

TRACK 28 0:46 **EXAMPLE 4**

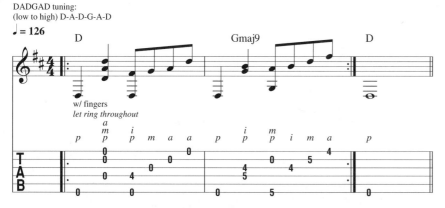

In this final example, we take advantage of the tuning's multiple open-D and open-A string drones, moving dyads along strings 3 and 4 while the open sixth, fifth, second, and first strings ring out.

TRACK 28 1:02 **EXAMPLE 5**

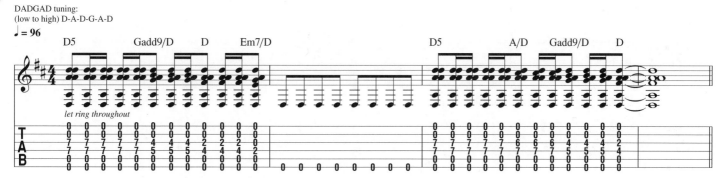

LESSON #30: DROP D TUNING

If you've never messed around in Drop D tuning, be warned: the hours can quickly get away from you. After pounding out a full, six-string open D chord for half an hour just because it sounds so good, you're likely to get seduced by the extra girth in your tone that results from the slackened sixth string. This tuning has been used by everyone from Delta bluesmen to Jimmy Page to Kurt Cobain. Needless to say, Drop D tuning is a whole lot of fun and can produce some inspiring sounds. So let's get our feet wet and check out Drop D tuning.

A Low-Maintenance Tuning

As far as alternate tunings go, you really can't get any easier than Drop D, which requires you to simply tune your low-E string down a whole step to D. If you don't have a chromatic tuner on hand, you can get pretty close by simply tuning the low-E string to an octave below your open fourth string (D).

Drop D tuning: D–A–D–G–B–E

That's it—you're in Drop D!

Feel the Power

The first thing that you'll likely notice is the power that you've gained in the bottom end. Now you can fret a basic D chord and strum through all six strings to get a huge sound. Go on… try it.

You'll also notice that, in this tuning, you can play power chords with one finger, which can sound nice and thick on the acoustic. Check out this example:

EXAMPLE 1

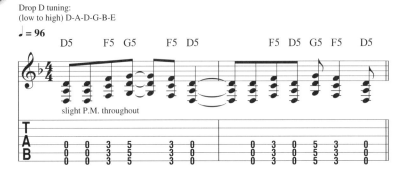

Exploiting the Octaves

Fingerstyle players love this tuning because it enables them to alternate octave bass notes without fretting. Consequently, you can create a droning bass and still have all four fingers available to play melodies on top.

EXAMPLE 2

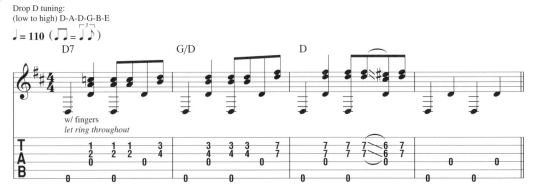

Here's a blues ditty that pairs a single-note melody on top with droning octaves in the bass:

 TRACK 29 0:25 **EXAMPLE 3**

And, if you do want to change chords, you can barre with your index finger and still access octave bass notes, leaving three fingers free for mischief on top.

 TRACK 29 0:48 **EXAMPLE 4**

This final example is in the key of D minor. A tricky position shift occurs at the end of beat 2 of measure 2, where you must shift with your index finger from a 5th-fret barre to the G note at fret 10 of string 2 in the space of a 16th note.

 TRACK 29 1:12 **EXAMPLE 5**

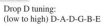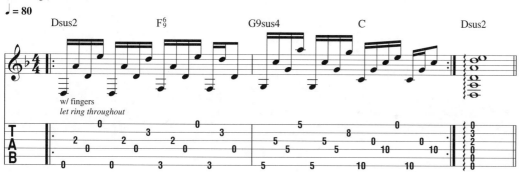

You'll hear Drop D tuning everywhere, from classical guitar to the most extreme death metal. Be sure to spend some time with it—you'll be glad you did!

DOUBLE DROP D TUNING

If you've dabbled in Drop D tuning, perhaps it's time to take the next step. Double Drop D tuning can open up even more possibilities for fresh sounds, without significantly altering the fretboard's architecture and causing strain to the left brain. So grab a frosty beverage, and let's take a closer look at Double Drop D tuning and what we can do with it.

A Logical Progression

Many players have fooled around with Drop D tuning (D–A–D–G–B–E), and Double Drop D is the logical next step. With Double Drop D, we tune both E strings (6 and 1) down a whole step to D. If you don't have a tuner, you can get there quickly by matching those strings to the pitch of your open D (fourth) string (though an octave below and above, obviously).

Double Drop D Tuning: D–A–D–G–B–D

Two Halves

Double Drop D is an interesting tuning because, if you play the bottom three strings open, they form a D5 chord. However, if you play the top four strings open, they form a G chord. You can exploit this fact to get some interesting sounds with little effort.

TRACK 30 `0:00` **EXAMPLE 1**

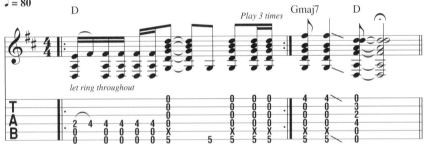

Unison Drones

Another attractive aspect of this tuning is the fact that you have three D strings in different octaves. By allowing these three strings to ring out among other fretted notes, you can create some colorful harmonies.

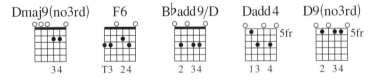

Let's check out some of those ideas in action. This first example moves a single shape down the fretboard three times to create an ear-opening chord progression.

TRACK 30 `0:23` **EXAMPLE 2**

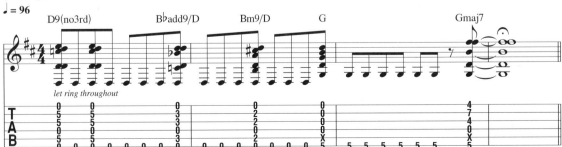

This example starts out kind of bluesy and gritty and works its way up the neck to finish off with a lush Cmaj9 chord.

EXAMPLE 3

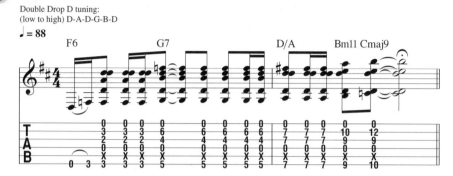

Fingerstyle Examples

Double Drop D tuning is also popular in the fingerstyle realm. The sixth and fourth strings enable you to keep an open bass drone going and the open high-D string enables you to access melodies that wouldn't be possible—or at least not practical—in standard tuning. In the following example, we're using the open high-D string to color the melody in a distinct way.

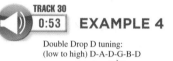

EXAMPLE 4

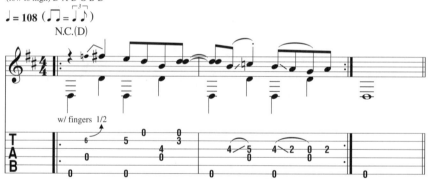

In this D minor example, we exploit some great minor-2nd rubs on the top two strings, made more accessible by the tuning:

EXAMPLE 5

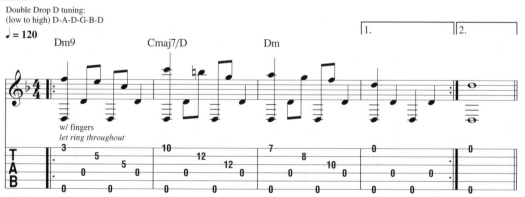

You can spend a lot of time experimenting with Double Drop D tuning and constantly come up with fresh ideas. The tuning is quick and easy to achieve and it sounds great. Enjoy!

LESSON #32: DADGAD TUNING

From Jimmy Page to Michael Hedges to Stephen Stills to Pierre Bensusan, DADGAD tuning has captivated guitarists for decades. In this lesson, we're going to examine some of its compelling qualities, and you'll learn some great-sounding riffs in the process. So loosen up those tuning pegs and let's get into DADGAD!

The Name Says It All

"DADGAD" literally spells out the tuning of the guitar's strings, from low to high. DADGAD requires you to tune your sixth, second, and first strings down a whole step.

DADGAD tuning: D–A–D–G–A–D

Dsus4

DADGAD is an alluring tuning that's extremely popular in the fingerstyle genre. The interval of a 2nd between strings 3 and 2 really adds a lot of possibilities for unique sounds. If you just strum all the open strings, you get a cool-sounding Dsus4 chord.

Let's check out some other interesting chords that you can generate with DADGAD tuning, chords that otherwise would be impossible or, at the very least, extremely difficult in standard tuning.

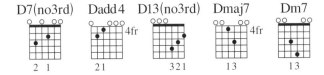

Examples

Now let's check out some examples to see what we can do with this tuning. Below is a mellow strumming example that moves a major seventh form down from D to C, adding a bit of variation on the C form. Check out the nice, big Cmaj9/D voicing at the end—definitely not possible in standard tuning.

TRACK 31
0:00 **EXAMPLE 1**

Next is a strummer that's inspired by the Goo Goo Dolls.

EXAMPLE 2

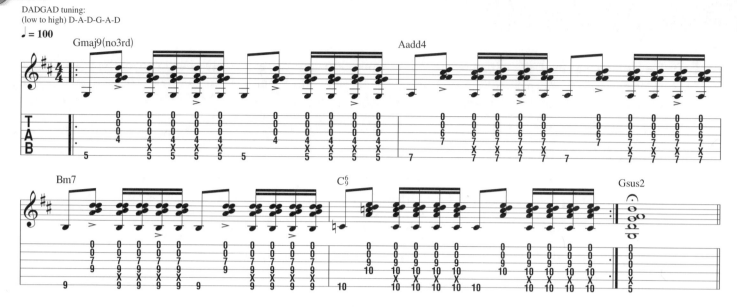

Here's a pretty fingerstyle example that uses the open high-A and G strings to create a descending scalar run (A–G–F#) that rings together:

EXAMPLE 3

And just because you have that honkin' low D string doesn't mean you have to use it. Here's an example that is played entirely on the top four strings and, like Example 3, uses the open high-A string to create a rolling phrase:

EXAMPLE 4

The more you mess with DADGAD tuning, the more you discover its magic. The tuning is subtle, but it can really generate some hauntingly beautiful sounds. Have fun with it and try to come up with your own DADGAD riffs.

OPEN G TUNING

From the bluesmen of the Delta to the Rolling Stones, Open G tuning has seen plenty of action over the years. The tuning not only enables you to play a chord (G major) with absolutely no fretting required, but also facilitates easy, one-finger barre chords anywhere on the neck. In this lesson, we'll talk about the ins and outs of Open G tuning and explore some cool riffs.

The Great Wide Open

To access Open G tuning from standard tuning, you'll need to detune your sixth, fifth, and first strings down a whole step, which is a relatively easy matter even without a tuner, because other open strings on the guitar match these pitches. .

▶ Tune your sixth string down a whole step so that it's an octave lower than your open fourth string.

▶ Tune your first string down a whole step so that it's an octave higher than your open fourth string.

▶ Tune your fifth string down a whole step so that it's an octave lower than your open third string.

For pitch stability, be sure to overshoot the mark, detuning below the destination pitch before reversing course and raising the string's pitch to hit your target.

Open G Tuning: D–G–D–G–B–D

It should be noted that the intervallic structure of this tuning is identical to Open A tuning. The only difference is that Open A tuning will sound a whole step higher. Consequently, any licks that you know in Open G will work in Open A as well, and vice versa.

Common Chord Shapes

Let's take a look at some chord voicings—both open-position and moveable forms—that are common in Open G tuning.

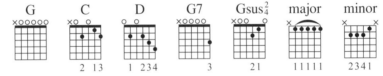

And below are a few voicings that aren't quite as common, but still illustrate the colorful possibilities that exist.

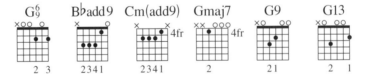

Examples

Now that you're familiar with the basics, let's check out what this tuning can do. Here's a classic rock take à la the Stones or John Mellencamp:

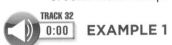

EXAMPLE 1

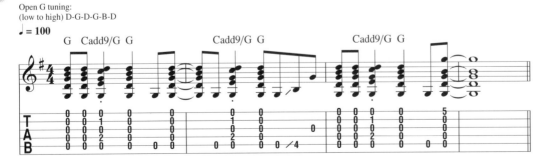

This example is more mellow and in the style of singer/songwriters like Joni Mitchell or the Indigo Girls.

EXAMPLE 2

The following example uses an arpeggio pattern and melodic movement on the D string to create a Black Crowes-inspired riff.

EXAMPLE 3

And, finally, here's a 6/8 romp that uses octaves on strings 4 and 1 to create a colorful melody among droning open strings:

EXAMPLE 4

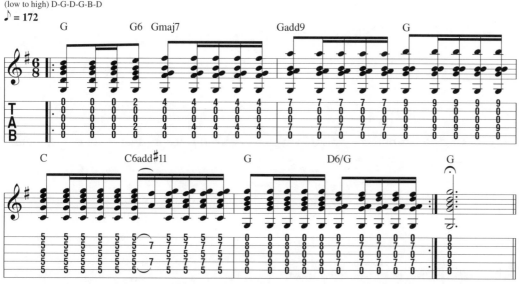

When you get a chance, take some time to really dig in to this tuning; it's a lot of fun and, in some cases, the only way to pull off some of the most classic riffs of all time. Open G tuning is quite often used in slide playing as well, but that's the subject of an entirely different lesson. Enjoy!

LESSON #34: OPEN D TUNING

Though not quite as common as Open G, Open D tuning has seen its fair share of use throughout the years as well. Open D shows up in the work of many Delta bluesmen and many slide players prefer it (or its sister tuning, Open E) for their bottleneck statements. Open D is a powerful tuning that often exploits the slackened sixth string, giving it a unique quality. In this lesson, we'll explore the structure of Open D tuning to see what we can do with it.

Open for Business

Open D tuning is so named because, when you strum all six strings, you get a D chord. From standard tuning, you'll need to retune four of your six strings: the sixth, third, second, and first.

▶ Tune your sixth string down a whole step so that it's an octave lower than your open fourth string.

▶ Tune your first string down a whole step so that it's an octave higher than your open fourth string.

▶ Tune your second string down a whole step so that it's an octave higher than your fifth string.

▶ Tune your third string down a half step so that it matches the pitch of the 4th fret of your fourth string.

For pitch stability, be sure to overshoot the mark, detuning below the destination pitch before reversing course and raising the string's pitch to hit your target.

Open D Tuning: D–A–D–F♯–A–D

It should be noted that the intervallic structure of this tuning is identical to Open E tuning. The only difference is that Open E tuning will sound a whole step higher. Consequently, any licks that you know in Open D will work in Open E as well, and vice versa.

Common Chord Shapes

Let's take a look at some chord voicings—both open-position and moveable forms—that are common in Open D tuning.

And here are a few voicings that aren't quite as common, but still illustrate the colorful possibilities that exist.

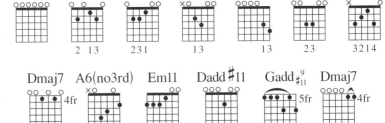

Examples

Now that you're familiar with the basics, let's check out what this tuning can do. Moving a chord shape along the inner strings while letting the outer open strings drone always produces some nice sounds.

EXAMPLE 1

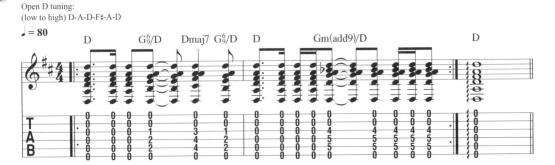

In the following riff, we're moving octave shapes along strings 4 and 1 while all the other open strings drone. The octaves make the melody sound big and majestic.

TRACK 33
0:23 **EXAMPLE 2**

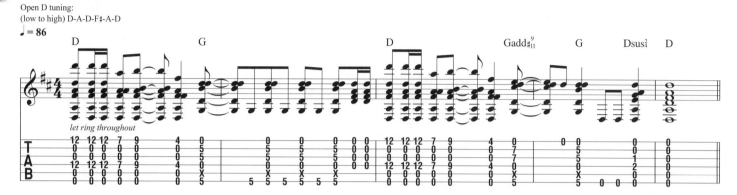

Here's a fingerstyle blues riff that maintains an alternating bass line played as octaves while a melody is performed on top:

TRACK 33
0:44 **EXAMPLE 3**

In this final example, we let the tuning do the work for us. Aside from the Gm chord, we're simply moving a first-finger barre-chord shape along the top four strings to create various harmonies above the open low-D string. To add a bit of interest, a few of the harmonies are anticipated by an 8th note.

TRACK 33
1:00 **EXAMPLE 4**

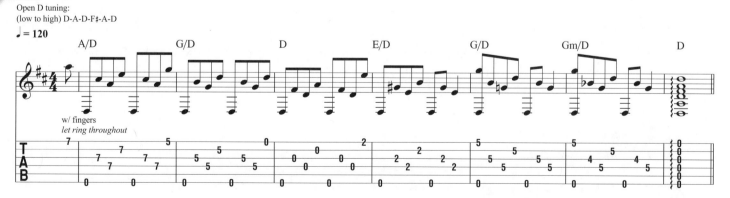

Open D is a great, full-sounding tuning that's a lot of fun to play in. That big, fat low-D string sounds really great on acoustic and the multiple open-D strings provide great opportunity for some easy octave phrases. Have fun exploring the possibilities.

LESSON #35: SLIDE RIFFS IN OPEN G TUNING

If you've never heard Robert Johnson, you need to! Though he played in numerous tunings, many of his classic slide songs used Open G tuning, and for good reason. This tuning makes so many classic slide licks and riffs lay out nicely along the neck. Even if you play the same notes with a slide in standard tuning, it's not quite the same. The resonance, the open-string possibilities, and the sound of the slackened strings all play a role in why slide riffs in Open G tuning sound so good.

DISCLAIMER

This lesson assumes that you're familiar with basic slide technique. If not, you should consult some instructional material before tackling the material here. If you insist on plugging on, please remember the following:

▶ For proper intonation, align the slide directly above the fretwire;

▶ Allow the fingers behind the slide to lightly touch the strings to help keep them quiet;

▶ The fingers of the plucking hand often mute strings that aren't being played, thereby keeping them quiet.

First Thing's First

First, we need to get into Open G tuning. To access it from standard tuning, you'll need to detune your sixth, fifth, and first strings down a whole step. If you don't have a tuner handy, here's a quick method to use:

▶ Tune your sixth string down a whole step so that it's an octave lower than your open fourth string.

▶ Tune your first string down a whole step so that it's an octave higher than your open fourth string.

▶ Tune your fifth string down a whole step so that it's an octave lower than your open third string.

Open G Tuning: D–G–D–G–B–D

It should be noted that the intervallic structure of this tuning is identical to Open A tuning—another popular slide tuning. The only difference is that Open A tuning will sound a whole step higher. Consequently, any licks that you know in Open G will work in Open A as well, and vice versa.

Common I, IV, and V Chord Shapes

Obviously, one of the most common applications for slide guitar in Open G tuning is a blues in G. Therefore, let's take a quick look at some common voicings within which to frame your slide licks.

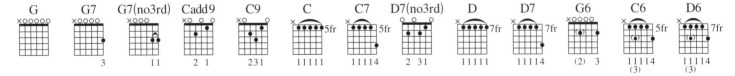

Examples

Below is a classic blues phrase that makes use of sliding double stops. Note that, although the C♯ note (fret 2, string 2) is out of key (it's the ♭5th), it still sounds great.

TRACK 34 0:00 **EXAMPLE 1**

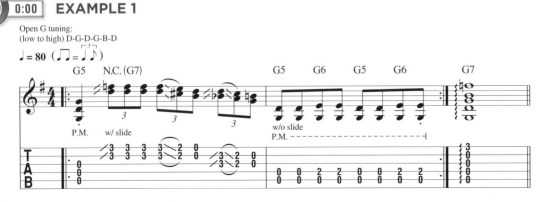

This next example is another Delta classic that works great as an intro. Notice the prevalence of half-step slides, which are actually more common in blues than whole-step slides.

EXAMPLE 2

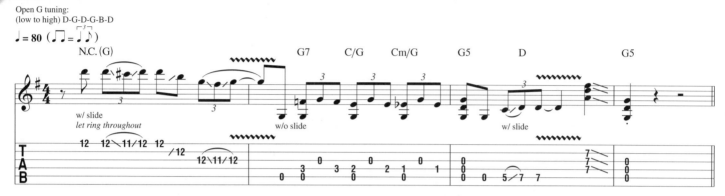

Though the following example borrows heavily from Delta blues, its technique is a bit more modern. On beat 4 of measure 1, you'll need to mute the B♭ note on string 1 by planting a pick-hand finger on it as you pick the E note on string 3. That way, the slide can keep on moving up the fretboard smoothly, without obscuring the melody as it moves from B♭ down to E.

EXAMPLE 3

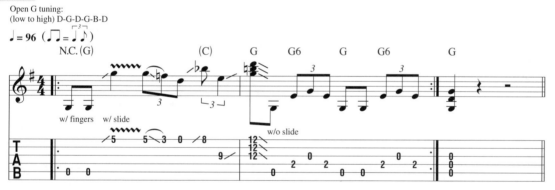

We'll close out this lesson with another example that is based on a classic Robert Johnson Delta move. You simply can't get any more soulful than Robert!

EXAMPLE 4

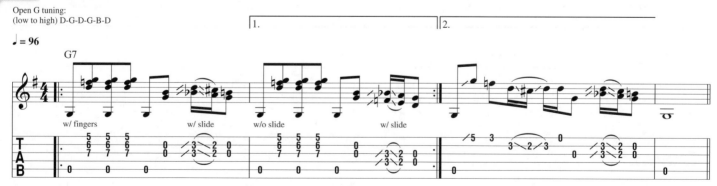

Again, with respect to Open G tuning, the man to check out is Robert Johnson, as well as Son House. For more modern examples, check out Bonnie Raitt, the Rolling Stones, and the Black Crowes, among others.

LESSON #36: SLIDE RIFFS IN OPEN D TUNING

If you've ever heard the brilliant slide playing of Duane Allman or, more recently, the virtuosic Derek Trucks, you've heard what Open D or Open E tuning can do with regard to slide. In this lesson, we'll look at the workings of Open D tuning to see what you can do with it slide-style.

Note: Be aware that the intervallic structure of this tuning is identical to Open E tuning—another popular slide tuning. The only difference is that Open E tuning will sound a whole step higher. Consequently, any licks that you know in Open D will work in Open E as well, and vice versa.

DISCLAIMER

This lesson assumes that you're familiar with basic slide technique. If not, you should consult some instructional material before tackling the material here. If you insist on plugging on, please remember the following:

▶ For proper intonation, align the slide directly above the fretwire;

▶ Allow the fingers behind the slide to lightly touch the strings to help keep them quiet;

▶ The fingers of the plucking hand often mute strings that aren't being played, thereby keeping them quiet.

First Thing's First

First, we need to get into Open D tuning. From standard tuning, you'll need to retune four of your six strings: the sixth, third, second, and first.

▶ Tune your sixth string down a whole step so that it's an octave lower than your open fourth string.

▶ Tune your first string down a whole step so that it's an octave higher than your open fourth string.

▶ Tune your second string down a whole step so that it's an octave higher than your open fifth string.

▶ Tune your third string down a half step so that it matches the pitch of the 4th fret of your fourth string.

For pitch stability, be sure to overshoot the mark, detuning below the destination pitch before reversing course and raising the string's pitch to hit your target.

Open D Tuning: D–A–D–F♯–A–D

Common I, IV, and V Chord Shapes

Obviously, one of the most common applications for slide guitar in Open D tuning is a blues in D. Therefore, let's take a quick look at some common voicings within which to frame your slide licks.

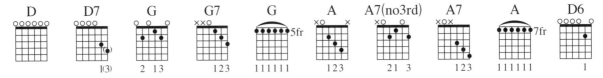

Examples

OK, now let's get to the licks. The first one uses the "3rd-fret trick"—a nice feature of this tuning that is kind of like playing Open G licks, but one string lower. First is a nice rhythm groove that can be used independently or as the backbone between other licks.

EXAMPLE 1

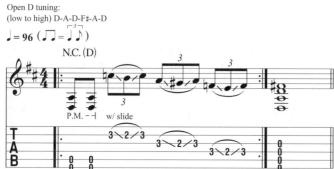

EXAMPLE 2

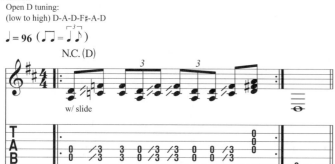

This next example commences in measure 9 of a 12-bar form, where the V (A) chord is introduced. Here a classic chromatic descent is used to move from the V chord to the IV (G) chord.

EXAMPLE 3

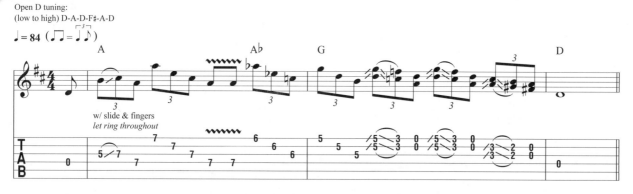

In this last example, we're starting from the IV chord in measure 10 before playing through a chromatic turnaround figure on the top three strings.

EXAMPLE 4

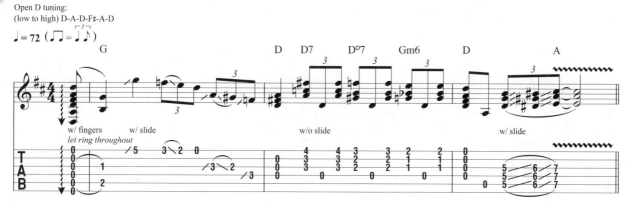

BLUEGRASS LICKS IN THE KEY OF C

The sound of a great bluegrass picker (Doc Watson, Tony Rice, etc.) tearin' it up is hard to beat. The bluegrass style is its own thing, really, and it takes a different coordination altogether to play really fast licks in open position, compared to moveable scale forms. In this lesson, we'll take a look at some classic bluegrass licks in the key of C and, in the process, have a little fun.*

Knee-slappin' is optional.

The Basic Idea

Bluegrass licks are usually played with a flatpick, which is another name for a standard plectrum (the term "flatpick" differentiates it from a thumbpick, which used to be much more popular). In the bluegrass style, open strings are part of the sound, so most of the licks are played in open position. That is not to say that bluegrass players never venture into the upper frets; it just means that, if a phrase can be played in open position, it usually is.

Also, with regard to picking, bluegrass is almost always played with alternate picking, as opposed to economy picking. Of course, that's not a law or anything…

Let's start off by ascending and descending an open-position C major scale to get a feel for it.

TRACK 36
0:00 EXERCISE 1

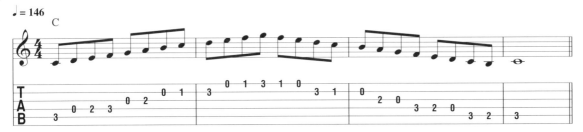

Try to minimize the picking motion as much as possible. Bluegrass is often played at breakneck tempos and your picking skills will definitely be put to the test!

Now let's try the same scale run, this time using legato technique (i.e., hammer-ons and pull-offs). Although picking every note is a little more common, legato is certainly used. Notice that hammering on from and pulling off to open strings feels a little different than doing so with two fretted notes.

TRACK 36
0:11 EXERCISE 2

Licks

OK, now that you have a basic feel for playing open-position scales, let's check out some licks in the key of C. This first one uses a sequence that's transferred down through the scale before finishing off with a short run straight through the scale.

TRACK 36
0:21 LICK 1

Below is an idea that moves from a G7 chord to a C chord. We're arpeggiating notes of the G chord (with a few additional notes) in an angular fashion, which makes the lick a bit unpredictable. Take this one slowly until you get the picking under control.

TRACK 36
0:27 **LICK 2**

Adding Chromatic Notes

Chromatic notes often are employed to give lines a slightly bluesy touch. Common additions are the ♭3rd and the ♭5th—E♭ and G♭ in the key of C. This lick features both of them:

TRACK 36
0:32 **LICK 3**

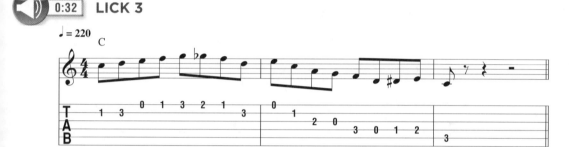

Here's a nice ending lick that features a downward jump from the 6th (A) to the ♭3rd (E♭):

TRACK 36
0:38 **LICK 4**

Beyond Open Position

In this final lick, we begin in eighth position with a moveable C major version of the Lester Flatt run. After reaching the high C note, we use the open E string to shift positions for the final descending phrase. The end result is a lick that spans over two full octaves.

TRACK 36
0:42 **LICK 5**

While the bluegrass style is a ton of fun, it's much better to hear these licks with some backup. So find some friends to jam with if possible. Learn a few standard tunes, search for a bluegrass jam in your area, and get out there and play!

BLUEGRASS LICKS IN THE KEY OF G

The bluegrass guitar style is really something to witness in the hands of seasoned pros like Doc Watson or Tony Rice. Bluegrass is its own thing, really, and it takes a different coordination altogether to play really fast licks in open position, compared to moveable scale forms. In this lesson, we'll take a look at some classic bluegrass licks in the key of G. So grab your axe and head for the front porch.

The Basic Idea

Bluegrass licks are usually played with a flatpick, which is another name for a standard plectrum (the term "flatpick" differentiates it from a thumbpick, which used to be much more popular). In the bluegrass style, open strings are part of the sound, so most of the licks are played in open position. That is not to say that bluegrass players never venture into the upper frets; it just means that, if a phrase can be played in open position, it usually is.

Also, with regard to picking, bluegrass is almost always played with alternate picking, as opposed to economy picking. Of course, that's not a law or anything…

Let's start off by ascending and descending an open-position G major scale to get a feel for it.

TRACK 37
0:00 **EXERCISE 1**

Try to minimize the picking motion as much as possible. Bluegrass is often played at breakneck tempos and your picking skills will definitely be put to the test!

Now let's try the same scale run, this time using legato technique (i.e., hammer-ons and pull-offs). Although picking every note is a little more common, legato is certainly used. Notice that hammering on from and pulling off to open strings feels a little different than doing so with two fretted notes.

TRACK 37
0:11 **EXERCISE 2**

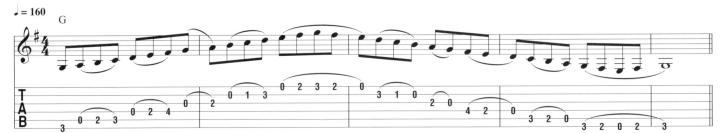

Licks

OK, now that you have a basic feel for playing open-position scales, let's check out some licks in the key of G.

TRACK 37
0:24 **LICK 1**

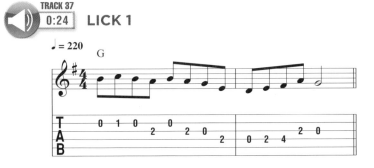

This next lick begins with a descending G major pentatonic sequence and finishes off with a line (C–B–A–F♯) that suggests a D chord before resolving to the open G string.

Adding Chromatic Notes

Chromatic notes often are employed to give lines a slightly bluesy touch. Common additions are the ♭3rd and the ♭5th—B♭ and D♭ in the key of G. We can't pass up the most famous bluegrass lick of all time: the Lester Flatt run, which uses the ♭3rd as a passing tone. Although we're using a few legato moves here, it's common to pick every note as well.

This next lick sounds like the descending version of the Lester Flatt run and uses a few pull-offs and a slide as well.

Beyond Open Position

In this last lick, we begin in fifth position with the high B note, though we use the open-E string to quickly shift back down to open position for the final descent, which includes a bluesy B–B♭–B–B♭ rub.

While the bluegrass style is a ton of fun, it's much better to hear these licks with some backup. So find some friends to jam with if possible. Learn a few standard tunes, search for a bluegrass jam in your area, and get out there and play!

BLUEGRASS LICKS IN THE KEY OF D

If you've never played in the bluegrass style, you may be a bit taken aback. Even accomplished pickers will find that it takes a different coordination altogether to play really fast licks in open position, compared to moveable scale forms. To hear stellar examples of this style, check out Doc Watson, Tony Rice, or Earl Scruggs. In this lesson, we'll take a look at some classic bluegrass licks in the key of D. So grab some lemonade and meet me on the front porch.

The Basic Idea

Bluegrass licks usually are played with a flatpick, which is another name for a standard plectrum (the term "flatpick" differentiates it from a thumbpick, which used to be much more popular). In the bluegrass style, open strings are part of the sound, so most of the licks are played in open position. That is not to say that bluegrass players never venture into the upper frets; it just means that, if a phrase can be played in open position, it usually is.

Also, with regard to picking, bluegrass is almost always played with alternate picking, as opposed to economy picking. Of course, that's not a law or anything…

Let's start off by ascending and descending an open-position D major scale to get a feel for it.

TRACK 38 **0:00** **EXERCISE 1**

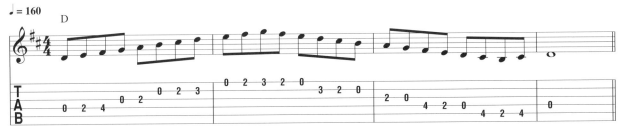

Try to minimize the picking motion as much as possible. Bluegrass often is played at breakneck tempos, and your picking skills will definitely be put to the test!

Now let's try the same scale run, this time using legato technique (i.e., hammer-ons and pull-offs). Although picking every note is a little more common, legato is certainly used. Notice that hammering on from and pulling off to open strings feels a little different than doing so with two fretted notes.

TRACK 38 **0:10** **EXERCISE 2**

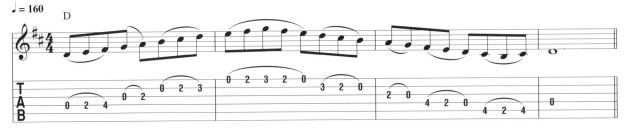

TRACK 38 **0:21** **LICK 1**

Licks

OK, now that you have a basic feel for playing open-position scales, let's check out some licks in the key of D.

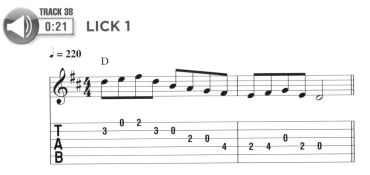

With its fleet triplets and major pentatonic vocabulary, this lick has a bit of an Irish bent:

Adding Chromatic Notes

Chromatic notes are often employed to give lines a slightly bluesy touch. Common additions are the b3rd and the b5th—F♮ and Ab in the key of D. This lick starts with a classic 2nd–b3rd–3rd move:

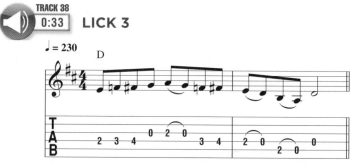

In addition to adding the b3rd (F) and b5th (Ab), this lick includes the b7th (C) for an extra bluesy sound:

Beyond Open Position

This last lick starts in fifth position and uses the open E string to quickly shift to open position. We continue with a classic move that surrounds the major 3rd (F#) with the 4th (G) and b3rd (F) before finishing off with a bluesy move similar to Lick 4.

Be sure to try to find someone with whom to play these licks, as it really helps to hear them played over their respective chords. Learn a few standard tunes, search for a bluegrass jam in your area, and get out there and play!

LESSON #40: BLUEGRASS LICKS IN THE KEY OF A

The sound of a great bluegrass lick is unlike any other. Open strings ringing throughout the lick lend a unique tone that sets it apart from more modern position-based playing. The bluegrass style is its own thing, really, and it takes a different coordination altogether to play really fast licks in open position, compared to moveable scale forms. To hear stellar examples of this style, check out Doc Watson, Tony Rice, or Earl Scruggs. In this lesson, we'll take a look at some classic bluegrass licks in the key of A. Overalls will help, but are not essential.

The Basic Idea

Bluegrass licks are usually played with a flatpick, which is another name for a standard plectrum (the term "flatpick" differentiates it from a thumbpick, which used to be much more popular). In the bluegrass style, open strings are part of the sound, so most of the licks are played in open position. That is not to say that bluegrass players never venture into the upper frets; it just means that, if a phrase can be played in open position, it usually is.

Also, with regard to picking, bluegrass is almost always played with alternate picking, as opposed to economy picking. Of course, that's not a law or anything…

Let's start off by ascending and descending an open-position A major scale to get a feel for it.

EXERCISE 1

Try to minimize the picking motion as much as possible. Bluegrass often is played at breakneck tempos, and your picking skills will definitely be put to the test!

Now let's try the same scale run, this time using legato technique (i.e., hammer-ons and pull-offs). Although picking every note is a little more common, legato is certainly used. Notice that hammering on from and pulling off to open strings feels a little different than doing so with two fretted notes.

EXERCISE 2

Licks

OK, now that you have a basic feel for playing open-position scales, let's check out some licks in the key of A. The first two licks work out of the upper range of the scale, with plenty of pull-offs and a repetitive slide move in Lick 1. Notice also in Lick 1 the unison E notes on strings 1 and 2.

TRACK 39
0:21 **LICK 1**

TRACK 39
0:29 **LICK 2**

Adding Chromatic Notes

Chromatic notes often are employed to give lines a slightly bluesy touch. Common additions are the ♭3rd and the ♭5th—C♮ and E♭ in the key of A. In the following lick, we're using both the ♭3rd and ♭5th, as well as the ♭7th (G), to create a bluesy major sound. We begin the lick in third position so we can slide from the ♭5th (or ♯4th [D♯], as it's notated here) to the 5th (E).

TRACK 39
0:37 **LICK 3**

Beyond Open Position

This final lick covers a lot of ground. We begin in ninth position with our middle finger on fret 10 of string 2. At the end of measure 1, we use the open E string to shift down to open position and begin using the A blues scale in measure 2. In measure 3, we climb back up the scale, once again mixing major and minor pentatonic sounds.

TRACK 39
0:44 **LICK 4**

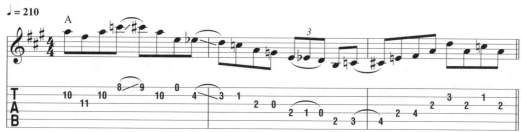

While the bluegrass style is a ton of fun, it's much better to hear these licks on top of a rhythm instrument, such as another guitar or a banjo. So find some friends to jam with if possible. Learn a few standard tunes, search for a bluegrass jam in your area, and get out there and play!

THE BASICS OF ARRANGING FOR SOLO GUITAR

One of the most enjoyable aspects of fingerstyle guitar is being able to play solo arrangements of songs. Solo guitar will test your pick-hand independence and your ability to creatively solve fingering issues that are bound to come up, which can range from simple to incredibly complex. In this lesson on arranging for solo guitar, we'll start at ground zero.

Choosing a Key

When arranging any song, the first item that needs to be addressed is choosing a key that sits well on the guitar. Due to the various idiosyncrasies and limitations of the instrument, it's extremely common to change the original key of a song when arranging for solo guitar. In the steel-string realm, the open string-based sharp keys (C, G, D, A, and E) are most common, although jazzers often play in flat keys. If you need the arrangement to sound in a different key for whatever reason, you can always use a capo.

THE MELODY

Along with deciding what key to play the song in, you should begin by taking a look at the melody. The melody will indicate up front whether you'll need to make special accommodations—a large range, harmonized melody notes, key changes, etc.

Getting Started

Due to space limitations, we'll choose a short melody to work on: the first phrase of "Twinkle, Twinkle Little Star." Our first two objectives are to find a key and play the melody. The melody has a range of a major 6th, and if we play it in the key of G, we can stay in open position and make use of the top three open strings.

Here's how the melody would look in the key of G:

Adding the Bass

The next step is to add some bass notes. A very basic version might look like this:

Filling in the Gaps

At this point, we need to fill in the gaps to give the arrangement some more substance and we have several options in this regard. One option is to simply add some arpeggiated chord tones in between the melody notes, like Example 2. (Note that we've changed the final D chord to a D/F♯ to accommodate our range.)

TRACK 40
0:38 **EXAMPLE 2**

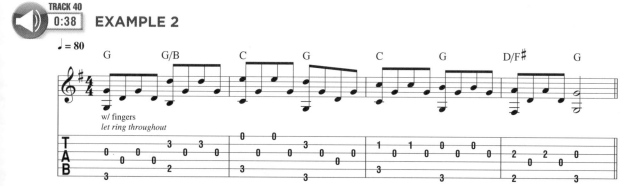

Or maybe we want to approach the melody from a block-chord style, in which we're sounding a bunch of notes simultaneously. That might sound like this:

TRACK 40
0:58 **EXAMPLE 3**

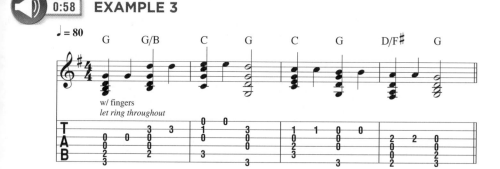

Another option is to create a Travis picking-style pattern that uses alternating bass notes played with the thumb. Here's an example of that idea:

TRACK 40
1:17 **EXAMPLE 4**

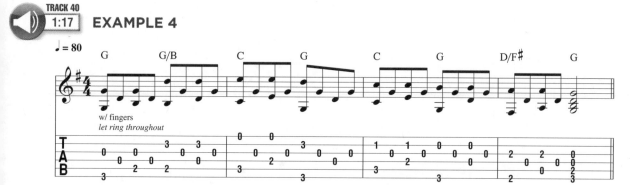

Or, if you're dealing with a longer example, you may choose to combine these approaches. For example, you could use one approach for the first verse and, for some variety, change it up for the second verse. Experimenting with different strategies is helpful, as certain melodies will tend to sound better with certain accompaniment styles.

That wraps up this lesson. We've just scratched the surface, so please continue to explore the world of arranging. It's a rewarding journey.

LESSON #42: ADVANCED TIPS ON ARRANGING FOR SOLO GUITAR

One of the most enjoyable aspects of fingerstyle guitar is being able to play solo arrangements of songs. Solo guitar will test your pick-hand independence and your ability to creatively solve fingering issues that are bound to come up. This lesson assumes that you have some experience with easier arrangements, so we'll focus on some more advanced tips on arranging for solo guitar.

Tip #1: Adjusting Melodic Rhythm

In many instances, when trying to arrange a song for solo guitar, players will get tripped up at a certain spot because of something the melody is doing rhythmically. However, often times these wasted hours can be avoided if you learn to be a bit flexible with the rhythm. Think about it: when was the last time you've ever heard a crooner sing a song exactly as it's written? Singers make changes to rhythms all the time, so why can't we?

For example, let's say that you're working on an arrangement of the Christmas hymn "Silent Night," and you want to do something special during the "round yon virgin" phrase, but the rhythm of the melody isn't jiving with what you want to do. No one is really going to pitch a fit if you change the rhythm of "virgin" melody from this:

To this:

Consequently, you can pull off this nice arrangement without much difficulty:

TRACK 41 **0:00** **EXAMPLE 1**

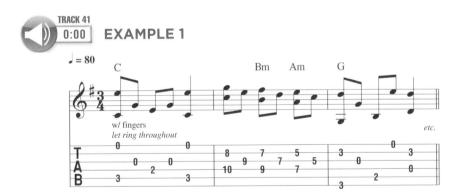

Tip #2: Be Flexible with the Voices

You don't always need a bass note on every beat (or on the first beat of every measure, etc.); you can bend the rules a bit if something's just not workable a certain way. In fact, you'll often discover that if you free yourself from these self-imposed limitations, the arrangement benefits. So try to be flexible with respect to the established roles of the voices in your piece.

Sticking with our "Silent Night" arrangement, let's say you're having trouble performing this section cleanly:

EXAMPLE 2

Well, who says that you have to keep the bass notes thumping throughout? The section actually sounds very nice when all but the first bass notes of each measure are eliminated.

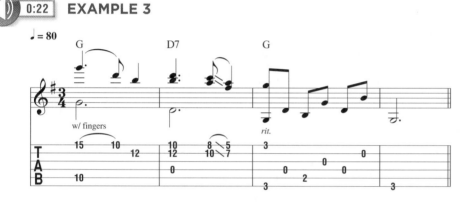

EXAMPLE 3

Tip #3: Reharmonization

Reharmonization is a great way to keep your arrangements sounding fresh, as well as to add a bit more of your own creativity. When reharmonizing a melody, we simply replace the original chord that is played beneath it with a new one. While the sky is the limit, most people generally don't use a chord that will clash with the melody note (e.g., using Gm [G–B♭–D] to harmonize a B♮ note). Your personal taste, knowledge of harmony, and patience to exhaust the many options will be the deciding factors.

For example, let's say that we have this phrase toward the end of the song form:

We could choose to reharmonize the final chord for a dramatic effect. Here's one option that I like:

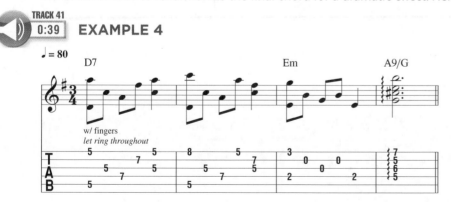

EXAMPLE 4

Arranging for solo guitar can be challenging, but the results are well worth the effort. Be sure to experiment in your own arrangements with all of these ideas. If you keep an open mind, you're sure to discover plenty of new possibilities that you'll enjoy.

LESSON #43: OPEN G RIFFS

If you've never spent much time experimenting with Open G tuning, you're missing out on some great riff opportunities. Timeless riffs have been generated throughout the years with this tuning, including "Start Me Up" (and plenty of other Stones tunes), "Pink Houses" (John Mellencamp), "Thorn in My Pride" (The Black Crowes), and many others. Open G tuning can yield some great, fresh sounds that are simply unattainable in standard tuning. To get a feel for the tuning's possibilities, let's check out some Open G riffs.

First Thing's First

To access Open G tuning from standard tuning, you'll need to tune your sixth, fifth, and first strings down a whole step, which is a relatively easy matter even without a tuner, because other open strings on the guitar match these pitches.

▶ Tune your sixth string down a whole step so that it's an octave lower than your open fourth string.

▶ Tune your first string down a whole step so that it's an octave higher than your open fourth string.

▶ Tune your fifth string down a whole step so that it's an octave lower than your open third string.

For pitch stability, be sure to overshoot the mark, detuning below the destination pitch before reversing course and raising the string's pitch to hit your target.

Open G Tuning: D–G–D–G–B–D

The Open Pivot-Chord Idea

One of the most attractive elements of this tuning is that the open strings form a G chord. Consequently, you can pivot off of this chord with other chord shapes to get sounds that are either unattainable or could only be faked in standard tuning.

Below is a classic example of the aforementioned idea that has the Stones written all over it. Notice that these particular add9 voicings are unattainable in standard tuning.

TRACK 42 0:00 **EXAMPLE 1**

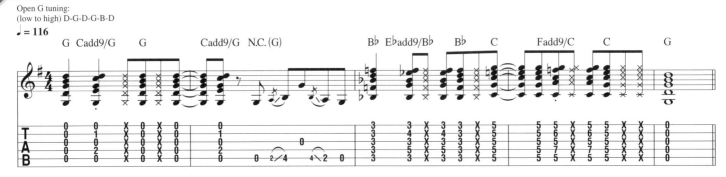

Below is a bluesy, somewhat demented riff that bounces Bb, B, and C chords against the open G chord. The riff is similar to something the Black Crowes might have played in their *Amorica* period.

TRACK 42 0:16 **EXAMPLE 2**

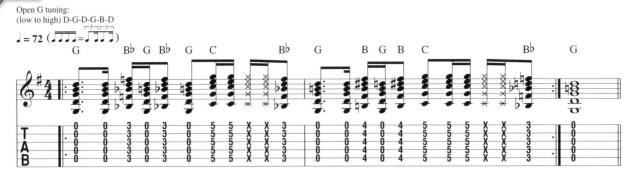

Normally Unplayable Chords or Riffs

If you've ever tried to figure out a Stones or Black Crowes riff, unaware of the fact that Open G tuning was used, you no doubt were left scratching your head at some point. Some guitar parts are simply impossible to play in standard tuning, but lay out easy as pie in Open G. (Of course, the opposite could be said as well.)

Let's take a look at some ideas that exploit that fact. The following is an arpeggio-based riff that's similar to Jimmy Page's Zeppelin days. The open high-D string is used to drone against a D–C#–D–B melody on string 2.

 EXAMPLE 3

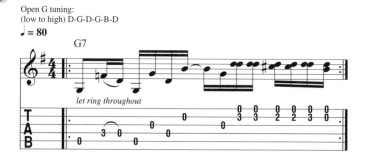

Below is another common device in this tuning. Here, we're moving 10th intervals played on strings 4 and 2 against the open fifth, third, and first strings. Go ahead, try to play these voicings in standard tuning!

 EXAMPLE 4

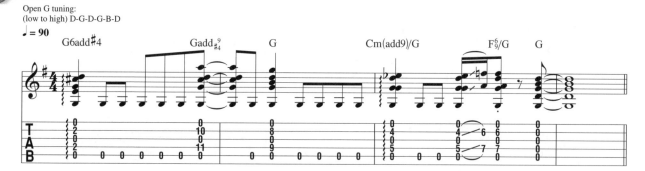

We'll close this lesson with a pretty fingerstyle riff that features a melody on the G string (for the G chord) and a colorful Cadd9#11 voicing—easy as pie in open G but extremely impractical in standard tuning.

 EXAMPLE 5

Well, that wraps it up. I hope that you've become aware of some of the exciting possibilities of Open G tuning and enjoy exploring them to the fullest.

LESSON #44: OPEN D RIFFS

Keith Richards spent a good amount of time using Open D tuning before settling (primarily) on Open G, and Derek Trucks plays exclusively in Open E (the same string intervals and fretboard layout—just a whole step higher). Rich Robinson of the Black Crowes has also used Open D and/or Open E to fuel some of his band's biggest hits, and scores of Delta bluesmen worked out of Open D on a regular basis. This lesson explores the riff possibilities that the tuning has to offer.

Open Up and Say "Ahhhh"

Open D tuning derives its name from the fact that, when all six strings are strummed, a D chord is produced. From standard tuning, you'll need to retune four of your six strings: the sixth, third, second, and first.

▶ Tune your sixth string down a whole step so that it's an octave lower than your open fourth string.

▶ Tune your first string down a whole step so that it's an octave higher than your open fourth string.

▶ Tune your second string down a whole step so that it's an octave higher than your open fifth string.

▶ Tune your third string down a half step so that it matches the pitch of the 4th fret of your fourth string.

For pitch stability, be sure to overshoot the mark, detuning below the destination pitch before reversing course and raising the string's pitch to hit your target.

Open D Tuning: D–A–D–F♯–A–D

It should be noted that the intervallic structure of this tuning is identical to Open E tuning. The only difference is that Open E tuning will sound a whole step higher. Consequently, any licks that you know in Open D will work in Open E as well, and vice versa.

Now that you're in Open D tuning, take a moment to strum that big, fat, open D chord a few times and revel in its beauty.

The Open Pivot-Chord Idea

One of the most attractive elements of this tuning is that the open strings form a D chord. Consequently, you can pivot off of this chord with other chord shapes to get sounds that are either unattainable or could only be faked in standard tuning.

Here is a classic example of the aforementioned idea. By adding the fingering for the standard E-chord shape, a lush Em11/D voicing is created in this tuning.

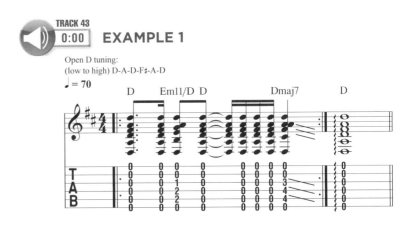

In this riff, we're volleying full, six-string, one-finger barre chords against the open D chord:

EXAMPLE 2

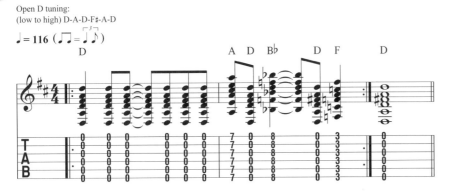

Normally Unplayable Chords or Riffs

If you've ever tried to figure out a song, unaware of the fact that Open D (or Open E) tuning was used, you no doubt were left scratching your head at some point. Some guitar parts are simply impossible to play in standard tuning, but lay out nicely in Open D.

Let's take a look at some ideas that exploit that fact. This first example features a big melody played in octaves on the fourth and first strings against droning open sixth, fifth, third, and second strings, resulting in the "bagpipe" effect that is produced by open tunings.

EXAMPLE 3

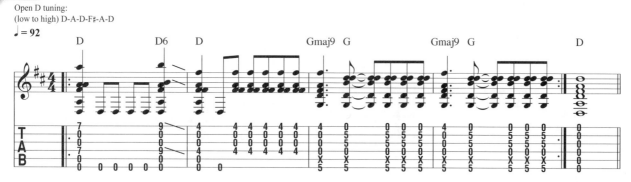

Below is a mellow fingerstyle example that pits several colorful harmonies atop a droning low-D bass note. For the "X" notes on the backbeats, forcefully plant your pick-hand fingers on the strings to produce a percussive "tick."

EXAMPLE 4

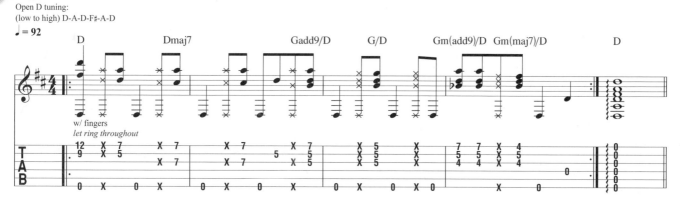

We'll close out the lesson with a groovy, swung riff that mixes D major and D minor sounds.

EXAMPLE 5

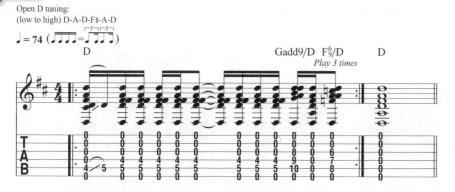

Well, that wraps up our look at Open D riffs. Take your time while exploring this tuning; you're sure to come up with some fresh sounds that you'll really dig.

LESSON #45: ADDING PERCUSSIVE ELEMENTS TO YOUR FINGERSTYLE TECHNIQUE

If you've ever sat in awe of the otherworldly sounds generated by acoustic virtuosos like Michael Hedges, you'll no doubt realize that what's going on is much more than traditional fretting and plucking. For example, you'll hear percussive noises that add a whole other dimension to the piece, which are especially effective in a solo format. These noises can be generated in many ways and that's the subject of this lesson: adding percussive elements to your fingerstyle technique.

The Percussive String Plant

We'll start with the most common trick of all, which is often used by many players—virtuoso or otherwise. I call it the "percussive string plant." This trick is accomplished by planting the pick-hand fingers (in preparation for the next chord) with great force, which results in a percussive "click" that simulates the sound of a snare drum in a full-band context.

TRACK 44 0:00 **EXAMPLE 1**

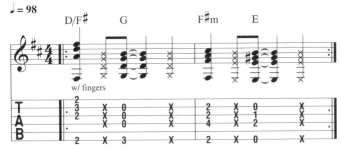

Of course, you can also randomly split up the bass and chords to create more texture. One of the most famous examples of this technique is found in Extreme's mega-ballad "More Than Words." Here, we expand on Example 1:

TRACK 44 0:16 **EXAMPLE 2**

Tapping the Soundboard

Another percussive technique involves tapping the face, or soundboard, of the guitar in rhythmic fashion in between notes. By using different techniques, you can generate a bass/snare effect. If you tap below the soundhole with your index and middle fingers, you can create a bass drum-like sound. To simulate a snare, tap above the soundhole with the side of your thumb.

EXAMPLE 3

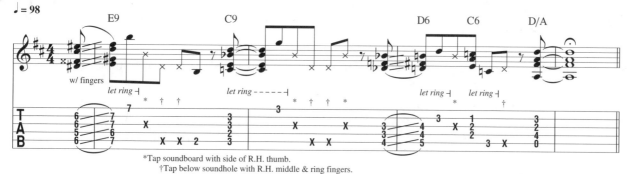

*Tap soundboard with side of R.H. thumb.
†Tap below soundhole with R.H. middle & ring fingers.

The Soundboard/Side Combination

Another commonly employed method to achieve the bass/snare effect is to hit the soundboard with the palm of the pick hand for the bass sound and tap the side of the guitar with the index and middle fingers for the snare sound.

Below is a sparse example that's deceptively tricky. Here, we're performing the bass hammer-on with a slap not only because it sounds good, but also because it helps to facilitate the transition from the tapped-soundboard bass-drum sound. For the chords, simply flick them with your index finger.

EXAMPLE 4

*S = Slap w/ R.H. thumb.
**Slap side of guitar w/ R.H. fingers.
†Tap soundboard with side of R.H. thumb.

You can also flail the pick-hand fingers to get a tabla-like effect, which can sound really cool.

EXAMPLE 5

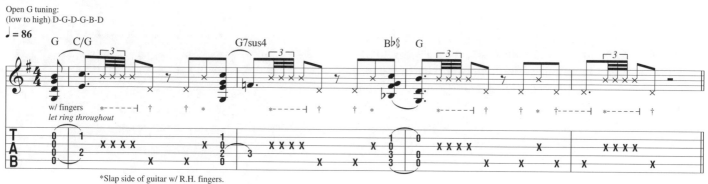

*Slap side of guitar w/ R.H. fingers.
†Tap soundboard with side of R.H. thumb.

THE BASICS OF SLAP AND POP FINGERSTYLE TECHNIQUE

Why should bassists get all the fun? As guitarists, we can take their "slap and pop" technique and add it to our bag of fingerstyle tricks for a different sound. When you unexpectedly break into slap and pop, you can really turn some heads. So let's get a bit funky and look at the basics of slap and pop fingerstyle technique.

The Basic Idea

Slap and pop technique is divided into two basic elements: the slap, performed by the thumb, and the pop, performed by the fingers.

The Slap

To perform the slap, use the side of your thumb to quickly and forcefully slap a bass string. A number of ways to hold the thumb while performing the slap exist, so you'll have to experiment to see what works for you.

You can check out numerous videos online to see different approaches to the slap. Slaps are indicated with an "S" between the notation and tab staves:

EXERCISE 1

Slap technique will probably take a bit of trial and error to perfect, but the more you work on it, the more you'll discover what you need to do to make it happen. On acoustic guitar, we can add another element to this technique by allowing the palm of the pick hand to thump the soundboard at the same time, which adds significant beef to the sound.

EXERCISE 2

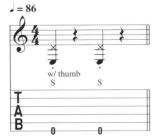

Once you get the hang of this technique, practice slapping different notes and on different strings.

EXERCISE 3

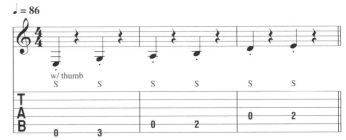

The Pop

If you're a country player, you've probably already messed around with this idea. The pop is easier to master than the slap. Simply pull the string up (away from the guitar) and release it, allowing it to snap back forcefully.

You should have a note that "pops." Pops are indicated with a "P" between the notation and tab staves.

Combining the Two Techniques

Now let's combine the two techniques in a few examples. Here's how a typical bass line that uses this approach sounds like when transferred to guitar:

The following example is good practice for learning to pop quickly after a slap, which can be challenging.

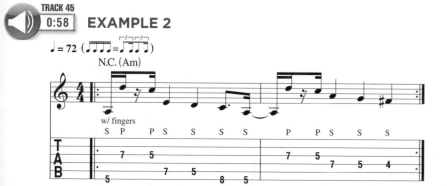

This final example is good practice for learning to quickly slap two notes in a row:

LESSON #47: ADVANCED SLAP AND POP FINGERSTYLE TECHNIQUE

If you've messed around with basic slap and pop technique and are looking for ways to take it to the next level, then this is the lesson for you! Here, we'll look at advanced slap and pop fingerstyle concepts and learn how to use them to create funky, interesting riffs that are guaranteed to get some booties shakin'!

This lesson assumes that you know how to produce basic slap and pop tones. If not, you should acquaint yourself with the basics before moving forward. In this lesson, we'll build on the basics of slap and pop with some companion techniques.

Slap and Pop: Only Half the Picture

Though "slaps" and "pops' give the technique its name, they really only comprise a portion of the full technique. Many other elements are involved, so let's take a look at some of them right now.

Muted Slap or Plant

This technique involves dead notes that are generated by either slapping a string that's muted by the fret hand or by simply planting your pick hand forcefully onto the strings. Both types are demonstrated here. The former is indicated between the staves with an "S" (slap) and in notation with an "X," while the latter is indicated with "R.H." (right hand) and an "X" note.

TRACK 46 `0:00` **EXERCISE 1**

Fret-Hand Muted Slap

Fret-hand muted slaps are created by slapping the fret hand against the strings hard enough to create a "tick," but not hard enough to sound any pitches. This technique is commonly used after a popped note and is indicated between the staves with "L.H." (left hand).

TRACK 46 `0:10` **EXERCISE 2**

Muted Pop

A muted pop is simply a pop that's muted by the fret hand. Muted pops are indicated between the staves with a "P" and in notation with an "X" note.

EXERCISE 3

TRACK 46
0:17

Examples

OK, now that you're familiar with slap and pop companion techniques, let's incorporate them into some riffs. Below is a funky A Dorian riff that uses single notes exclusively. The riff is played mostly on the bottom strings, occasionally popping as low as the fifth string.

EXAMPLE 1

TRACK 46
0:24

The following is an A dominant idea that includes some chord punches, which can really add another dimension. As you can see, a harmony can be implied with very few notes.

EXAMPLE 2

TRACK 46
0:38

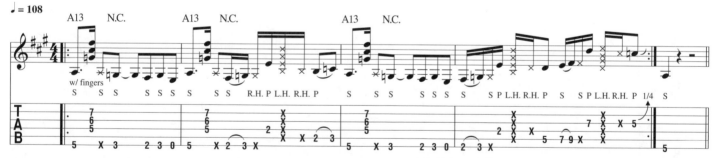

This final example demonstrates that you don't have to go crazy with all these techniques. A few well-placed slaps and pops within a nice groove can go a long way.

EXAMPLE 3

TRACK 46
1:01

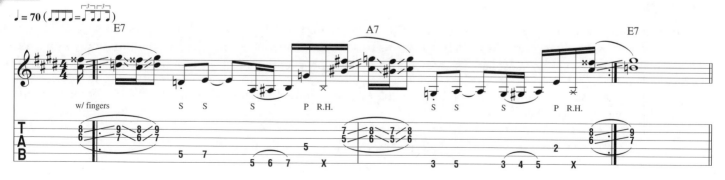

LESSON #48: OSCILLATING HAMMER-ONS AND PULL-OFFS

If you haven't checked out Michael Hedges yet, be prepared to have your mind completely blown when you do. His playing will completely redefine what you thought was possible on an acoustic guitar. Many of his contemporaries have achieved similar technical mastery, but Hedges was one of the true pioneers in the solo acoustic genre, as well as its most lauded practitioner, and the world lost a truly brilliant musician with his passing. In this lesson, we're going to take a look at oscillating hammer-ons and pull-offs—a technique that Hedges used in more than a few of his compositions.

The Basic Idea

With this technique, the idea is to repeatedly hammer-on and pull-off a combination of fretted notes and open strings while you perform other maneuvers beneath (or above) them. Double stops are commonly used for the hammers and pulls, and it should be mentioned that this type of idea is almost always performed in an alternate tuning in order to facilitate harmonious combinations of fretted and open strings.

Here's a basic example of oscillation in Open G tuning (D–G–D–G–B–D, low to high):

Changing fretted notes during the oscillation is common as well.

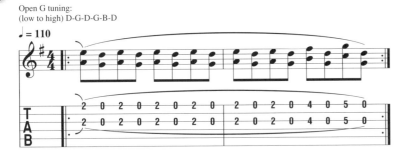

Adding Other Elements

Once you get a feel for the aforementioned techniques, you can add other melodic elements—bass notes, melodic notes on other strings, harmonics, etc.—to create a fuller texture. Those elements are not easy to perform and you have to be extremely accurate with your oscillations so as not to infringe on events that may be occurring on neighboring strings.

Next is a relatively simple example that only involves changing bass notes beneath the oscillations. Watch for the one variation in pitch among the oscillations.

EXAMPLE 1

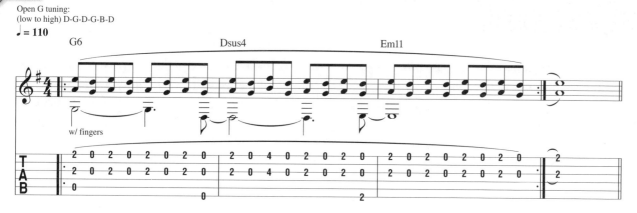

In this next example, we're adding not only bass notes beneath the oscillations, but a second-string melody as well. The biggest challenge here is avoiding nudging the B string with your hammer-ons and pull-offs.

EXAMPLE 2

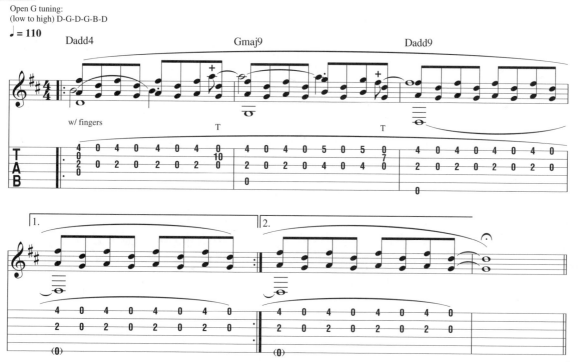

In this final example, we're plucking and tapping mostly whole notes in the bass due to the increase in intensity of the hammer-ons and pull-offs.

EXAMPLE 3

To hear Hedges' mastery of this technique, check out "Aerial Boundaries" or "Because It's There." When performed properly, this technique truly sounds like more than one instrument playing. Plus, it's a whole lot of fun!

LESSON #49: HARP SCALES

The acoustic guitar is a beautiful-sounding instrument capable of many brilliant sounds. One of the traits that we can exploit in this regard is the creative use of open strings. By combining certain fretted notes with certain open strings, we can create cascading scalar lines that simulate the sound of a harp or a piano with the sustain pedal down. I like to call these lines "harp scales," the subject of this lesson.

The Basic Idea

With this technique, we're going to try to find ways to play a scale (descending or ascending) in which we can let the maximum number of notes ring together. This approach creates a lush, dense sound that's hauntingly beautiful.

Below is a simple exercise in which we descend an E minor scale. Notice that we have to fret two pairs of 2nds (D–C and F#–E) during the run—a common occurrence with this idea. You really must keep your fingers arched in order to stay out of the way of neighboring strings. Also, pick-hand fingering is critical in order to achieve fluidity. Therefore, I've included suggested fingerings (*p* = thumb, *i* = index, *m* = middle, and *a* = ring) for each example.

 EXERCISE 1

Examples

To see what else we can do with this basic technique, let's take a look at some examples. This first example expands on Exercise 1 by creating a four-note sequence that works its way down the scale. Notice that we reposition the fingering for the D–C group the second time it appears in order to maintain maximum sustain. (If we hadn't done that, the open B string would be immediately cut off by the fretted D note on beat 3.)

 EXAMPLE 1

Below is a triplet run up the C major scale. Notice that we use the exact same pattern for the second beat (F–G–A) as we did for beat 1, just moved up one string group.

 EXAMPLE 2

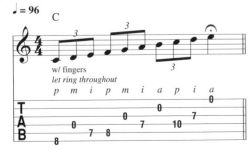

Incorporating Alternate Tunings

When alternate tunings are brought into the picture, the possibilities greatly expand. Let's check out a few examples in this regard. In the first example, played in E–B–D–G–B–D tuning, we're able to run up and down the first five notes of a G major scale with ease. Then, we descend the E minor hexatonic scale, facilitated by the fifth string's new pitch, B.

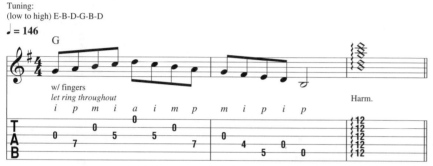

The following is an E Dorian triplet run in the same tuning as Example 3. You can hear the 16th century minstrels frolicking about…

For this final lick, we've altered the previous tuning by detuning the second string from B to A, resulting in an E–B–D–G–A–D tuning. This lick is another E Dorian run, with lots and lots of open strings.

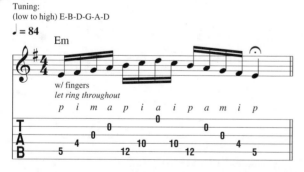

Harp scales are a lot of fun to mess around with and you can generate some truly stunning results. Remember to keep your fingers arched and stay out of the way of those open strings!

LESSON #50: USING PARTIAL AND/OR MULTIPLE CAPOS

The capo is a guitarist's best friend. Its usefulness cannot be overstated. Nevertheless, the capo can become an even more powerful tool if you explore it further. Numerous options exist, including partial and multiple capos, both of which we'll explore in this lesson.

Partial Capos

A partial capo is one that's designed to cover only certain strings. Common models include the "Drop D" capo, which only covers strings 5–1, leaving the sixth string open, and the "short cut" capo, which normally covers only strings 5–3.

So, what can we do with them? Well, the following are a few ideas.

Note: While partial and/or multiple capos can produce some great sounds, they're not the easiest methods in the world to notate on paper. In the following examples, all the notes are written in their actual-sounding pitch, and the capoed frets are non-bold in tab.

DROP D CAPO

Drop D Capo

Perhaps the most obvious use for the Drop D capo is to place it on fret 2. This approach simulates Drop D tuning—albeit a whole step higher in pitch—with one caveat: you don't fret the sixth string. Although this method feels a lot like Drop D, when you fret the sixth string, you realize that you're still in standard tuning. Several of the chords in the following example would require serious stretches in Drop D tuning.

SHORT CUT CAPO

TRACK 49 `0:00` **EXAMPLE 1**

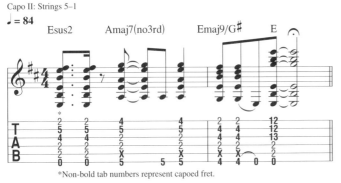

*Non-bold tab numbers represent capoed fret.

Of course, you also can move the capo to higher frets, which allows for interesting possibilities including fretting "behind the capo."

TRACK 49 `0:13` **EXAMPLE 2**

Short-Cut Capos

With a short-cut capo, the fifth, fourth, and third strings are typically capoed, while the others ring free.

EXAMPLE 3

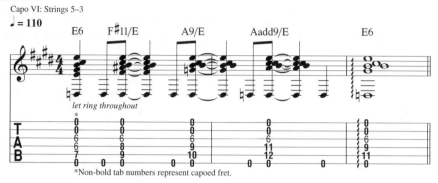

In the next example, we've turned the short-cut capo upside down and placed it on the 4th fret. Check out how easy it is to play these lush chords.

EXAMPLE 4

Multiple Capos

When you combine any of the aforementioned capos, the possibilities expand exponentially. In this final example, we've placed a full capo on fret 2 and an upside down short-cut capo on fret 4 (strings 4–2).

EXAMPLE 5

INTRODUCTION TO CLASSICAL GUITAR, PART 1

Classical guitar is played on a nylon-string acoustic and involves plucking the strings with your fingers, rather than with a pick. This approach enables melody and accompaniment to be played simultaneously. A few formalities make playing classical guitar different from playing "regular" guitar, so let's discuss those first.

Posture, Posture

Classical guitarists, more than any other stylists, play their guitars in optimum playing position. Proper posture requires you to sit on the edge of your chair and then place your left foot on a footstool while resting the guitar on your left leg. Alternatively, you may want to use a guitar support, which attaches to the side of your guitar via suction cups and "lifts" the guitar into optimum playing position, without having to use the footstool.

Once you're in proper playing posture, it's time to place your hands in proper position. Your left hand should fret the strings with your thumb behind the neck, much like you normally would do; however, you'll want to fret the notes more with your fingertips than you would on a "regular" acoustic guitar, as you'll need to let notes ring clearly.

Your right-hand technique, however, will be quite different. In classical technique, you use an arched-wrist and curled-fingers approach, with your wrist a few inches from the guitar's top. If you choose to play with your nails—the accepted method for classical guitar—keep them just slightly longer than your fingertips and well-manicured. You may opt to pluck with your fingertips, but your tone will suffer.

PROPER POSTURE WITH FOOTSTOOL

Rest Strokes and Free Strokes

Classical guitar uses two basic strokes: the rest stroke and the free stroke. In a rest stroke, your finger plucks the string with a slightly downward motion, or push toward the guitar, and then comes to rest on the next string. To achieve the best tone, pluck slightly across the string. Using a few different fingering combinations, let's try some rest strokes. Right-hand fingers are labeled as follows: *p* (*pulgar*) for thumb, *i* (*indicio*) for index, *m* (*medio*) for middle, and *a* (*anular*) for ring finger.

EXAMPLE 1

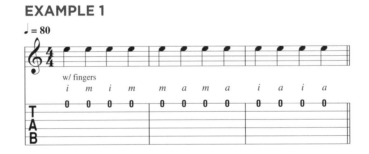

Be sure to practice those strokes on the B, G, and D strings, as well.

Now let's play Beethoven's popular "Ode to Joy" melody, using all rest strokes. Alternate between your index and middle fingers throughout and strive for consistent, even volume.

TRACK 50
0:00 **EXAMPLE 2**

The basic movement of the free stroke is the same as the rest stroke, except in the final phase. Instead of coming to rest, the finger just clears the adjacent string and stops in the air above it. Play the second half of Beethoven's "Ode to Joy," using all free strokes:

TRACK 50
0:30 **EXAMPLE 3**

Now, you may be wondering just what the difference is between these two strokes, aside from the physical action. The rest stroke typically produces a more full-bodied and richer tone and thus, is often used for single-note melodies, whereas the free stroke is used more frequently in counterpoint, where you want notes to ring out.

You also will use both rest strokes and free strokes with your thumb. Let's try a melody that uses thumb-based free strokes.

TRACK 50
1:00 **EXAMPLE 4**

Now let's add free-stroke bass notes to Beethoven's "Ode to Joy."

TRACK 50
1:20 **EXAMPLE 5**

INTRODUCTION TO CLASSICAL GUITAR, PART 2

This lesson on the basics of classical guitar requires that you have at least a general understanding of playing single-note melodies with rest strokes and free strokes. Part 2 addresses playing chords in a simple, two-note dyad form, eventually adding a bass line as well. We'll also add the essential slur technique to your single-note repertoire.

Chord Technique

When two or more notes are sounded simultaneously, the outcome is referred to as a chord. When playing chords, you should use free strokes, performed with your fingers and thumb. Be sure the *i* and *m* notes sound at precisely the same time.

It's important to note that, when you play chords your plucking hand should not move up and down; instead, it should remain stable with the movement originating at your finger joints. Let's play Beethoven's "Ode to Joy" melody using chords.

TRACK 51 `0:00`   **EXAMPLE 1**

In addition to playing chords with your fingers, you will also use your thumb to add a bass note, giving the chord a fuller and more complete sound. When adding the thumb, it becomes more difficult to get the notes to "speak" at the same time, so pay close attention to making all of the notes in the chord sound simultaneously.

TRACK 51 `0:30`   **EXAMPLE 2**

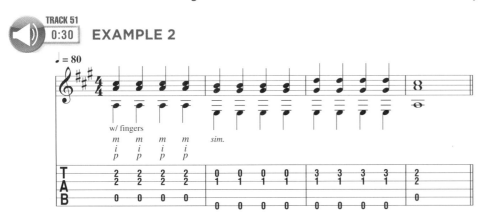

Smooth Lines

Sometimes, linking two notes together in a manner that is smoother than simply plucking both of them individually is desired. This technique is called a slur. Slurs can occur in both ascending and descending directions. In the case of an ascending slur, or hammer-on, you pluck the first note and then hammer onto the second note. In a descending slur, or pull-off, you'll strike the first note and then pull that fretting finger off the note to sound a note lower in pitch.

Below is an exercise that incorporates all four fret-hand fingers to help you build strength and precision in your slur technique. Be sure to continue the pattern all the way back down the first string, and then practice it on the remaining five strings, as well.

EXAMPLE 3

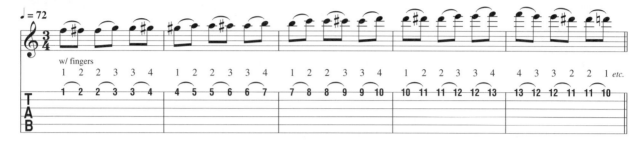

Here's a short etude to put the slur technique into a melodic context:

TRACK 51
0:47 **EXAMPLE 4**

Now, to bring it all together, here's "Ode to Joy" with chords, bass notes, and slurs:

TRACK 51
1:12 **EXAMPLE 5**

LESSON #53: COUNTERPOINT

Counterpoint? Uh-oh, boring, "old people" music alert! *Au contraire, mon frère*. A little classical training can go a long way toward helping you become a better musician, regardless of what musical style you prefer. Remember, many of the compositional and arranging tools and techniques that we use in pop, rock, and country music stem from classical theory and harmony, so put away those preconceived notions and dig in for a deeper understanding of how the music that you love works.

Music in Motion

The term counterpoint is often misunderstood. Among musicians with little or no formal music education, counterpoint frequently is thought of as "contrary motion." Although that is true, contrary motion is only one form of counterpoint. The basic definition of counterpoint is "the combination of two or more melodic lines played simultaneously." Whenever you have two or more voices in a piece of music, both vertical (chords, harmony) and horizontal (melody) components exist. Counterpoint refers to analysis of the latter aspect. In this lesson, we're going to explore three commonly used types of counterpoint.

PARALLEL MOTION

Take a look at the following example:

EXAMPLE 1

Harmonic analysis of the first measure yields a C–Dm–Em–F chord progression. But if you look at those note groupings as three separate melodic voices—rather than as triads or chords—you'll find three voices that move melodically (horizontally) up the C major scale in intervals of diatonic 2nds.

That movement brings us to the first type of counterpoint: parallel motion, which is defined as two or more melodic lines moving in fixed intervals. You can hear this type of counterpoint in the first three beats of the Beatles' classic "Blackbird," in which Paul McCartney applies parallel motion to 10th (octave plus a 3rd) intervals in the key of G. Here is a similar musical passage with, and without, an open-G pedal tone:

TRACK 52
0:00 **EXAMPLE 2**

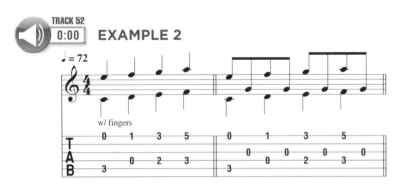

OBLIQUE MOTION

The pedal point in that last example also can be interpreted as adding oblique motion—the second form of counterpoint covered in this lesson. Oblique motion is defined as two simultaneous melodic lines in which one remains stationary while the other is in motion. In the previous example, the open G note remains static while the upper and lower voices move in parallel.

One of the most famous two-voice examples of oblique motion in guitar music is heard in Isaac Albeniz's "Leyenda."

EXAMPLE 3

In this passage, the upper voice (open B note) serves as the stationary melody while the lower voice, or melody line, moves within the E minor scale.

CONTRARY MOTION

A third commonly used form of counterpoint is contrary motion, which is defined as two melodic lines moving in opposite directions; that is, one line moves *up* in pitch while the other moves *down*. One of the most famous examples of contrary motion is the opening figure in Johann Sebastian Bach's "Bourrée," from *Lute Suite No. 1.*

EXAMPLE 4

Those first three dyads constitute quite possibly the most famous instance of contrary motion in music history, with the lower voice descending G–F♯–E while the upper voice simultaneously ascends E–F♯–G. Then, Bach immediately reverses direction on beat 2 of measure 1, and continues to weave back and forth in masterly fashion throughout.

Other famous uses of contrary motion in the popular music realm include the opening Am–Am(add9)/G♯–C/G chord salvo of Led Zeppelin's epic "Stairway to Heaven" and the legendary C–G/B–Am progression that begins the verses of the Kansas classic "Dust in the Wind." This next musical example puts contrary motion to good use in a minor-key rock setting.

EXAMPLE 5

Here, the lower voice descends diatonically, following the chord roots while the upper voice ascends the E minor scale, staying on chord tones for each change. Measure 4 offers a bit of a change-up, adding the major 7th (B) on top for tension within the measure while simultaneously creating a V–I (B–E) move when the melody returns to E on the repeat.

These forms of counterpoint can be very helpful tools when composing acoustic music, be it classical, folk, Celtic, pop, or rock. Experiment with these types and research others to help you get the most out of your arrangements.

LESSON #54: POWER CHORDS

When you think about all the wonderful chords with which you can take advantage of the acoustic guitar's brilliant ringing strings, power chords are probably the last ones to come to mind. But power chords do indeed have a place in your acoustic guitar repertoire. In this lesson, we'll explore various power-chord shapes and voicings and how you can use them in acoustic settings.

The Perfect Pair

By definition, a power chord comprises just two chord tones: the root and its perfect 5th. Although that simple harmonic arrangement is frequently used on the guitar, by doubling up on one or both chord tones, power chords can be approached many ways.

To begin, let's review the most commonly used basic two-note shapes, in both open position and movable grips.

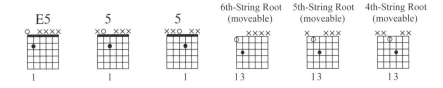

Even though these shapes may appear "boring" on an acoustic guitar, they're likely the power-chord grips that you'll most often encounter, whether in a straight rock or pop context (Example 1) or a blues shuffle (Example 2).

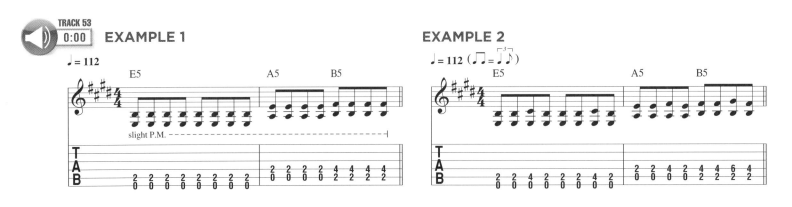

Three of a Perfect Pair, Four, and More!

The easiest way to get more mileage from a power chord is to add the octave of the root note, thus creating a three-note voicing.

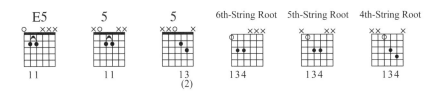

Here's one of the more popular power-chord rock rhythm patterns that utilize this form:

EXAMPLE 3

Note how the added octave notes give the chord stabs a bigger, fuller sound than if you were to use just the two-note version.

Just as we added the octave of the root, we also can add the lower octave of the 5th to power chords rooted on the fifth or fourth string. The resultant "inverted power chord" on the lowest two strings of the voicing, with the 5th in the bass, gives the chord a dark and heavy sound. Try this unplugged, grunge-style riff on for size:

EXAMPLE 4

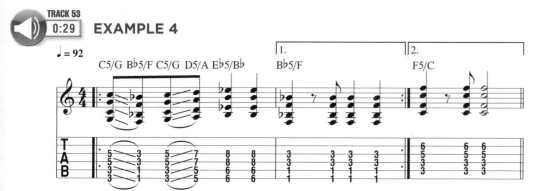

As you would expect, most power chords emphasize the bass register of the guitar, but the following is a pair of power chord shapes that enable you to take advantage of the shimmering sound of the top two (B and E) strings of the acoustic guitar.

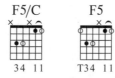

The first voicing is a movable shape with the 5th in the bass. The second voicing, also movable, inserts the root on the 6th string, fretted with your thumb. In our final example below, those two power-chord voicings are presented in a chord riff that might be heard as a "big rock intro" or a post-solo interlude. The first two measures feature the slash chord voicing, whereas the last two measures include the thumb-fretted root to raise the intensity of the chords.

EXAMPLE 5

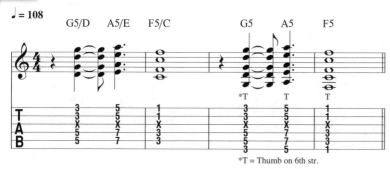

In addition to the ideas presented in this lesson, other even more exciting ways to use power chords on the acoustic guitar exist, like playing them against drones (open, ringing strings). To work out your own power-chord voicings, just remember that if you mute the 3rd interval in any major or minor triad, the remaining notes form a power chord!

Open tunings and acoustic guitar go together like peanut butter and jelly. But for some reason, the tunings that are almost always used are open *major* tunings, like Open D, Open G, and Open E. Given the great quantity of minor-key songs in the world, you'd think that open *minor* tunings would get a little more attention. Well starting now, they do. In this lesson, we'll explore the dark, brooding world of Open D minor tuning.

Tune Up

Open D minor tuning might sound a bit complicated—at least until you see it printed in its alternate name: "DADFAD." Yep, it's simply DADGAD tuning with the third string lowered a whole step. As a result, many of your favorite DADGAD licks and riffs will transpose quite simply to DADFAD, only they will now have a distinctly minor tonality, as opposed to that lovely modal airiness that DADGAD imparts.

Since strumming all six open strings produces a Dm chord, placing a one-finger barre across any fret will produce the minor chord named for the sixth-string root. To create a *major* chord, all you need do is fret the third string with your middle finger, one fret in front of the barre.

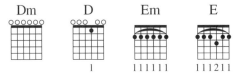

The Saddest of All Keys

Well, OK, maybe that's E♭ minor (nothing that a capo at the first fret can't cure!), but still, Open D minor tuning lends itself very well to creating ominous-sounding riffs. This first dirge-like example takes full advantage of the key's morose tone, compounded by its lumbering tempo (60 bpm):

TRACK 54 | **0:00** | **EXAMPLE 1**

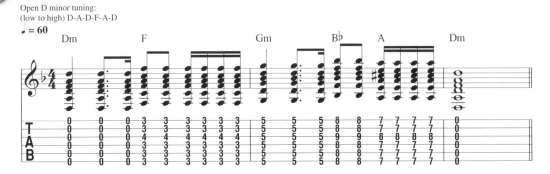

One advantage of the one-finger barre chords that open tunings produce is the ease with which you can add embellishments to the chord voicings. This next example depicts a Jimi Hendrix-like minor-key rock ballad, similar in vibe to "Little Wing."

TRACK 54 | **0:18** | **EXAMPLE 2**

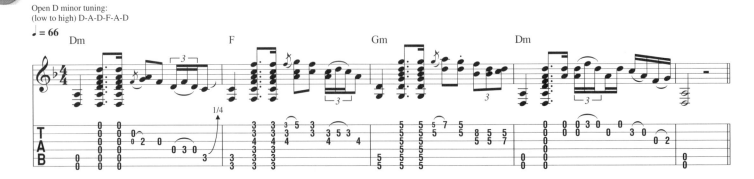

And while we're on the topic of "sad keys," let's take a look at a fingerstyle blues in DADFAD. Bluesman Skip James frequently used open minor tunings, including Open E minor, Open E♭ minor, and Open D minor. Despite being in a minor tuning, James would often play in major keys, hammering onto the major 3rd on the third string. Bukka White also took this approach quite a bit. Here is an example inspired by James:

EXAMPLE 3

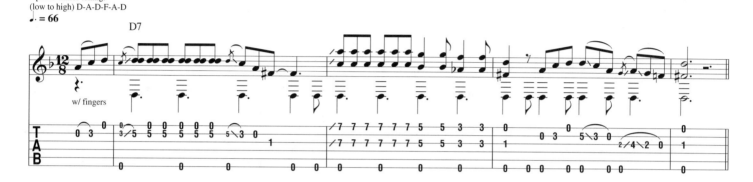

Minor Drones

Of course, no lesson on an open tuning would be complete without touching on drones. Whether performed in arpeggio fashion or via strumming, drones in DADFAD tuning ring just as true—if a bit darker—as those in DADGAD or major tunings.

This next example is an arpeggio riff in 6/8 time, featuring droning D and F notes against rising and falling B♭, C, and D octaves. Feelin' a little proggy, perhaps?

EXAMPLE 4

This final example conjures the mystical power of Led Zeppelin's "Kashmir," with 6th intervals descending the neck against a droning two-octave D5 chord.

EXAMPLE 5

LESSON #56: DOUBLE PLUCKING

Many varied ways to strike the strings on an acoustic guitar exist, including strumming, flatpicking, fingerpicking, Travis picking, hybrid picking, and slap techniques—all of which are covered in this book. But another rather obvious yet rarely used technique exists that, when used in the right places, can add an extra special dash to an arpeggio or fingerstyle pattern. In this lesson, we're going to take a look at the hybrid picking approach called double plucking.

Double Down

The technique of double plucking involves playing two notes simultaneously within a chord or arpeggio pattern. Although this technique can be performed in a fingerstyle manner, it's presented here by way of hybrid picking, whereby a flat pick is used to sound the lower note while your middle or ring finger sounds the upper note.

Our first example, shown below, uses double plucking to play a G major arpeggio in ascending and descending fashion. Use your pick and middle finger to pluck these dyads. Once you're accustomed to the technique, move on to the Example 2, which requires you to jump back and forth a bit between string sets. Practicing these examples will help to "teach" your pick hand how to make these moves with precision.

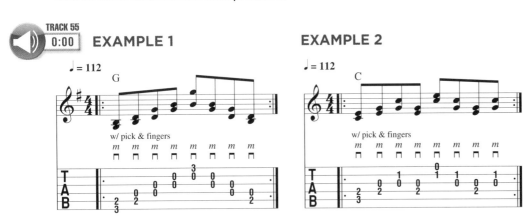

Next, try using double plucking to play this common pop and rock progression:

Go Wide

Double plucking certainly is not limited to adjacent strings; in fact, it's most effective when you mix things up. But for now, let's work on plucking non-adjacent strings, with one string in between. For the following exercise, pluck with your pick and middle finger initially, and then try using your pick and ring finger.

Our next example, an acoustic progressive-rock riff that changes from 3/4 to 4/4 time, is a more practical, musical use of double-plucking technique. The riff maintains the same string spacing (one string between plucked notes) as the previous example, but the change in time and feel makes it a more challenging prospect.

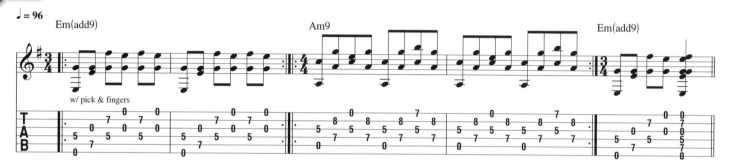

Spaced Out

The example below is where we get deeper into the technique's practical use. Here, double-plucked dyads of varying "spacing" intermingle with single-plucked notes. Though the example may appear somewhat similar to Travis picking, differences exist, particularly in the dyads, which are more unconventional than those found in more traditional fingerstyle patterns.

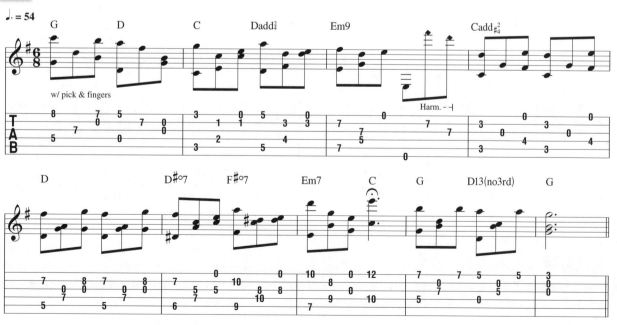

For more on double plucking and other rock-focused fingerstyle techniques in the styles of Jeff Buckley, Nick Drake, Elliott Smith, John Frusciante, and others, check out *Power Plucking* (Hal Leonard) by ace instructor Dale Turner, who inspired this lesson.

LESSON #57: OPEN-STRING BARRE CHORDS

Nearly everyone learns chords in a similar manner when they first pick up the instrument. First, open-position "cowboy" chords featuring lots of open strings are learned; then you get to barre chords, with no open strings; and finally, you learn power chords, wherein open-position forms have open-string roots and movable shapes have no open strings.

Yet some of the coolest and most colorful sounds that you can create on an acoustic guitar involve a combination of barre chords, power chords, and open chords. In this lesson, we'll examine those tools of sonic delight that we'll collectively call open-string barre chords.

The "E" Shape

The first barre chord that most students learn is a movable form of the open E chord. Although these six-string barre chords offer access to a wide variety of key centers, they just don't seem to sound as good on an acoustic guitar as open chords do. Thankfully, a simple solution exists. Simply play an open E major chord with your middle, ring, and pinky fingers, and then slide the form up one fret, placing your index finger on the 1st fret of the low-E string. Then strum the resultant chord, leaving the top two strings, B and E, free to ring. The delightfully complex-sounding chord that results is Fmaj7#11.

EXAMPLE 1

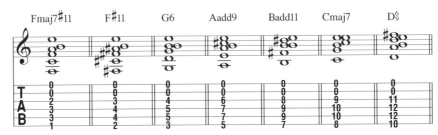

As you can see in Example 1, as you slide the E major shape up the neck, you get some very cool-sounding chord voicings. You'll also notice that we skipped a few positions; although you can use the ones we skipped, unless you're playing some truly "out there" material, they most likely won't fit comfortably into many songs.

Example 2 uses some of these shapes to create a colorful chord progression.

TRACK 56
0:00 **EXAMPLE 2**

The "A" Shape

Typically, the next barre-chord shape that students learn, following the E shape, is the one based on the open A chord (and the parallel Am shape). Of course, we have some dandy open-string versions of these chords as well.

EXAMPLE 3

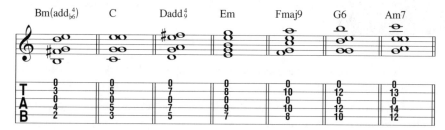

Notice that, for these five-string voicings we've opted to allow the open high-E and G strings to drone, as opposed to the open E and B strings, as in the E shape. This is done because the 3rd degree of the chords, which determines major and minor tonality, falls on the B string in this shape and we want to include that all-important chord tone.

Here's a pianistic ballad riff that uses several of these A-shape open-string barre chords:

EXAMPLE 4

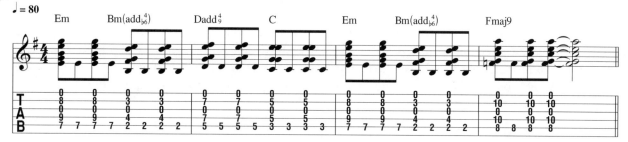

Power Drones!

Let's revisit the A-shape open-string barre chords, but this time we're going to fret the G string and allow the top two strings, B and E, to ring freely. The result is a movable power-chord shape in which the droning B and E strings determine the overall tonality of the chord.

EXAMPLE 5

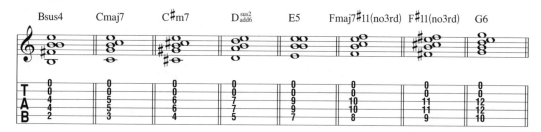

Those voicings are especially useful when you're faced with playing power chords but want to fill out the sound. Just make sure the resultant extensions and alterations jell with the song that you're playing.

EXAMPLE 6

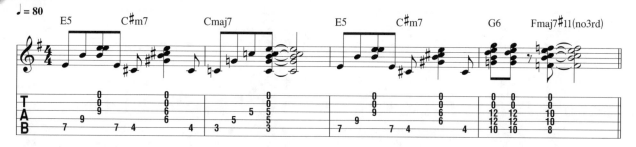

Many of the lessons in this book conclude with advice to experiment further with the lesson's content on your own, but few will result in as much fun as playing around with all the open-string barre chord shapes presented here. Start by mixing and matching the three basic shapes; for example, in the final measure of Example 6, you might want to substitute the power chord-based G6 and Fmaj7#11 chords for the A-shape voicings. From there, just keep exploring. Soon you'll be creating chords so colorful that you'll earn the nickname "Crayola."

LESSON #58: "ADD" CHORDS

Western music is based on tertian harmony; that is, chords built on the 3rd interval. In other lessons in this book, you can learn about how to extend chord harmony past basic major and minor triads, building seventh chords, and even extended chords like 9ths and 13ths. However, another way to *add* color to those basic triads exists, and that's precisely what we're going to explore in this lesson—the world of "add" chords.

More Art Than Math

First, let's review basic triad theory. Major triads contain three notes—the root, 3rd, and 5th. Minor triads contain the same three notes, with one small, yet critical, difference—the 3rd is flatted: 1–♭3–5. One way by which we can color those basic triads is to "suspend" the 3rd, replacing it with either the 2nd for a sus2 chord, or the 4th for a sus4 chord. The result in both cases is a chord that is neither major nor minor. "Sus" chords have their advantages, particularly in modal settings; however, what if you want to maintain that major or minor tonality, yet still subtly "color" the sound? Enter "add" chords.

While maintaining the basic triadic structure, an add chord adds a scale tone to the chord. For example, if we begin with a C major triad, C–E–G, and add the scale tone D to it, we get C–E–G–D, or a 1–3–5–9 formula. The C major triad is now a Cadd9 chord. Now let's give the same treatment to a G major triad. If you add the scale tone A to it, you get G–B–D–A, which is also a 1–3–5–9 formula, or a Gadd9 chord. Here are what those chords, along with an Eadd9, look like in grid form:

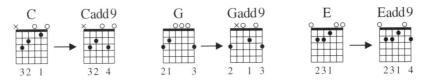

> ### IF 2 WAS 9?
> You might be wondering why in the examples above I labeled the chords as "add9" instead of "add2," when we added the 2nd of each respective chord's major scale. Technically speaking, the chord could be named either way, Cadd2 or Cadd9, depending on the octave in which the added note falls. In the aforementioned Cadd9 chord, the added D note falls an octave plus a 2nd above the root, C; therefore, we call it Cadd9. If instead you were to play a basic open C major chord and remove your second finger from the E note on the fourth string, so that the open D note is allowed to ring out, you'd be playing a Cadd2 chord. Generally, in most guitar music it doesn't matter in which octave the added note appears—unless it serves as the bass note, but more on that later in the lesson.

Now let's check out some add chords in action to hear how they can liven up a basic chord progression. This first example is one of the most popular chord progressions in pop rock music over the past 25 years:

TRACK 57
0:00 **EXAMPLE 1**

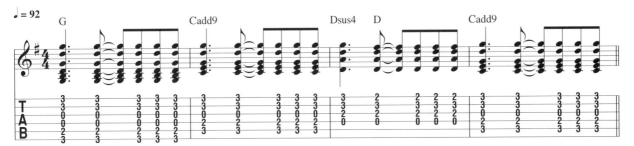

While the underlying G–C–D progression is quite commonplace, using the Cadd9 in place of a normal C triad, along with the brief appearance of the Dsus4, provides some cool voice-leading via the droning G5 dyad on the top two strings.

The next example, based on an E–D–A (I–♭VII–IV) progression, introduces another kind of voice-leading whereby an E–F♯ melody on the high-E string follows the same rhythmic motif across all three chords, resulting in add and sus chords, including an A chord in measure 3 that features both a suspended 2nd and an added 6th.

EXAMPLE 2

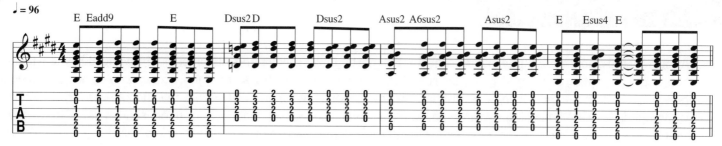

Adding Open Strings

Another way to create cool-sounding add chords is by adding open strings to barre chord shapes. This approach is especially common among modern acoustic guitarists who know how to take advantage of those ringing strings. In the next example, open strings are incorporated into fifth string-rooted Bm and D barre chords to create Bm(add4) and Dadd2/4, respectively. Yes, that D chord has *two* added notes—a common result when building chords with open strings.

EXAMPLE 3

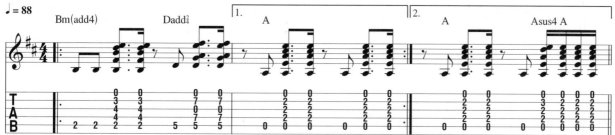

The next example utilizes discordant sounds similar to those you might hear from Ani DiFranco. Again, both of the add chords in this progression feature two added notes.

EXAMPLE 4

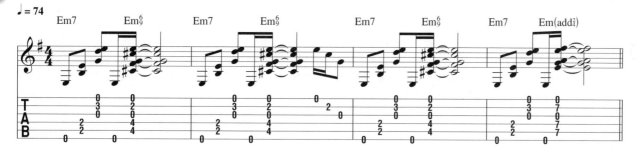

"Add" Notes in the Bass

In the sidebar at the beginning of the lesson, I alluded to placing added notes in the bass. This type of add chord most frequently occurs in the jazz realm, where you may see a triad with the added 9th (or 2nd) in the bass to provide hip voice-leading. When that occurs, we label the chord in "slash" fashion with the triad name first, followed after a slash by the bass note. So a Gadd9 with the 9th (A) in the bass would be written as G/A. In the next example, a G/A serves as a substitute for the ii chord (Em7) in a ii–V–I (G/A–A7♭9–Dmaj13) progression.

EXAMPLE 5

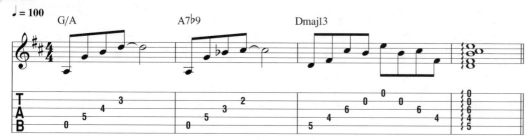

LESSON #59: INTERVALLIC COMPOSITION

Aside from the piano, the acoustic guitar is arguably the most popular songwriting instrument in the world. But when guitarists approach songwriting on the guitar, they typically dive right into chord strums or arpeggios, occasionally working out a single-note riff as well. These approaches work just fine, but they tend to limit creativity. One way to expand those creative horizons is through intervallic composition. A fancy phrase for a simple concept, intervallic composition is much easier to use than it sounds. In this lesson, we'll explore basic intervals and a few of the ways that you can use them to energize your song craft.

Interval Basics

Before we delve into how to use intervals to create cool riffs, let's take a moment to review the basics of musical intervals. Example 1A, shown below, illustrates the naturally occurring intervals in a C major scale. A capitalized "M" indicates a major interval, and a capitalized "P" a perfect interval. Example 1B comprises the non-diatonic intervals. A lowercase "m" indicates a minor interval, with "aug" and "dim" representing augmented (sharp) and diminished (flat), respectively.

To get a feel for how these intervals sound, pluck each intervallic pair in Example 1A in unison and then separately. A great ear training exercise is to sit with a friend back to back and have him play an interval, and you guess it. Then you play a random interval, and he guesses.

Static Intervals

You can approach intervallic composition in two basic ways. You can choose either a single interval, like a 6th, and adhere to that sound, or you can choose a key center and create dynamic intervals against it. First, we're going to explore the former approach, which we'll call static intervals.

Here, we're going to use 3rd intervals, arguably the most important interval in Western music because the 3rd determines major and minor tonality. The first example is a very simple I–vi–iii–IV (G–Em–Bm–C) progression that uses the root and diatonic 3rd of each chord to form a riff. Notice that the two major chords, G and C, are expressed with major 3rd intervals, whereas the two minor chords, Em and Bm, use minor 3rd intervals.

EXAMPLE 2

Let's expand that riff to include droning open strings, which will both fill out and color the progression.

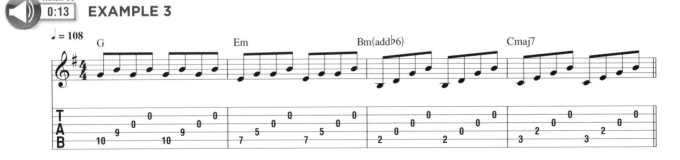

EXAMPLE 3

Now, we're going to take that 3rd interval to a whole new level—literally. In the next example, we're going to place an octave between the root and the 3rd. The result is a fingerstyle riff constructed from 10th intervals. You might recognize this sound and shape from the Beatles' acoustic classic "Blackbird" or the Red Hot Chili Peppers' smash hit "Scar Tissue."

TRACK 58
0:26 **EXAMPLE 4**

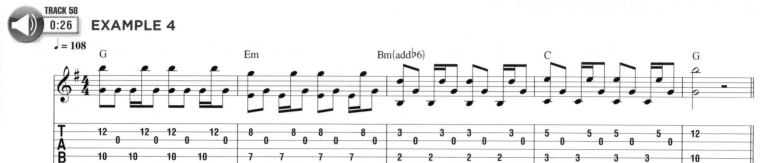

Dynamic Intervals

In this section, we'll examine intervallic composition that uses dynamic intervals, which essentially is the practice of crafting a riff with various diatonic intervals against a static key center. This approach to composition is most easily achieved by using a droning note.

The riff in this next example is in the key of A, but with a ♭7th degree, thus making it an A Mixolydian riff. We keep things simple: just a static root note, A, against a dynamic interval. This starts with a perfect 5th (E), climbs to a major 6th (F♯), and then sits on the ♭7th (G)—which creates the Mixolydian sound—before climbing to a 10th (C♯) (an octave plus a major 3rd), then travels back down to the octave A with a 9th (B) embellishment for a touch of color.

TRACK 58
0:41 **EXAMPLE 5**

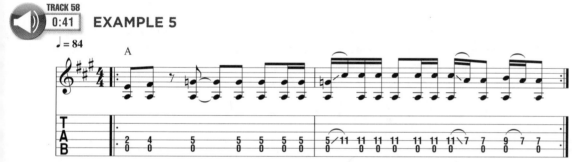

Now let's take that same basic riff and add a perfect 5th interval to the moving (i.e., dynamic) interval, as well as open B and E strings, to further fill out the arrangement.

TRACK 58
0:57 **EXAMPLE 6**

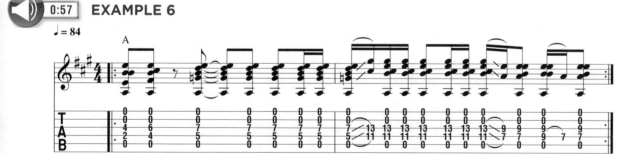

Up to this point, all the examples in this lesson have been fairly "ear-friendly." But with intervals, the real fun comes when you begin to explore more dissonant sounds, like 2nds and 7ths. In our final example, octave G notes are separated by F and F♯ notes, which can be classified as either major and minor 2nds or minor and major 7ths, depending on which note pair you examine.

TRACK 58
1:14 **EXAMPLE 7**

LESSON #60: 6TH INTERVALS

A thorough knowledge of musical intervals is a powerful tool when playing guitar, whether writing or improvising, but when it comes to acoustic guitar, 6th intervals have special appeal—particularly when combined with droning open strings. In this lesson, you'll learn where 6ths lay across various string sets and how to use them in conjunction with ringing open strings.

Intervallic Roadmap

The 6th interval is defined as two notes, five diatonic steps apart, played either consecutively or simultaneously.

Though you need to be able to identify the two notes that compose a 6th interval anywhere on the fretboard, the real fun is when you harmonize a scale in 6ths, so you can play melodic phrases using the interval. Here is a one-octave C major scale harmonized in 6ths, beginning with the C root on the fifth string:

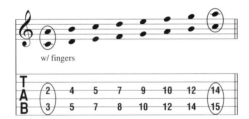

Here is the harmonized C major scale on string set 4–2. Note that it begins on the 3rd (E):

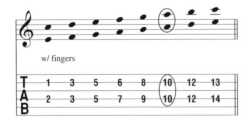

And finally, on string set 3–1, this time starting on the 6th (A).

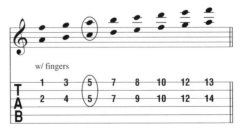

Droning in 6ths

Although 6th intervals most often are associated with soul or country guitar, they can sound downright huge on an acoustic guitar when paired with droning open strings.

Example 1 is a I7–IV7 (E7–A7) blues progression arranged in diatonic 6th intervals and pedaled against the open-E string root. This type of riff is more common in old-time acoustic country blues than you might expect, and one worth revisiting.

TRACK 59 0:00 **EXAMPLE 1**

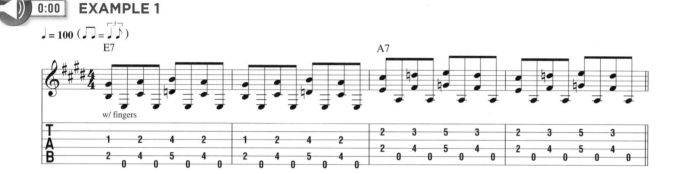

This next riff takes its uptempo acoustic-rock cue from the acoustic work of Led Zeppelin's Jimmy Page, who is rather fond of droning strings, though normally in an altered or open tuning. Here, even the droning open G and E strings are a 6th apart!

TRACK 59 0:14 **EXAMPLE 2**

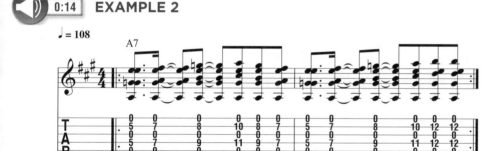

The final example is a modern modal-droning arrangement of the children's classic "Itsy Bitsy Spider." To beef it up even more, tune your low A and E strings down one step to G and D, respectively, and strum those on select beats, turning that itsy-bitsy spider into one big, scary arachnid!

TRACK 59 0:27 **EXAMPLE 3**

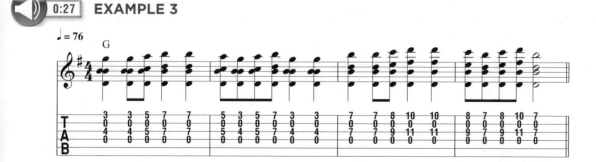

Although the examples in this lesson stayed true to diatonic harmony, half the fun of moving predetermined intervallic shapes, like 6ths, around the neck in conjunction with open, droning strings is discovering all of the beautiful "accidents" that occur as a result. Start with the diatonic strategy until you get comfortable with the various minor and major 6th interval shapes and locations, but then turn it loose and have fun!

LESSON #61: DRONES

Acoustic guitarists—even ones with many years of playing experience—always go back to open-position chords for a reason: those open, ringing strings just sound so darned good! However, you don't have to be in open position to use those open strings. Moreover, ringing notes don't have to be from open strings, either. In this lesson, we'll explore various ways in which you can combine ringing, or droning, notes with other notes or chords, anywhere on the neck.

Open Strings

A precursor to modern counterpoint, the drone originally was developed to help define the key center of a song or melody. Most often associated with that noblest of instruments—the bagpipes—a drone is a constant pitch, typically in a lower register, that is maintained beneath a melody line. The modern use of drones, however, has shifted to include droning notes that are higher in pitch than the melody line, as well. We'll begin with the classic use: a lower-pitched drone.

Our first example is an acoustic rock riff in Drop D tuning that features a double dose of droning notes. As you can see, a big, open D5 power chord is struck on every other beat, while the open D string accompanies the descending D Mixolydian melody. Be sure to let that power chord ring throughout.

EXAMPLE 1

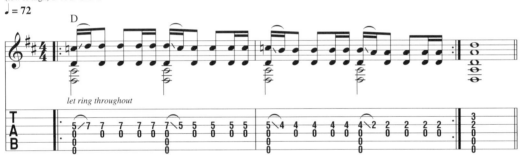

In the second example, the open, low-E string is played against octaves that are diatonic to the key of E, beginning on the major 7th (D♯), to create cool tension.

EXAMPLE 2

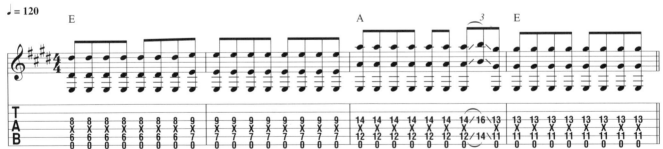

As was alluded to earlier, the droning notes do not have to sound in a lower pitch. One of the great uses of drones in acoustic pop and rock music is heard in Paul McCartney's brilliant piece "Blackbird," in which the open G string serves as a counterpoint to the melody and bass lines. Here is a similar riff:

EXAMPLE 3

Altered Tunings

Altered tunings, particularly on acoustic guitar, provide a fabulous means by which to be creative with drones. Take, for example, the popular use of the modal tuning DADGAD to play Celtic music. Those ringing modal notes help to mimic the sound of bagpipes, albeit in a typically softer manner.

This next riff is an example of how Jimmy Page might interpret a Celtic approach to DADGAD. Let all the notes ring as long as possible, particularly the open low-D and high-A strings.

EXAMPLE 4

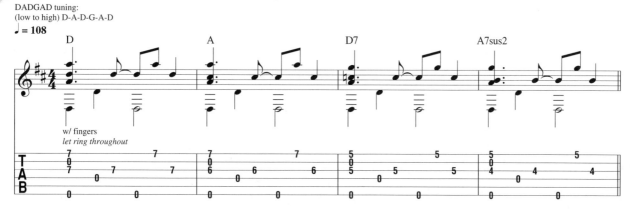

This next riff takes its cue from Johnny Rzeznik of the Goo Goo Dolls. The figure is in D5 tuning, which is essentially DADGAD, but with the third string (G) tuned down to D so it's in unison with the open fourth string.

EXAMPLE 5

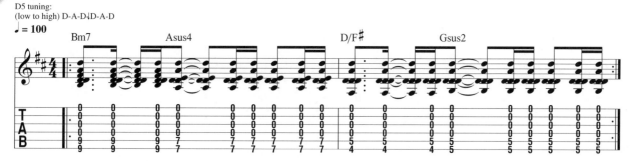

Wonder-Drones

As mentioned in the introduction, drones can also be played with notes higher in pitch than the melody or the chord motion. Back in the mid-nineties, British rockers Oasis struck paydirt with this technique on the smash hit "Wonderwall." Countless other acoustic pop and rock artists have had great success with this approach as well.

Our final example, in the style of "Wonderwall" as well as the Indigo Girls' "Closer to Fine," another mid-nineties acoustic hit, features a droning G5 dyad (G/D) on the top two strings of every chord strum.

EXAMPLE 6

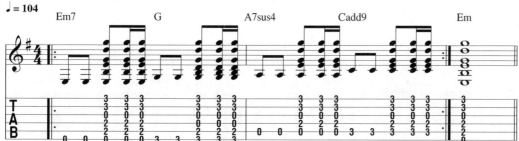

Drones are a nearly inexhaustible compositional tool, especially when you pair them with altered or modal tunings. Artists ranging from the aforementioned Rzeznik to virtuosos like Preston Reed and Michael Hedges have made careers out of using them. All it takes is a little tweak in your approach and a big sense of adventure. Have fun!

Believe it or not, many guitarists go nearly their entire careers counting to four, and nothing more. The simple 4/4 time signature is so commonplace in pop and rock music these days that finding songs written in other meters is a challenge—and a treat. Nevertheless, a whole world of rhythmic variety exists out there in the form of compound meter, better known as 6/8, 9/8, and 12/8 time signatures, among others.

Compound Basics

The top number of compound meter time signatures has two distinguishing characteristics: 1) it is 6 or higher, and 2) it is a multiple of 3 (most commonly 6, 9, or 12). Compound time signatures are also to be counted in groups of three, rather than as individual beats. So instead of quarter notes receiving the beat, in compound meter dotted quarter notes get the beat.

6/8 Meter

Our first compound meter is 6/8, which indicates that six 8th notes comprise each measure. But as previously mentioned, the pulse is felt as two dotted quarter notes. This type of two-beats-to-the-bar feel is referred to as duple meter, and since it's a compound time signature, it's classified as compound duple.

One of the musical forms most commonly associated with 6/8 time is the Irish jig. This beloved traditional form thrives not only on the two-beat feel, but also places the main emphasis on the backbeat, which means the fourth 8th note in each bar gets the accent, with beat 1 also receiving a slight accent as the downbeat.

EXAMPLE 1

Of course, 6/8 is not confined to Irish dancing; you may also hear it in lilting pop or rock ballads, as in this riff:

EXAMPLE 2

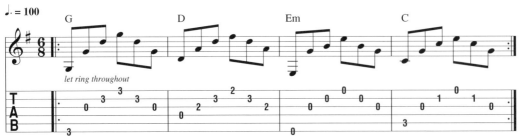

And here's a "must-know" acoustic strum pattern in 6/8 time:

EXAMPLE 3

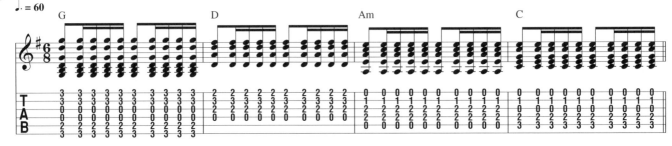

9/8 Meter

Our next compound meter is 9/8. Although 9/8 meter contains nine 8th notes per bar, it's felt as three dotted quarter notes, making it compound triple meter. The most common song form in 9/8 is the Irish slip jig, like "The Butterfly," played here in E minor.

TRACK 61
0:37   **EXAMPLE 4**

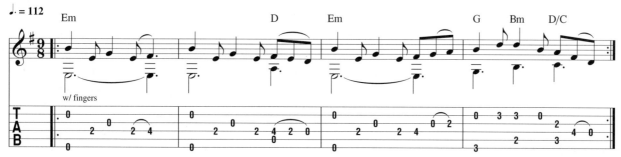

12/8 Meter

Our final compound meter is 12/8. Although 12/8 meter contains 12 8th notes per bar, it's felt as four dotted quarter notes, making it compound quadruple meter. Now, because you're feeling this one as four beats per measure, you may be wondering why it isn't notated as triplets in simple 4/4 time. The answer is that, because the rhythm is felt as three pulses per beat, it is by definition, compound meter.

You'll hear 12/8 in two primary musical contexts: fifties-style doo wop ballads and slow blues. Below is a classic I–vi–IV–V (G–Em–C–D) example of the former. Note the doo wop-style 16th notes in the first beat of each chord.

TRACK 61
0:54   **EXAMPLE 5**

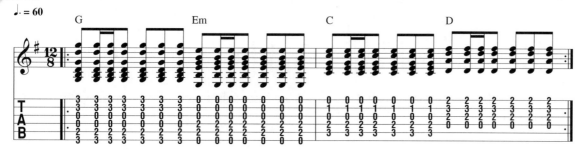

This final example is a I7–IV7 (E7–A7) slow blues change in 12/8:

TRACK 61
1:15   **EXAMPLE 6**

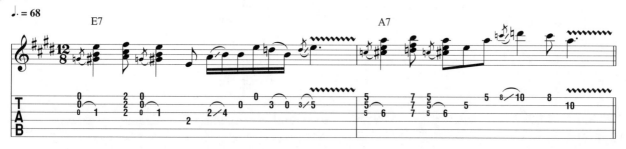

Experimenting with compound meter is an excellent way to break out of the 4/4 rut and broaden your songwriting horizons. Compound meters also provide a smooth transition into the exciting world of complex time signatures like 5/4 (Dave Brubeck's "Take Five") or even shifting time signatures, as heard in the Beatles' "Strawberry Fields Forever" and especially in progressive rock music.

LESSON #63: 6/8 STRUM PATTERNS

From the Beatles to Queen to the Red Hot Chili Peppers to countless Irish jigs, 6/8 time signature has become an enduring component of acoustic guitar playing. Drawing on examples from the masters, in this lesson we'll take a look at some of the most useful strum patterns for playing in 6/8 time.

Compound Interest

The 6/8 time signature is a compound meter in which each measure contains six 8th notes. Each measure is simply counted: "1, 2, 3, 4, 5, 6." The pulse, however, is felt as two dotted quarter notes. This type of two-beats-to-the-bar feel is known as duple meter, and since it's also a compound time signature, we call it compound duple.

So now that the theory lesson is over, let's talk about what makes 6/8 meter special. Simply put, it's a versatile alternative to common 4/4 time—one which easily can be made into a hard-driving rhythm, a lilting one, or even accompaniment for a ballad.

Get Jiggy with It

Our first example is a straightforward one-strum-per-8th-note example in the style of an Irish jig. Although the rhythmic counting is straightforward, other key components give the example its Irish jig feel. For starters, the strum pattern itself is not strictly alternating; instead, it's "down-up-down, down-up-down." If you're not used to hitting two consecutive downstrokes in the middle of the measure, it can be challenging—particularly at the high tempos of some jigs—but it's absolutely essential to the sound. Second, note the accent on beat 4 of each measure, which establishes the backbeat feel of the jig.

TRACK 62 `0:00` **EXAMPLE 1**

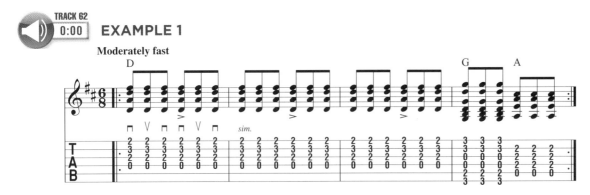

This next strum pattern is also used in Irish jigs. Here, beats 1–2 and 4–5 are essentially tied to create a quarter/8th rhythm, like an exaggerated shuffle. Again, note the accent on the backbeat.

TRACK 62 `0:11` **EXAMPLE 2**

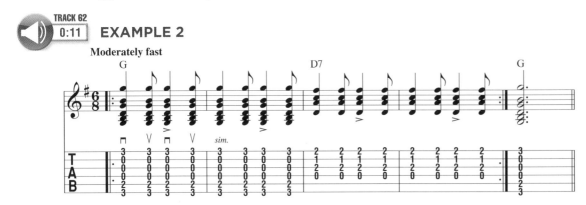

Subdivisions

The next step in creating strum patterns in 6/8 requires subdividing some of the beats into 16th notes. Staying with the Irish jig theme, the next example divides beat 2 of each measure into two 16th notes. You'll count this as "1, 2-and, 3, 4, 5, 6." Played with an accented backbeat, it's a minor-key jig; played without an accent, it could be an accompaniment for a 6/8 quasi-rock ballad.

EXAMPLE 3

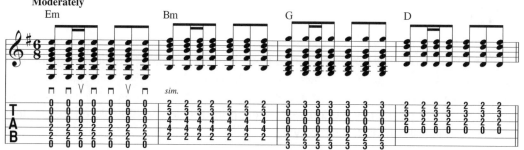

The strum patterns in the next two examples—which can be heard in the Beatles' 6/8 classic "Norwegian Wood"—feature additional 16th-note subdivisions. In the first pattern, both beats 2 and 3 are subdivided into 16th notes, while the backbeat portion of the measure (beats 4–6) remains as 8th notes.

EXAMPLE 4

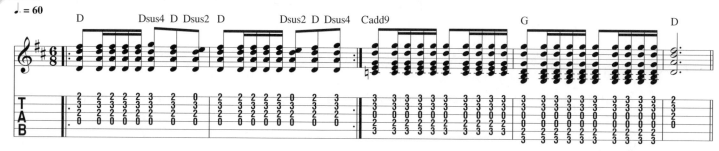

And here, only the strong beats, 1 and 4, remain as 8th notes. This pattern also works well in a 6/8 ballad.

EXAMPLE 5

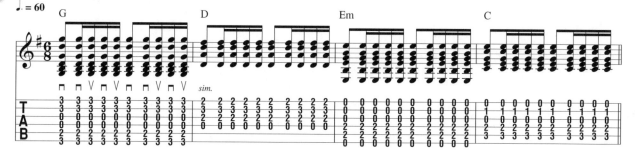

Syncopated 16ths

Finally, you can further manipulate those subdivided 16th notes with syncopation. The syncopated strum pattern in this next example, inspired by John Frusciante's funky acoustic riff in the Red Hot Chili Peppers' "Breaking the Girl," is counted: *1-and, 2-and,* 3-*and,* 4-*and,* 5-*and, 6-and.*

Practice this pattern using just the opening A chord until you feel the rhythm properly. Be sure to keep your pick hand relaxed while strumming in steady 16ths, only striking the strings on the italicized portions of the beat, as shown above.

EXAMPLE 6

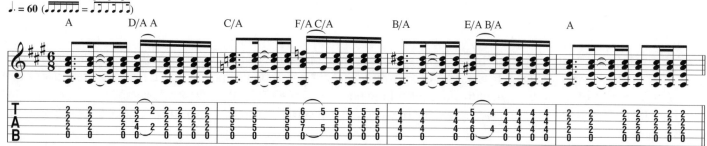

As you can see by just this small sampling of strum patterns, 6/8 has lots to offer. We encourage you to explore 6/8 strum patterns to break out of the 4/4 rut and spur those creative juices in your own songwriting.

LESSON #64: TWISTED TUNINGS

About a century ago, country and Delta blues guitarists often turned to open tunings to facilitate their slide guitar playing. Then, in the late sixties and early seventies, artists like John Fahey, Joni Mitchell, and Leo Kottke began to explore modal tunings like DADGAD, and with the emergence of experimental acoustic artists like Will Ackerman, Michael Hedges, and Preston Reed in the eighties, virtually all tuning barriers were forever broken. In this lesson, we'll explore those wide-open sounds as we twist your tuning pegs to previously uncharted territory.

A Bit of a Stretch

As you embark on the journey down the road of extreme altered tunings, keep in mind that some tunings may require re-stringing, for fear of snapping strings or leaving them so slack that you can't play in tune. Michael Hedges went so far as to replace his low-E string with a bass string when dropping that string's pitch a 5th, down to A, and Goo Goo Dolls guitarist Johnny Rzeznik uses identical string gauges on the top two strings for his "Iris" tuning. The examples presented here were conceived while using .013–.056 gauge strings, and I'm proud to say that no strings were harmed during the writing.

Modal Mayhem

Although DADGAD is the most commonly mentioned modal tuning, it's not the only one. British guitarist Richard Thompson—one of the most underrated guitar geniuses of all time—was one of the early adopters of varied tunings, including Drop D (D–A–D–G–B–E), DADGAD, and Cmaj9 (C–G–D–G–B–E). The tuning that we'll examine here is essentially a G modal tuning, only with an F on the lowest string: F–G–D–G–C–D.

This example kicks off with a Celtic-flavored riff (Thompson has said he was highly influenced by traditional Irish music) that exploits the low F in the B section.

TRACK 63 `0:00` **EXAMPLE 1**

Singer-songwriter Patty Larkin is another aficionado of altered tunings and cites Richard Thompson—specifically his F–G–D–G–C–D tuning—as an influence. In fact, she's even written four songs in Thompson's tuning. But here, we'll take a look at how she applies one of her favorite tunings—a G modal tuning: C–G–C–G–C–D. In the following example, based on one of her tunes that uses the tuning, "Carolina," playing the opening Am11 chord in arpeggio form results in the scalar line B–C–D on the top three strings.

EXAMPLE 2

Unison Notes

The next three tunings make use of some fairly extreme twisting of the tuning pegs and feature unison-tuned strings in varying degrees.

The first tuning, C–G–D–D–A–E, comes from experimental master Michael Hedges and his landmark composition "Breakfast in the Fields." Here, the third string—normally tuned to G—is tuned *down* to match the open D note of the fourth string. The accompanying example includes one of Hedges' signature techniques, in which you "hammer on from nowhere" to sound the D5 dyad in measure 3, and then, with your pick-hand index finger lightly touching all six strings at the 12th fret, you "violently" pull off those two notes in a downward motion, plucking the top four strings along the way to sound the harmonics.

EXAMPLE 3

*Hammer on from nowhere.
**Pull off from previous chord w/ R.H. index finger over 12th fret to sound harmonics.

Guitarist Johnny Rzeznik used our final—and most extreme—tuning on the Goo Goo Dolls' smash hit "Iris." Featuring three octaves of open D strings, including two unison pairs, this tuning is spelled: B–D–D–D–D–D. The fifth string is tuned down a 5th, the third string down a 4th, the second string *up* a minor 3rd, and the first string down one whole step.

EXAMPLE 4

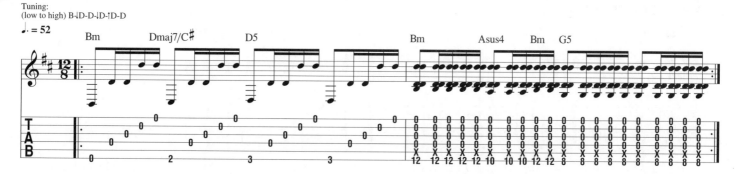

As you can see, from the experimental sounds of Michael Hedges to the mellifluous musings of Patty Larkin to the unabashed acoustic pop of the Goo Goo Dolls, extreme guitar tunings have made an indelible mark on acoustic music. When it comes right down to it, the number of altered tunings that you can explore or invent is limited only by the fact that you've got six strings, so start twisting those pegs, ignore those boundaries, and make some music!

LESSON #65: NASHVILLE TUNING

Picture this: you're sitting in the studio, strumming away on your trusty dreadnought. The engineer is twisting EQ knobs like crazy, trying to contain that big, boomy low end when someone says, "Can't we replace the low strings and tune them up an octave?" Voila! Nashville tuning is born.

High Strung

Nashville tuning has had an indelible impact on recording acoustic guitar and can be heard in such classic tunes as the Rolling Stones' "Wild Horses," Pink Floyd's "Comfortably Numb," and Tom Petty's "Free Fallin.'"

Nashville tuning requires you to re-string the bottom four wound strings (E–A–D–G) of your guitar with a lighter gauge and tune them up one octave. The string gauges are generally as follows, from low to high:

Sixth-String E:	.025
Fifth-String A:	.017
Fourth-String D:	.012
Third-String G:	.010

The top two strings, B and E, are strung normally—for example, with .016 and .012, respectively. Several guitar-string manufacturers offer specially packaged Nashville tuning sets.

Let's Take It Higher

The notation in this first example illustrates the difference between standard- and Nashville-tuned chord voicings. You can clearly see that now at least one doubled (or unison) note is present in each voicing, which helps to fatten the overall sound—a desired effect in the studio.

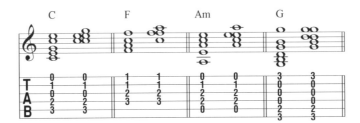

Now let's put those chords to work in a bouncy 3/4 chord progression.

TRACK 64
0:00 **EXAMPLE 1**

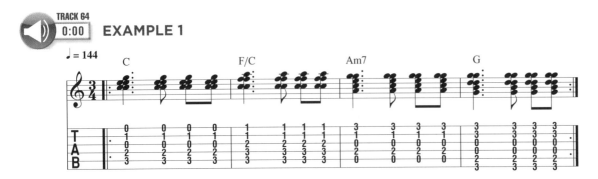

Although its origins are apparently unknown, we do know that Nashville tuning was originally conceived in the studio to replace the boomy low end of an acoustic guitar. These days, the tuning is often paired with standard tuning to create layered guitar parts. For example, if you record the progression in Example 2 on a Nashville-tuned guitar and then play it back while performing the same progression on a standard-tuned guitar, you can hear the huge sound it creates. But you can take it even further—and higher—by adding a third part that is composed of Nashville-tuned chord inversions that are played up the neck, like this:

EXAMPLE 2

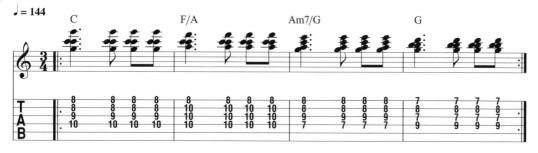

Yet another way to use Nashville tuning for layering purposes—or even simply for a cool accompaniment effect—is to add a capo to the mix.

EXAMPLE 3

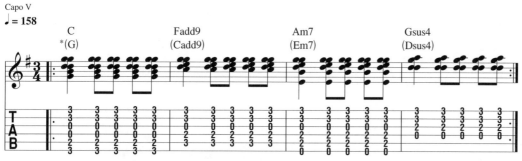

*Symbols in parentheses represent chord names respective to capoed guitar.
Symbols above reflect actual sounding chords. Capoed fret is "0" in tab.

Even good old-fashioned fingerpicking takes on a whole new and interesting sound when performed in Nashville tuning. Because of the change in tuning, you get all sorts of cool octave displacement and thus, wild melodic contours. This next example uses a pretty stock picking pattern, yet it sounds vastly different than when played in standard tuning.

EXAMPLE 4

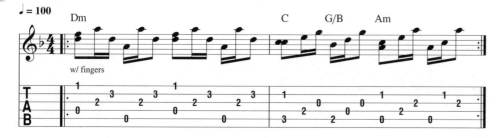

These days, with all the digital modulation, harmonizing, EQ, and other tone-shaping effects available to guitarists in the recording studios, organic methods for achieving new sounds might be easy to overlook. Although Nashville tuning isn't as simple as slapping a capo on the neck, its radical retuning might just be what your song is looking for.

Few names are more influential in the world of traditional country music than the Carter family of Virginia. Such timeless classics as "Wildwood Flower," "Can the Circle Be Unbroken," "Diamonds in the Rough," and "Bury Me Under the Weeping Willow," among others, were either written by or made popular by A.P. Carter, his wife Sara, and sister-in-law Maybelle. In this lesson, we're going to examine Maybelle's pioneering guitar approach, presently known as "Carter strumming" or "Carter picking."

Two Voices Are Better Than One

As the sole instrumentalist in the Carter Family group, Maybelle Carter was responsible for providing accompaniment to the vocals of A.P. and Sara. To better fill out the arrangements, Maybelle developed a then-unique style of picking in which she combined single-note bass melodies with chord strums on her trusted Gibson L-5 archtop. This clever approach produced the illusion that listeners were hearing two instruments instead of just one.

The Root–5th Pattern

The most basic Carter strumming approach is to create a bass line with just the root and 5th of each chord, with those two notes occurring on the downbeats (beats 1 and 3, respectively), and chord strums—usually on the top few strings of the chord voicing—falling on the upbeats (beats 2 and 4).

Now, if you're wondering why we're referring to beats 1 and 3 as "downbeats" and beats 2 and 4 as "upbeats," it's because this style of traditional country, folk, and bluegrass is typically played in cut time, in which each "beat" has a half-note duration.

Here's the basic root–5th idea, using an E chord:

 EXAMPLE 1

Depending on the particular chord voicing, the pitch of the 5th may fall *below* the root. For example, when applying the Carter strum technique to an open-position A major chord, the root (A) falls on the open fifth string, whereas the 5th (E) is played as the open sixth string.

 EXAMPLE 2

The Root–3rd Pattern

For some chords, such as open G and open C, you'll find that you've got the option of using either the root–5th approach or a root–3rd tack. The following examples show both approaches.

EXAMPLE 3

EXAMPLE 4

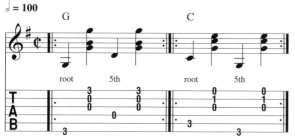

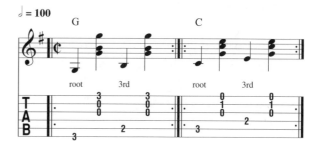

Double Up

So far, all the examples have used quarter-note rhythms, with one bass note and one chord strum every two beats. This seemingly simplistic approach is quite common when songs are played at fast tempos; however, when presented with some rhythmic "space," a popular variation is to play two 8th-note strums on each upbeat (beats 2 and 4).

EXAMPLE 5

Carter Country Stomp

Now we're going to add some bass-line melodies to the strum patterns to create a complete cut-time, 24-bar country stomp in the style of Maybelle Carter. The tempo is 100 bpm (cut time), which is cookin', but only on medium-high heat. Still, if this style is new to you, try playing the example at approximately 70 bpm (cut time), and then gradually work your way up. You should also try to use 8th-note strums on some of the upbeats to work on that strum pattern as well.

EXAMPLE 6

Even if you're an accomplished strummer or fingerstylist, you can always find something to add to your bag of licks and tricks to round out your sound—like say, techniques typically reserved for a stringed instrument such as the banjo.

Banjo Basics

The five-string banjo is tuned to open G (G–D–G–B–D), with the "low" G string (that short one with a tuning peg around the 4th fret) actually sounding the highest pitch. Short of restringing your guitar with a super light-gauge string (e.g., an .008) in the normal fifth-string slot, you won't be able to perfectly duplicate true banjo tuning, but for the sake of simplicity, we're going to begin this lesson in Open G tuning (low to high: D–G–D–G–B–D). Although the top five strings are now tuned to the same notes as the banjo, that fifth-string G sounds two octaves lower.

The Banjo Roll

The most commonly adopted banjo technique for the guitar is the banjo roll, which comes in two general varieties: forward rolls and reverse rolls. The three-finger forward roll is played with the thumb (*p*), index (*i*), and middle (*m*) fingers, in that order (*p–i–m*). This first example features the melody from the traditional tune "Lily of the Valley," played with a forward roll in Open G tuning.

EXAMPLE 1

Now, sticking with Open G tuning, let's flip the pattern. When playing reverse rolls, the three-finger pattern moves from high strings to lower ones, using your middle (*m*), index (*i*), and thumb (*p*), in that order (*m–i–p*). This next example uses the reverse-roll pattern and a single fretted shape to move down, and then back up, the neck chromatically.

EXAMPLE 2

Without a doubt, the all-time king of down-home banjo pluckin' is Earl Scruggs. One of his favorite picking patterns was *p–i–p–m–i–p–m–i*, which you can hear in the banjo roll-based bluegrass line that he made famous, shown here:

TRACK 66
0:15 **EXAMPLE 3**

Frailing

Banjo techniques aren't all about barn-burnin' pickin' and grinnin'. One of the more important banjo-style rhythm techniques that's worth checking out on acoustic guitar is called frailing. If you're a practiced Travis picker, frailing may seem counterintuitive, but with practice you'll get it. When performing the basic frailing pattern, the thumb plays on the upbeat and the fingers play the melody notes. Let's take a look at a basic I–IV (G–C) frailing pattern.

TRACK 66
0:24 **EXAMPLE 4**

In Example 4, you play beats 1 and 3 by picking upward with your index finger, as you normally would. Beats 2 and 4, however, are played by striking downward with the nail on your middle finger, followed by your thumb on the "and" of those beats. Try not to think of it as fingerpicking; rather, generate momentum by moving your whole hand. Further, the thumb doesn't "pluck"; instead, it performs a push-and-release maneuver, pushing down on the string and releasing with an abrupt upward motion.

Ending Lick

Finally, having the ability to pull a classic ending out of your straw hat, like the banjo-style chromatic line below, courtesy of super-picker Jerry Reed, is always nice. This example uses a picking pattern that is similar to the previous Scruggs lick, so it should feel vaguely familiar.

TRACK 66
0:32 **EXAMPLE 5**

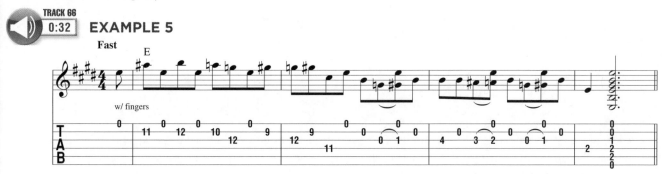

In addition to the aforementioned Earl Scruggs, check out six-string pickers like Jerry Reed, Albert Lee, and John Jorgenson, all of whom have borrowed mightily—and successfully—from the guitar's five-string cousin, to ignite new ideas for banjo-based lines for guitar.

COUNTRY TAG LICKS

If you've ever sat in, or just watched and listened to, an open jam, one of the sillier things that you'll witness is how often the musicians have no idea how to end a tune. Unless of course, you're talking about country musicians—those good ol' boys know how to go out in style, using what is known as a tag, or a tag lick. So to help you dot the "i" in lick and cross the "t" in tag, this lesson will cover four open-position country tag licks for acoustic guitar.

Tag! The Major Pentatonic Scale Is It!

Not surprisingly, the tag licks presented here are based on the major pentatonic scale—the go-to tones for country twang. The major pentatonic scale contains five notes, the formula being: 1–2–3–5–6. Below are the notation and tab for the G, C, and A major pentatonic scales, which are three of the most commonly used keys in country music. We've also provided fretboard diagrams that depict where all the notes of those scales fall in open position.

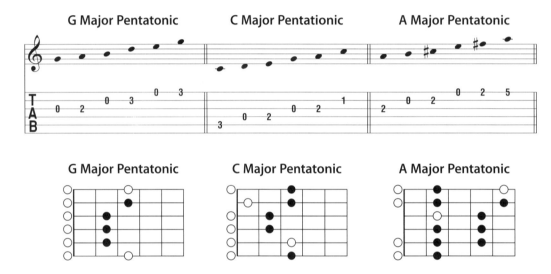

With a Side of Cornbread

Although the major pentatonic scale forms the basis of these tag licks, if you want to sound authentically country, you're going to need to add some Southern flavor. One of country guitar's must-know moves is to lead into the major 3rd from the minor 3rd, so if you're playing in the key of G, you'll want to slip some B♭–B moves into the lick, like the one in measure 2 of the first lick below. Note the B♭ contained in the 16th-note triplet of measure 1; rather than resolving to the major 3rd (B), its presence here serves strictly as ornamentation, or a dash of greasy tension.

TRACK 67
0:00 **EXAMPLE 1**

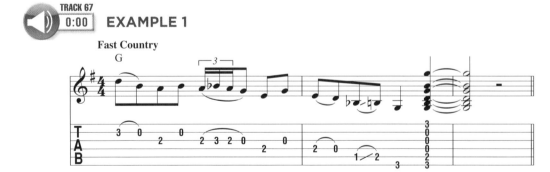

Next is a tag in the key of C that also exploits the ♭3rd–3rd (E♭–E) movement. This one starts in third position, and then performs a rapid position shift via the open high-E string, as opposed to the fretted E note at the 5th fret of the second string. The open string provides the opportunity to make the shift without missing a beat.

EXAMPLE 2

Another way the ♭3rd is used in country music is as a passing tone between scale tones, resulting in a cool bit of chromaticism. This next lick demonstrates this approach perfectly, as made evident by the ascending and descending A–B♭–B lines. To really bring this lick to life, swing the 8th notes a bit to impart a jazzy country sound.

EXAMPLE 3

Finally, no country guitar lesson is complete without a banjo-roll lick. For the A major lick below, we're once again dipping into the ♭3rd–3rd (C–C#) well; this time however, it's more for the twangy dissonance of the minor 2nd interval than for its properties as a leading tone. You'll want to use either hybrid picking or a fingerstyle approach to tackle the roll. In measure 2, the ♭3rd–3rd move serves its more traditional country purpose, resolving to the root A, and a twangy A13 voicing.

EXAMPLE 4

As a final tip, if you're not familiar enough with the *major* pentatonic scale to experiment with your own licks, remember that it's the exact same scale and shape as its relative minor pentatonic scale. In other words, if you know the A minor pentatonic box shape in fifth position (unless you're an absolute beginner, you almost certainly do), all you need to do to play the A *major* pentatonic scale is slide that box shape down three frets to second position and—*voila!*—you've got it. Just remember to resolve to the root!

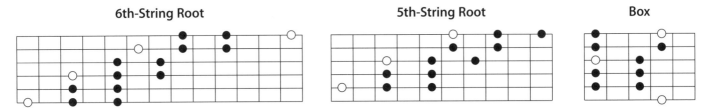

LESSON #69: COUNTRY SOLOING

When it comes to country guitar solos, the man with the Tele usually gets the spotlight, while the acoustic guitarist strums cowboy chords behind him. But what if it's an acoustic jam? If you know some basic country soloing constructs, you can rest assured that you won't have to skip over the solos. In this lesson, we'll examine some of the key techniques and approaches to country soloing, applied to acoustic guitar.

Major Pentatonic

If country guitar soloing has a defining sound, it is the major pentatonic scale, which has a formula of 1–2–3–5–6. In the key of C major—a popular country key—the scale is spelled: C–D–E–G–A. Other popular country keys are G, A, and E. To make things easy, here are three commonly used major pentatonic scale patterns: a position-shifting version with its root on the sixth (E) string, one with its root on the fifth (A) string, and a box pattern with its root on the sixth string.

6th-String Root	5th-String Root	Box

Note that the box pattern is the same as the popular *minor* pentatonic scale box used by rock and blues guitarists. Although the fingerings are the same, phrasing will differentiate the sounds.

This first example is drawn from the C major pentatonic box at the 5th fret, using a combination of pull-offs and 4ths intervals in a descending pattern to create a hip country "cascading" sound. Note the ♭3rd–3rd (E♭–E) move on the final beat in the first measure, setting up the resolution to the root. This is a classic country move.

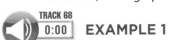

EXAMPLE 1

Like many country licks, that one's a bit of a barn-burner, so take your time and work your way up to tempo.

6ths Licks

If country guitar soloing has a defining interval, it's the 6th. Whether it's played in the context of a hot country lick or a ballad, the sound is unmistakably country.

This next lick climbs the fifth string-rooted C major pentatonic scale, leading to a highly melodic phrase that is played in 6ths. This phrase is useful over the I chord in a mid-tempo country shuffle.

EXAMPLE 2

When playing 6ths in dyad form, you should pluck the two strings simultaneously using either your thumb and index finger (fingerstyle) or a plectrum (or thumbpick) and one of your pick-hand fingers (i.e., hybrid picking).

This next example is a great 6ths lick for making a I–IV chord change. It's presented in two octaves; although it sounds more "classic country" in the higher octave, accessing those frets on a non-cutaway acoustic can be difficult. In that case, try the lower octave.

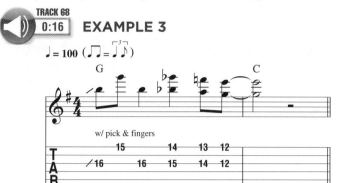

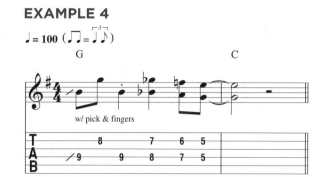

Below is a 6ths lick that is tailor-made for an up-tempo country boogie in the key of A. This one includes pull-offs to the open high-E string—another key country technique—and a dash of chromatic movement to exploit the minor 3rd/major 3rd tension.

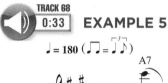

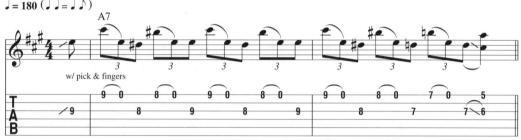

Make It Cry and Sing

Finally, few things sound as "country" as pedal-steel licks. The problem is, pedal-steel licks can be really—*really*—hard to bend on an acoustic guitar, much less holding bends to create the pedal-steel effect. Nonetheless, we're going to try a couple.

This first one includes a classic country pedal-steel move and works great over a V chord that resolves to the I chord; in this case, D to G. Bending the G string up a whole step and holding it there will require a heavy-duty team effort from your ring, middle, and index fingers. If you think you'll be bending regularly on your acoustic, try light-gauge strings.

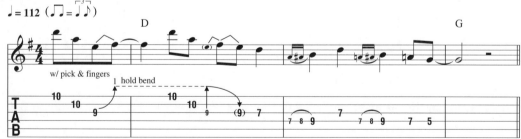

This final lick poses quite a challenge: bending an entire triad at once! The good news is, to get that greasy, bluesy, pedal-steel sound, you're only going to bend the triad up a quarter step. Using a G6 triad gives this lick a light jazz-blues flavor.

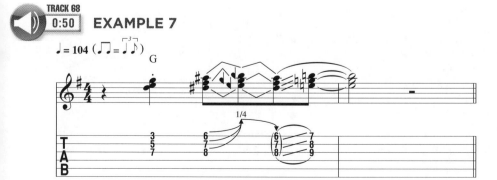

LESSON #70: CHORD EMBELLISHMENT

So much acoustic folk, pop, and rock music is composed from basic open-position major and minor triads—and there's nothing wrong with that. But, if you're looking to breathe life into a stale progression, or perhaps alter the mood of a progression, one way to do so is through chord embellishment. In this lesson, we'll explore various ways in which you can embellish basic triads to craft unique and moving chord progressions.

Add a Note Here, Extend a Chord There

One of the easiest ways to liven up a basic "cowboy chord" progression is to either add a note to or subtract a note from the basic major and minor triads. Example 1 contains a simple, strummed F–C chord progression.

TRACK 69
0:00 **EXAMPLE 1**

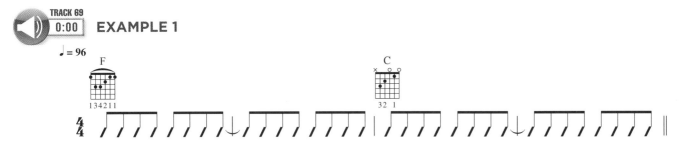

To breathe a little life and melodic movement into that progression, we're going to mix in some "sus" (suspended) and "add" chord shapes. The result is a much more interesting rhythm part.

TRACK 69
0:14 **EXAMPLE 2**

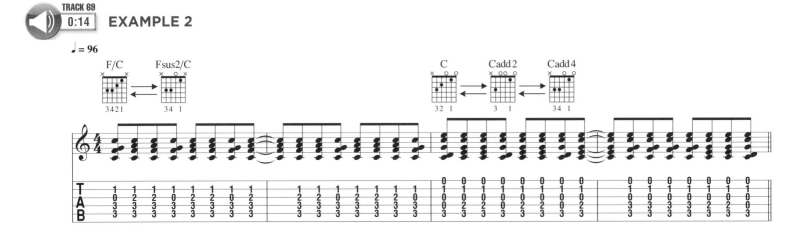

You can use similar embellishments in arpeggiated acoustic parts as well. This next example depicts a fairly common G–C riff.

TRACK 69
0:29 **EXAMPLE 3**

To spice that one up, we've changed the G chord to Gadd9 and the C chord to Cmaj7.

TRACK 69
0:44 **EXAMPLE 4**

WHICH CHORD WHERE?

So how do you know which chord embellishments can be used on which chords? Here's a brief "cheat sheet" table:

Chord Type	Embellishments
Major	add9, sus2, 6, 6/9, maj7, maj9, maj13
Minor	m7, m9, m(add9), sus2
7th	9, 13, 7♯9, 7sus4

Sticking with the G–C progression, our next example employs an implied harmony of Gadd9–Cmaj13. We say "implied" because the chord tones that make up those chords are achieved via hammer-ons and pull-offs and, thus, are not static. The result is a highly melodic arpeggio riff.

TRACK 69
1:00 **EXAMPLE 5**

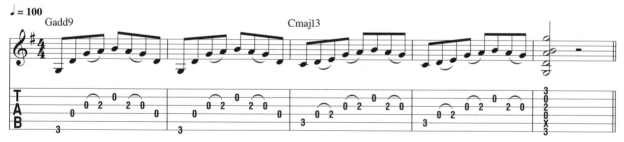

In our final example, we're going to take a common G–C–Em–D progression and embellish the chords in such a manner that we get some cool voice leading via the droning G5 dyad on the top two strings.

TRACK 69
1:16 **EXAMPLE 6**

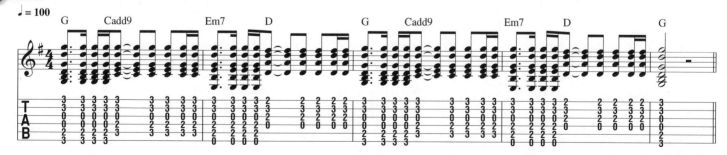

Chord embellishment really has only one overriding rule: it needs to *sound* good. Whether you achieve that goal via pure chance or through thoughtful harmonic analysis really doesn't matter. So get busy experimenting with those major 7ths, minor 7ths, extended chords, sus chords, and add chords to hear what beautiful music you can make together.

LESSON #71: RAGTIME GUITAR

So many styles can be played on an acoustic guitar, but if you long to be "the entertainer" with your instrument, learning how to play ragtime music is a requisite course. Ragtime music is the primary antecedent to jazz and widely considered the first truly all-American music. Ragtime originated in African-American communities in the mid-South, particularly St. Louis and New Orleans, and combined the march with the polyrhythms of African music. The genre's earliest and key composers include Ernest Hogan, Scott Joplin, Joseph Lamb, and Jelly Roll Morton, among others. In this lesson, we'll apply ragtime's stomping bass and syncopated melody to the guitar.

Piano Roots

Ragtime music originally was played on the piano, with the left hand pounding out a steady bass line on the strong beats (1 and 3) and chords on the weak ones (2 and 4), while the right hand played the melody often with accents on the upbeats to create that "ragged time" feel. Adapted to the guitar, you'll play a steady quarter-note bass line in the traditional or Travis-picking style, simultaneously striking chord tones, with melody notes filling in the spaces. To begin, we'll stick with a fairly consistent picking pattern while weaving through a four-bar ragtime-style phrase.

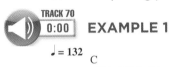

EXAMPLE 1

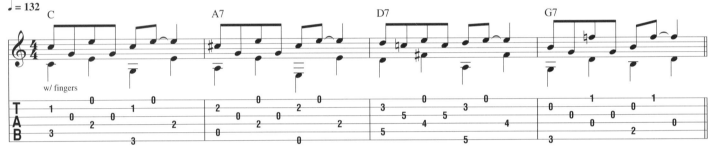

The Ragtime Progression

The most popular chord progression in ragtime guitar music, I–VI7–II7–V7, was established in the early 1900s and is similar to the later, popular "rhythm changes" of the jazz music world, except the minor vi and ii chords are substituted for their respective dominant-seventh qualities, which helps to give ragtime its bouncy feel. The full 16-bar progression, which was later heard in Robert Johnson's "Hot Tamales" and Arlo Guthrie's "Alice's Restaurant," among others, is shown here in the key of C. Use the picking pattern from Example 1.

EXAMPLE 2

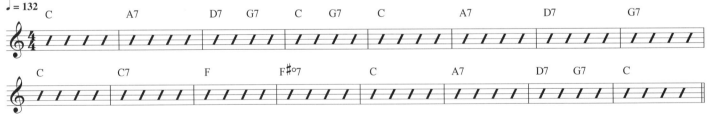

A popular technique in ragtime guitar is changing chords on the "kick," or an 8th note early. In the example below, the changes from D7 to G7, G7 to C, and C back to G7 are all heralded with the open G string on the "and" of beats 2 and 4.

EXAMPLE 3

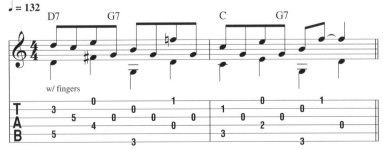

The following are a couple of simple ways to break the monotony of a single picking pattern and to give the piece a little breathing room. The first one shows a new pattern for bars 9–10.

TRACK 70
0:52 **EXAMPLE 4**

EXAMPLE 5

Example 5 shows how you might play bar 4.

Entertain Yourself

To wrap up this lesson on ragtime guitar, below is the ever-popular first section of Scott Joplin's "The Entertainer," arranged in Drop D tuning (the way Chet Atkins famously played it). Ragtime's melodic syncopation and driving bass really stand out in this classic. Start slowly and work your way up to the stately tempo of 116 bpm.

TRACK 70
1:05 **EXAMPLE 6**

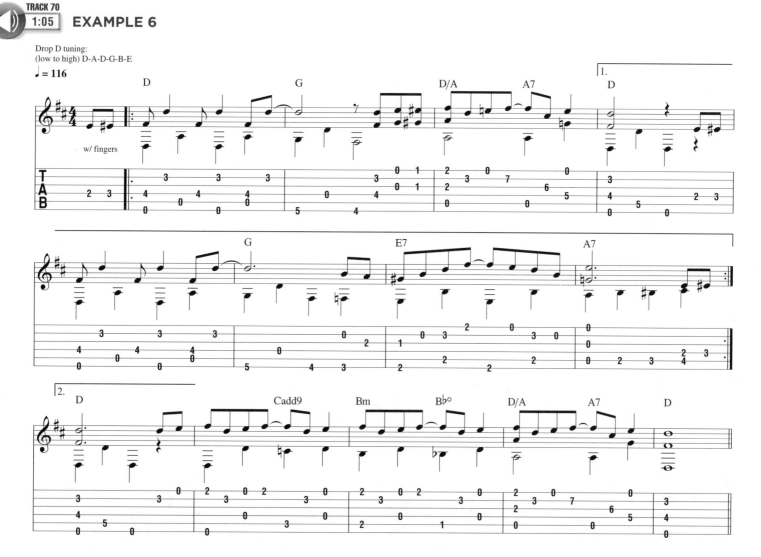

Using a single picking pattern like the one used for most of this lesson will help you to get the basic feel of ragtime fingerpicking, but relying on a single pattern—or even two or three—can paint you into a corner. As you become comfortable and confident with the pattern approach, begin to experiment with upper chord tones and melody notes, adding fills or licks and using ornamentation such as hammer-ons and pull-offs, but remember that maintaining a steady, alternating quarter-note bass line is critical.

It began with the field hollers of 19th-century slaves in the South, evolved in the hands of itinerant country blues musicians like Charley Patton, Skip James, and Son House, and reached its zenith with the mythical story and chops of the great Robert Johnson. For the past 100 years, the blues forged in the Mississippi Delta during the early 20th century has proven to be among the most influential and inspirational music we've ever known. In this lesson, we'll explore the essential sounds and techniques of this timeless form.

Went Down to the Crossroads...

Of all the Delta blues stories, none is more legendary than that of Robert Johnson, whose guitar technique was so otherworldly for its time that many people speculated that the bluesman went down to the crossroads and sold his soul to the devil in exchange for those prodigious chops (more on him in a bit).

Before Mr. Johnson worked his magic, other Delta-based country blues guitarists like Charley Patton, Willie Brown, and Son House were spreading the good word of the blues in juke joints all across the South.

Charley Patton

Widely considered to be the "Father of the Delta Blues," Charley Patton also was a pioneering "showman," playing the guitar between his legs, behind his head, and even on the floor. Among the contributions he made to the Delta blues guitar sound were his offbeat accents, percussive attack, and descending bass runs. This first example, in Open G tuning with a capo at the 3rd fret, features the latter two elements.

TRACK 71 | 0:00 | **EXAMPLE 1**

*Symbols in parentheses represent chord names respective to capoed guitar.
Symbols above reflect actual sounding chords. Capoed fret is "0" in tab.

**Hit top of guitar and string simultaneously on downstemmed notes in first two bars.

This next example, in standard tuning, shows another side of Patton's playing. Here, a single-note riff in the top voice drives the tune. Note his early use of the now-classic (and essential) "train-whistle" lick in the second ending.

TRACK 71 | 0:13 | **EXAMPLE 2**

Son House

Nearly as influential as Patton—and for a while, his playing partner—Eddie James "Son" House was one of the most sure-handed bottleneck sliders in the South in the thirties. A downright physical player, House stamped his foot to keep time and the rest of his body always seemed to follow suit. Here, we encounter a House-worthy riff that is played in Open G tuning and combines a fretted descending phrase with a classic slide lick that closes the phrase.

EXAMPLE 3

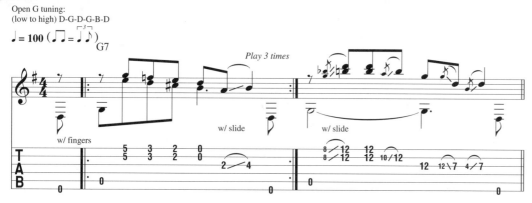

Robert Johnson

And finally, we come to the man, the myth, the legend—Mr. Robert Johnson. The King of the Delta Blues possessed prodigious skills on the guitar, confounding for decades those who tried to cop his tunes. And though much of the mystery of his technique has now been unraveled, good luck with trying to replicate his parts as cleanly and effortlessly—unless of course, you're willing to sell your soul to do so. Only two photos of Johnson are known to exist, and one clearly shows him wearing a thumbpick on his right hand, which leads us to believe that he employed one primarily on bass notes, with his index and middle fingers likely handling the upper strings.

The shuffle rhythm of this next example is by far Johnson's most famous. Immortalized in his tune "Sweet Home Chicago," the boogie rhythm shown below is the most pervasive rhythm approach in the history of blues and rock music. Although the boogie shuffle is pretty straightforward, incorporating the open-G and open-E string notes is the key to Johnson's Delta sound.

EXAMPLE 4

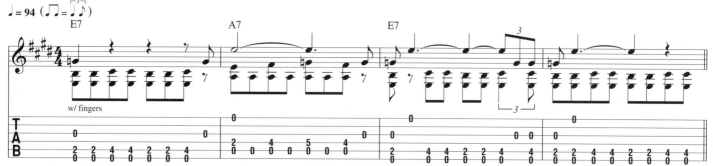

Finally, no lesson on the Delta blues would be complete without a turnaround, and Johnson was an absolute master of the device. This one—just one of his many enduring turnarounds—features the tonic note (A) as a pedal tone on the top string, while the bass descends from the ♭7th (G) to the 5th (E), setting up the V7 (E7) chord in bar 12 (here, bar 2).

EXAMPLE 5

LESSON #73: DELTA BLUES TURNAROUNDS

All other things being equal, a quality turnaround can be the difference between a memorable blues experience and a forgettable string of choruses. And nearly every turnaround commonly heard in the blues today has its roots in the acoustic Delta blues of the early 20th century. In this lesson, we'll examine several essential turnarounds that sound as fresh today as they did in the twenties and thirties.

Turn Yo' Blues Around

A turnaround is a short phrase at the end of a progression that ends on the V (or V7) chord. In the blues, the turnaround occurs in measures 11–12. Some of the blues' most enduring turnarounds came from the spidery fingers of Delta legend Robert Johnson. In his boogie shuffle "Sweet Home Chicago," Johnson offers up not one, but two of today's most popular blues turnarounds.

Though you may be more accustomed to hearing variations of this first turnaround in the electrified fingers of Texas blues artists like Stevie Ray Vaughan, Johnson played this open-position chromatically descending turnaround fingerstyle (or with a combination of thumbpick and fingers) on his old, battered acoustic guitar. Note the F♯ (5th) in the bass voice of the B7 (V chord) in the second bar. That voicing may require some getting used to, but for authenticity's sake, it's worth the effort, as this is a classic Johnson move.

EXAMPLE 1

The second turnaround that Johnson gave the blues world in "Sweet Home Chicago" actually serves as the tune's intro —a common way to begin a blues. The version presented here consists of the tonic on the high E string—in this case, an E note—with a chromatic walk down from the ♭7th (D) to the 5th (B), setting up the V7 (B7/F♯) chord in the next measure.

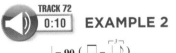

EXAMPLE 2

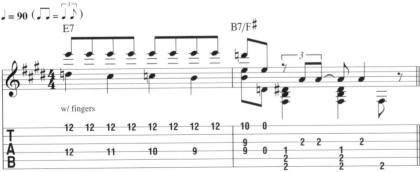

Because all of the notes are fretted, the previous turnaround is movable. To determine where to play it, simply plant your pinky finger on the first string on the fret of the song's key (e.g., if the song's in the key of A, your pinky goes on the 5th fret), then walk it on down.

This next turnaround is essentially the same as Johnson's classic, only this time it's in 12/8 time and both voices have been dropped an octave. The figure also leads into the V7 (B9) chord from a half step above (C9), which is an essential turnaround move.

TRACK 72
0:20  **EXAMPLE 3**

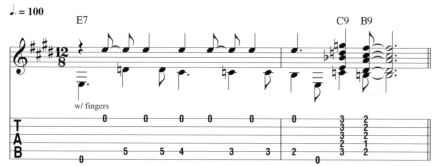

The next example is yet another classic turnaround in the key of E. In this one, an open high-E string is once again a pedal tone, but the intervals of the descending bass voice are much closer, starting with a unison E on beat 1. Further, rather than descending from the ♭7th to the 5th, this version walks stepwise down the E blues scale (E–D–B–B♭–A–G–E) over the course of the first three beats. Check out the hip ♯9th/♭3rd (D) that ends the phrase on the B7 chord!

TRACK 72
0:29  **EXAMPLE 4**

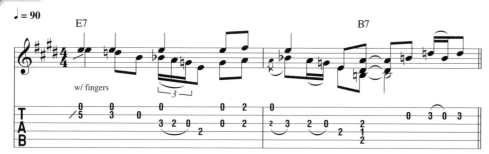

Fillin' the Gaps

While essential, the turnarounds presented so far are also somewhat sparse, harmonically speaking. But, if you take that basic "descending bass line against a higher pedal tone" structure and add another layer of harmony to it, you get a slightly more complex turnaround, as heard in the fingerstyle blues of the twenties, thirties, and forties. This turnaround features fretted 6th intervals bookended by a ringing high E string and a palm-muted low E:

TRACK 72
0:39  **EXAMPLE 5**

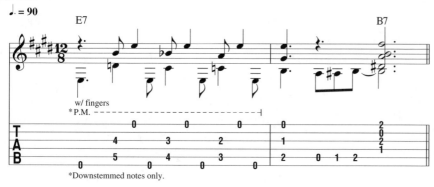

*Downstemmed notes only.

Don't underestimate the importance of having many—and varied—blues turnarounds in your arsenal. If you play the same two turnarounds every time, it's very easy to sound repetitive—or worse, boring. Look at this lesson as a good start, with a nice selection of essential moves, but keep exploring.

LESSON #74: DADGAD BLUES

Say "DADGAD" and most guitarists immediately think of either Celtic or New Age instrumental music. With DADGAD tuning's intervallic relationships and soft, lilting sound, Celtic and New Age are logical deductions. However, the tuning's wide-open sound is also easily manipulated for a down-home Delta blues vibe, as you'll see here.

Blues Tunings Refresher

Standard tuning (E–A–D–G–B–E) has been, well… standard on the six-string guitar since the early 1800s. With the rise of blues guitar in the early 1900s, however, alternate tunings like Open G (D–G–D–G–B–D) and Open D (D–A–D–F♯–A–D) became popular. Several arguments can be made as to this evolution, each as plausible as the next. First, in an open tuning, you can barre all six strings with one finger, which makes for not only easier harmonic embellishment, but also slide playing. Second, with a poorly made instrument, which was the case for many poor, itinerant bluesmen of the day, the slack tunings made fretting much easier on the fingers.

Then, in the early sixties, alternate tunings on acoustic guitar exerted their first influence in popular music. During this period, British folk guitarist Davey Graham is said to have "invented" DADGAD tuning, which has since become synonymous with fingerstyle players like Pierre Bensusan, Patty Larkin, and Al Petteway.

DADGAD Blues? Sure, Why Not?

So, even though it's nowhere near the first altered tuning that comes to mind when you think of acoustic blues, DADGAD actually offers some interesting advantages for the style. Two of the most important sounds in the blues are the "blue notes" that lie between the minor and major 3rd and between the dominant and major 7th tones. If you play a D blues in open position with DADGAD tuning, you'll soon discover that the ♭3rd (F) falls at the 3rd fret of all the D-tuned strings (6, 4, and 1), and the ♭7th falls at the 3rd fret of the two A-tuned strings (5 and 2). This architecture provides comfortable and familiar access to those "true blue notes" via just a gentle quarter-step nudge on five of the guitar's six strings. Now that's a blues gold mine!

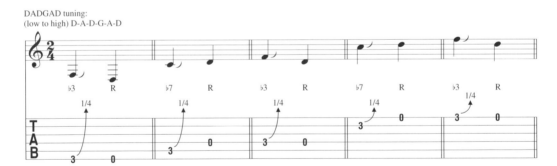

"Lucky Charms Blues"

To most effectively see how DADGAD tuning can work in a blues context, on the next page is a 12-bar blues arrangement titled "Lucky Charms Blues." From the start, we exploit those blue notes at the 3rd fret in what will likely be a familiar-sounding blues motif. Measure 2 offers a low-register response to the high-register call in measure 1. In true blues fashion, measure 3 repeats the initial call before measure 4 adds some 16th-note triplet sizzle, calling on the ♭5th (A♭) for extra-bluesy oomph. A variation on the main motif introduces the IV chord in measure 5, while measure 6 answers the call with bluesy slurs in a similar statement.

Back at the I7 chord in measure 7, we repeat the original motif, whereas measure 8 offers a classic take on the ♭3rd–3rd (F–F♯) blues move. The introduction of the V7 (A7) chord offers a moment to gather your breath for the fiery, Celtic-tinged descent over the IV7 (G7) chord, which leads back to the I-chord motif in measure 11. Don't let the 32nd notes intimidate you; the DADGAD-friendly pattern lies quite comfortably under the fingers and the open strings allow for easy string switching. Finally, the 12-bar form ends with a simple turnaround.

TRACK 73
0:00

As you can see, DADGAD makes for some fabulous down-home acoustic blues guitar fun. Take some time to explore more blues phrasing in this fun tuning. You might find DADGAD so fun and easy, you may never go back to standard-tuning blues again!

LESSON #75: OPEN-POSITION BLUES LICKS IN E

Because the guitar's standard tuning is bookended by open E strings that are two octaves apart, and because the acoustic guitar shines brightest when played in open position, with plenty of open strings, the key of E is the friendliest of musical keys for the blues. As a result, you can never have too many open-position blues licks at your disposal. In this lesson, you'll learn five cool and useful blues licks in E.

Open-Position Blues Scale

You most likely are already familiar with the standard blues-scale box pattern, whether in open position, as shown below, or in its movable shape. To review, here is the pattern, both in grid form and in standard notation and tab:

E Blues Scale

Although you may make adjustments as particular licks dictate, you'll generally stick to a positional fingering for the scale; that is, index finger on the 1st fret, middle finger on the 2nd fret, and ring finger on the 3rd fret.

Lick Your Chops

Now let's get started on those licks. This first one draws solely from the E blues scale and features a couple of bluesy 4th–♭5th–4th moves, played in 16th-note triplet rhythms.

TRACK 74
0:00 **EXAMPLE 1**

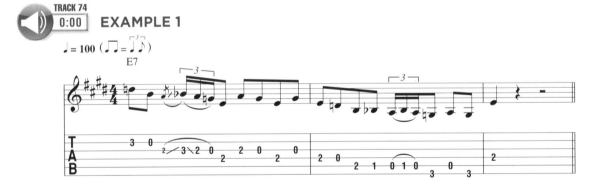

This second lick highlights the bluesy quarter-step bend on many of the ♭3rd (G) and ♭7th (D) notes, thus attaining what we call the "true blues notes," which are located midway between the minor 3rd and major 3rd and between the minor 7th and major 7th.

TRACK 74
0:09 **EXAMPLE 2**

For this next lick, we shift to a 12/8 meter. The two highlights of this lick are the initial ♭3rd–3rd (G–G♯) hammer-on and the inclusion of the 2nd (F♯) for a dash of Mixolydian pizzazz.

EXAMPLE 3

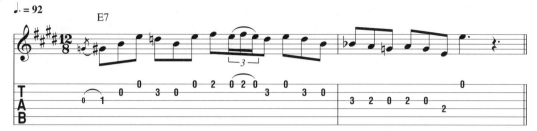

Dandy Double Stops

Bluesy double stops are especially delicious on an acoustic guitar, as seen in our next lick. To play this one, barre the G and B strings at the 2nd fret with your index finger. For the ensuing hammer-on/pull-off move, you can use either a middle finger barre on the 3rd fret or your middle finger on the G string and ring finger on the B string, whichever is more comfortable to you.

EXAMPLE 4

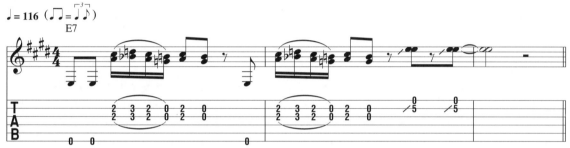

Don't Forget the Down-Low

In general, guitar licks are most often played on the top three or four strings, but the low strings, especially on an acoustic, are sometimes just what a phrase needs. The application of this final lick is more as a fill, say over bars 3–4 of a standard blues, than as a lick in the middle of a solo, but you get the idea.

EXAMPLE 5

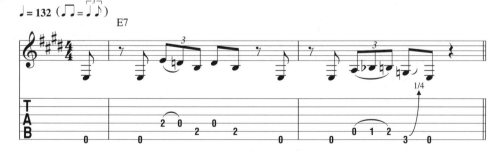

The licks in this lesson merely scratch the surface of what's possible when playing a blues in E in open position. When trying to discover your own licks, be sure to mine the incredible supply of electric blues licks, as well, as many of those licks are easily translated to acoustic guitar. Although you may need to occasionally substitute slides for bends, electric blues licks are a treasure trove that you simply can't ignore.

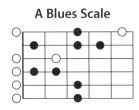

LESSON #76: OPEN-POSITION BLUES LICKS IN A

Although the key of E is by far the most popular blues key on acoustic guitar, the key of A isn't far behind. And while the A blues scale fingering in open position doesn't lay as conveniently on the fretboard as the E blues scale does, it's a solid second-best. In this lesson, we'll explore some of the licks and patterns that you need to know for acoustic blues' second most-popular key.

Open-Position Blues Scale

Whereas the open-position E blues scale is the same pattern as the movable box shape that every guitarist learns early on, the pattern for the A blues scale is based on the lesser-used "box 4," with its root on the fifth string. You also need to be aware that the open second (B) string is not used in the scale. Here's the A blues scale both in grid form and in standard notation and tab:

Although you may make adjustments as particular licks dictate, you'll generally stick to a positional fingering for the scale; that is, index finger on the 1st fret, middle finger on the 2nd fret, ring finger on the 3rd fret, and pinky on the 4th fret.

Get Your Licks

Now let's get started on those licks. This first one draws solely from the A blues scale, using a half-step bend to achieve a bluesy 4th–♭5th–4th move, played in a 16th-note triplet rhythm (measure 2). Bending on an acoustic guitar can be a challenge. Fret the D note with your ring finger, using your index and middle fingers to reinforce the bend. Also, hook your thumb over the fretboard to provide coupling force. Note the quarter-step bends of the ♭3rd (C) to reach that magical "blue note" that's located between the ♭3rd and major 3rd.

EXAMPLE 1

This next lick commences with the same half-step bend/16th-note triplet move that's found in the previous example, followed by a descent of the blues scale in a sequence of threes.

EXAMPLE 2

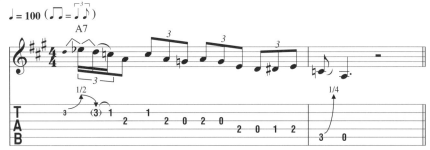

This next lick exploits the chromatic 4th–♭5th–5th sequence of the blues scale in a country fashion.

EXAMPLE 3

Major-Minor Fun

One of the signature sounds of the blues is tension that is caused by playing the minor 3rd from the blues scale over dominant 7th chords that contain a major 3rd. The great blues guitarists understand that you can play either note, depending on the mood that you're going for, as well as which chord is in the harmony. For example, in a 12-bar blues in the key of A, you play A7, D7, and E7 chords. Over the A7 chord, you might try the following lick, which hammers home the major tonality via the two C♯ (major 3rd) notes.

EXAMPLE 4

When you get to the IV7 (D7) chord, however, you could try the version below, which still features the ♭3rd–3rd rub in the first half of the lick, but then reinforces the ♭3rd (C) in the second half. This approach works well over D7 because C is the ♭7th of the D7 chord.

EXAMPLE 5

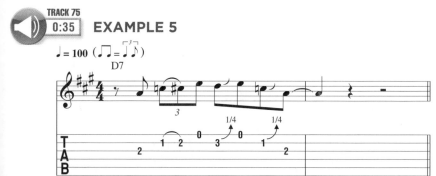

Turn It Around

The final lick in this lesson is a turnaround that is derived from the extended pattern of the open-position A blues scale. The open low-E note in bar 2 offers just enough time to get your hand up to the F9 chord at fret 8.

EXAMPLE 6

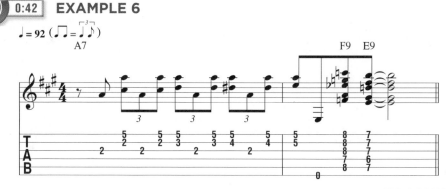

LESSON #77: BLUES SOLOING

When it comes to blues soloing on acoustic guitar, most people immediately think of open-position licks in E, in the style of the Delta blues greats—which you should. But acoustic guitars generally have 20 frets, 15 of which are usually easily accessible, so what's to prevent you from playing electric-style blues licks and solos on the ol' wooden box? That's right: nothing. In this lesson, we'll take a look at some cool acoustic blues licks that are inspired by electric blues guitar.

Pentatonic Blues

The fact that we'll be mining the minor pentatonic (1♭3–4–5♭7) and blues (1♭3–4♭5–5♭7) scales for some of these licks should come as no surprise, but we're also going to borrow from the Mixolydian mode (1–2–3–4–5–6♭7), as well as the "hybrid," or "composite," blues scale (1–2♭3–3–4♭5–5–6♭7).

This first lick comes straight from the classic blues-scale box pattern in the key of A. It has a bit of a rock flavor to it and works great as a solo closer.

TRACK 76
0:00   **EXAMPLE 1**

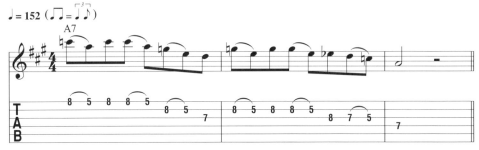

This second lick, inspired by B.B. King, fits nicely over the first two bars of a quick-change blues. The first phrase is straight out of the minor pentatonic box pattern, but instead of bending the 8th-fret G up to the root, A, we slide à la B.B. (not to mention that it's easier to slide than bend on an acoustic, but we'll get to that in a bit). In measure 2, we place another classic B.B.-ism into a cycling syncopation pattern for a more modern, "stuttered" effect, before resolving to the root.

TRACK 76
0:07   **EXAMPLE 2**

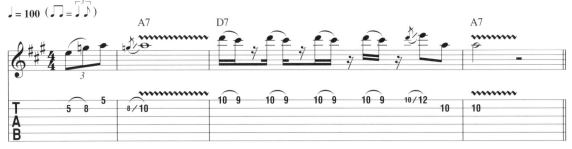

The 6th interval is a key sound in the blues and sounds particularly nice on acoustic guitar. This 6ths lick, which works nicely as a lead fill, draws from the E composite blues scale.

TRACK 76
0:18   **EXAMPLE 3**

Train-Whistle Blues

One of the blues' most distinctive sounds is the "train-whistle" lick, which has its roots in the acoustic Delta blues of the early 20th century. This lick is composed of double-stop 3rds and bluesy quarter-step bends. This train-whistle lick works great as a fill.

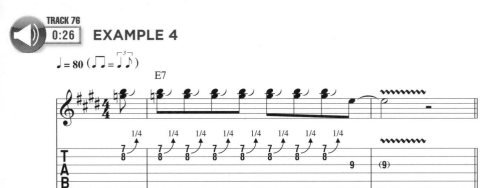

Bend 'Em, Baby!

Finally, no blues soloing lesson—even on acoustic—would be complete without some talk about bends. Bending on acoustic strings is indeed a challenge, but with hard work (and calluses), it can "separate the men from the boys," so to speak.

The following lick is also based on the train-whistle double stop; however, in this example, you'll bend the second string up a half step and hold it for each triplet. Although you'll need to give the string some extra juice, strive to keep it in tune.

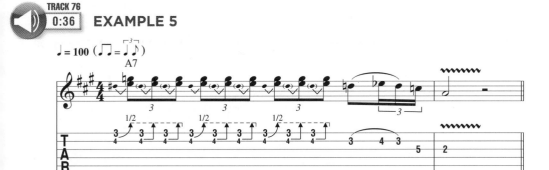

The final example, a blues-rocker in the style of Jimmy Page, features two full-step bends! Be sure to reinforce your ring (bend) finger with your middle and index fingers to provide some extra oomph.

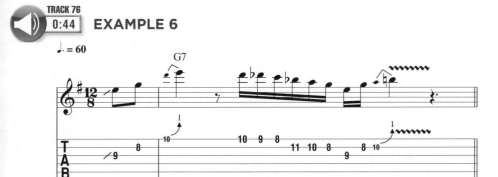

If you think that you'll be regularly bending strings on your acoustic, you may want to consider using light-gauge strings, which for acoustic guitars are typically .012 sets.

LESSON #78: OPEN-POSITION ROCK LICKS

Even acoustic guitarists get to rock out once in a while, and there's nothing like having a store of handy licks and fills—especially in open position—on call for such occasions. And just because legendary rockers and masters of open-position licks like Jimi Hendrix, Jimmy Page, and Angus Young made their bones by defiling electric guitars, it doesn't mean those licks can't—or don't—translate to the steel-string box that you have in your hands. If you play hard and with plenty of 'tude, these licks will jump off the fretboard.

Scales

When playing in open position on the guitar, certain keys—and thus, scales—offer a friendly layout, namely the keys of E, A, and G. When you factor in the rock aspect of open-position playing, you'll find that you'll quite often be playing over E, Em, E5, or E7 chords. Therefore, we'll focus on licks in the key of E in this lesson. Below are three essential scale patterns in E: the minor pentatonic, blues, and blues hybrid.

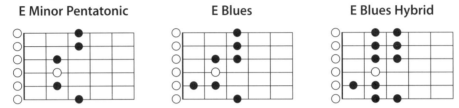

When you play scales or licks in open position, fingerings often come into question. If you choose to use strict positional playing, your fret hand's index finger should play every note on the 1st fret, your middle finger on the 2nd fret, and so on. But because so few notes are played on the 1st fret of the blues scale, most players use their index finger on the 2nd fret and middle finger on the 3rd fret, making adjustments as the music or your comfort dictates.

Lickety-Split

The licks in this lesson can of course be used in solos, but they're intended more for the purpose of fills or transitions between chords. And a couple of them are presented in this context.

Not surprisingly, a lot of the greatest open-position rock licks are adaptations of blues licks. Our first lick is pretty much a straight descent down the E blues scale in a triplet rhythm. This one works nicely as a song-ending flourish.

TRACK 77 0:00 **EXAMPLE 1**

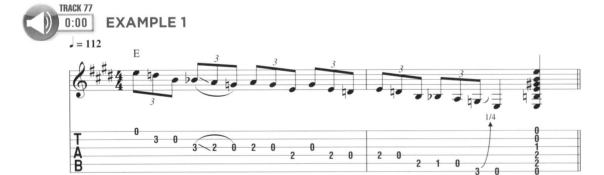

This 12/8 lick is in the style of Jimi Hendrix, one of the most exciting open-position rock guitarists of all time. While Jimi would have bent that grace-note slide move on beat 3 of measure 1, it's much easier—and sounds better—to use slides on an acoustic.

TRACK 77 0:08 **EXAMPLE 2**

Led Zeppelin's Jimmy Page is another master of short, bluesy open-position rock licks. Because the next lick is such a recognizable phrase, it works great as a quotation device and will perk up the ears of most any audience. Again, we substitute Pagey's bends for the easier slides.

Major Licks

Rock licks may tend to fall into minor, blues, or ambiguous key types, but plenty of major-key rock and pop songs are sure to come across your music stand. But rather than look at the parallel key, E major, we're going to switch to G major—by far the most popular major key on acoustic guitar.

G major is also the relative major to E minor, which means that the E minor pentatonic fingering that you know in open position is exactly the same for G *major* pentatonic—it just starts on a different note.

G Major Pentatonic

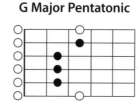

The Allman Brothers Band is famous for their major-pentatonic soloing (as is Southern rock, in general). The two G major pentatonic licks shown below are inspired by that sound and style. The first one works over either a G tonic or its V chord (D), leading back to G. The second lick also sounds great over G, particularly as a turnaround between song sections that end and begin on G.

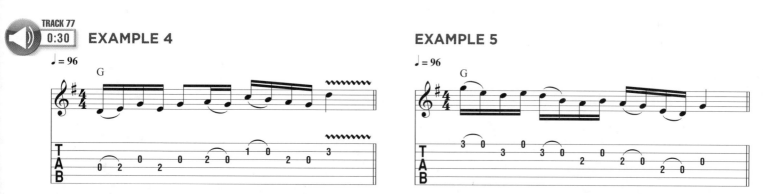

Below is another example presented in a rhythm context. Both licks are based on G major pentatonic, but the first one includes an added 4th (C), which helps lead to the pending Am chord.

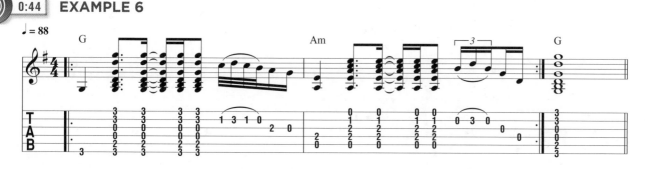

Keep in mind that licks are only one half of the recipe to successful fills—you also need to play them *in time*. As you practice these and other licks, play them over chord progressions with a metronome or drum track so you can perfect that timing. *Rawk!*

LESSON #79: ACOUSTIC ROCK RHYTHM

From the Beatles, Led Zeppelin, and Heart to Dave Matthews, Goo Goo Dolls, and Sheryl Crow, the acoustic guitar often has found the spotlight on rock's biggest stages. In this lesson, we'll take a look at some easy and effective ways to use your acoustic guitar to play a rock rhythm role.

Acoustic Arpeggios

One of the most frequently heard acoustic devices in rock music is the arpeggio—the notes of a chord played one note at a time. Instead of playing strict arpeggios, we're going to take a look at a more "free-form" rock approach in which you may strike one, two, three, or more notes at a time.

The first example uses the popular rock progression G–D–Am–C. When attempting to use this approach on your own, look at the picking pattern shown here as a general guide rather than a hard-and-fast rule—let the feel and groove lead the way.

 EXAMPLE 1

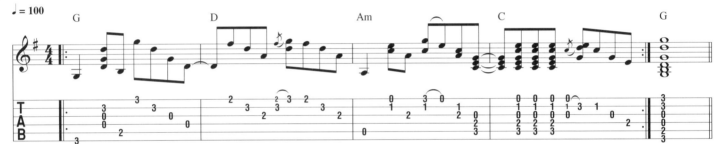

Power-Chord Rock

As anyone who's ever played or even listened to Chuck Berry knows, the power-chord boogie rhythm pattern (e.g., A5–A6) first employed by early blues pianists also has a rich history in rock guitar. In terms of acoustic rock rhythm guitar, you'll likely encounter patterns similar to the one shown below in styles like Americana, folk-rock, and country alt-rock. Employ a slight palm mute throughout.

 EXAMPLE 2

This next example uses power chords in a more straight-ahead rock context. While the use of two-note power chords isn't real common on the acoustic guitar, it is nonetheless an essential tool.

 EXAMPLE 3

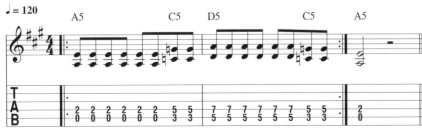

Now let's step back into a more comfortable acoustic arena and rework that A5–C5–D5–C5 progression from the previous example. In a rock setting, an electric guitarist might cover the straight power-chord version while an acoustic guitarist doubles the progression with chords that better exploit the instrument's acoustic benefits—ringing strings. Here, we slap a capo on the 2nd fret and slide an open G5 chord shape up and down the neck, adding harmonic color to a basic riff.

EXAMPLE 4

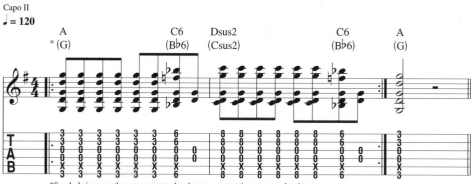

*Symbols in parentheses represent chord names respective to capoed guitar.
Symbols above reflect actual sounding chords. Capoed fret is "0" in tab.

Inversions

A thorough knowledge of and ability to use inversions is essential to any rock guitarist—electric or acoustic. The following chord riff in the key of A draws from such disparate sources as Pete Townshend, Eddie Van Halen, and John Mellencamp. Try to play the chord stabs both with and without palm muting.

EXAMPLE 5

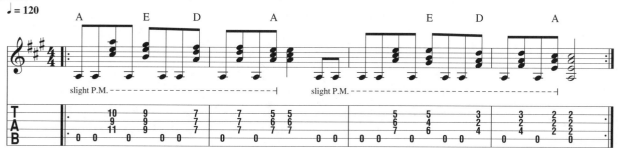

Drum Up Some Rhythm

Rock 'n' roll is a highly percussive style and the acoustic guitar is particularly well-built for that purpose. When playing rhythm guitar on acoustic, many rock players use an aggressive muting technique wherein they slap down onto the strings with the "blade" side of the pick hand while simultaneously hitting the top, or soundboard, with the side of the pinky finger to produce a drum-like sound.

In this final example, the string mutes occur on beats 2 and 4 of each measure, thereby simulating the snare drum in a 4/4 beat.

EXAMPLE 6

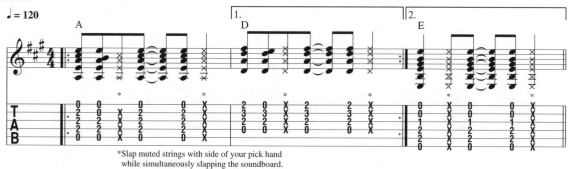

*Slap muted strings with side of your pick hand
while simultaneously slapping the soundboard.

In addition to that basic muting technique, you might also want to try tapping or "rolling" your fingers on the soundboard between chords to create drum-like percussive fills. This approach is particularly effective when you're playing solo or in a small ensemble that doesn't have a drummer.

ACOUSTIC ROCK SOLOING

In the realm of rock guitar soloing, the electric guitar reigns supreme. But, as rock guitar heroes from David Gilmour and Eric Clapton to Eddie Van Halen and Slash have proven in such classic solos as "Wish You Were Here," "Layla," "Spanish Fly," and "Patience," respectively, the acoustic guitar can be a very effective rock soloing tool. In this lesson, we'll explore some of the techniques and phrases of these sometimes-acoustic rock guitar heroes.

Blues Roots

Given rock guitar's heavy blues pedigree, the fact that one of the primary approaches to acoustic rock soloing is a blues-based one should come as no surprise, as it draws largely from the major (1–2–3–5–6) and minor (1–♭3–4–5–♭7) pentatonic scales, as well as the blues scale (1–♭3–4–♭5–5–♭7).

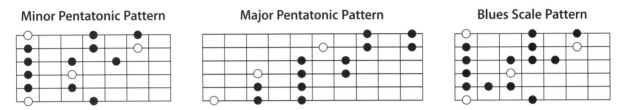

Minor Pentatonic Pattern　　**Major Pentatonic Pattern**　　**Blues Scale Pattern**

Our first example comes from one of the greatest rock guitarists of all time, who also just happens to be one of the finest blues guitarists in history—Eric Clapton. When "Slowhand" released his monumental acoustic album, *Unplugged*, in 1991, the disc contained an acoustic arrangement of his 1969 hit "Layla," when he was a member of Derek & the Dominos. In his acoustic version, Clapton puts on a clinic for blues-rock acoustic soloing, with licks from the minor pentatonic, blues, Mixolydian, and natural minor scales. Here's a phrase that captures his use of the minor pentatonic and blues scales:

TRACK 79
0:00 **EXAMPLE 1**

The blues also influenced Pink Floyd guitarist David Gilmour's soloing style to a large extent. But blessed with one of the greatest ears for melody in rock history, Gilmour took the common blues tools of the pentatonic scales and, via his unique phrasing, made them sound, well… not all that bluesy. In Pink Floyd's classic hit "Wish You Were Here," Gilmour offers up powerful, yet restrained, pentatonic lines rife with double stops—a very acoustic-friendly soloing weapon.

TRACK 79
0:13 **EXAMPLE 2**

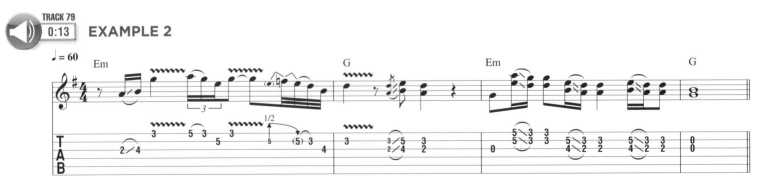

In the mid-to-late eighties, Guns N' Roses brought an edgy, angry, and raw rock 'n' roll sound to the glitz and glam hair-metal scene. But for all their gutter glory, GN'R still had a sensitive side, as made evident by their acoustic smash, "Patience." Guitarist Slash, who eschewed the fretboard flashiness of the era for a more classic-rock approach on his Les Paul, carried over his bluesy bends and slides to his Guild acoustic as well.

The following example demonstrates Slash's use of full-step bends. If you're not used to bending on an acoustic, this example might hurt a bit. Note the eighties-style rake that kicks off the major pentatonic-based phrase.

 TRACK 79 `0:35` **EXAMPLE 3**

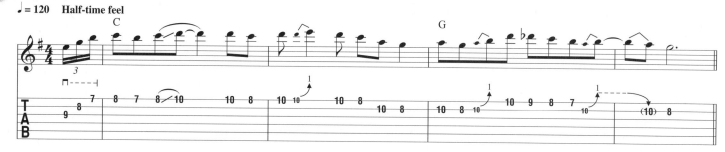

Double Stops 'n' Drones

Depending on the harmonic and dynamic context of the song, a single-note acoustic guitar solo can sound a bit thin or even get lost in the mix. One way to bolster your acoustic lines is to use double stops in conjunction with droning notes. Here's an example in the popular rock key of E that makes convenient use of the open-B and open-E strings as drones:

 TRACK 79 `0:47` **EXAMPLE 4**

The Extremists

Although the previous examples may have mined the obvious outcroppings of blues-based rock guitar, a handful of rock guitar heroes have plied their shred-style super-chops on the steel-string to great acclaim as well. Among them is the great Eddie Van Halen, who hammers, pulls, and taps his way to fretboard glory in "Spanish Fly," which is essentially the acoustic-shred answer to his iconic electric masterpiece, "Eruption."

Though you most likely won't find much use for Eddie's two-hand tapping work in the typical acoustic rock solo, you might occasionally wish to put the pedal to the metal via some rapid-fire three-notes-per-string licks like this one:

 TRACK 79 `1:04` **EXAMPLE 5**

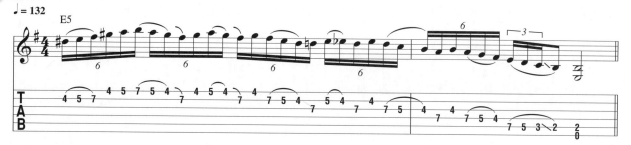

Just as in the world of electric rock guitar, when you're playing acoustic rock, half the fun is breaking the rules. And although the instrument presents tougher physical challenges, if you approach it with the aggression and drive that the greats do, you'll be rockin' the "box" in no time!

If you're new to Irish or Celtic music, the rhythm guitar parts may, upon first glance, appear to be quite simple. But the truth is that proper accompaniment in Celtic music is an art. Therefore, to help you avoid being smacked on the arm with a fiddler's bow or bopped with a bodhrán, we will explore some of the fundamental aspects of Irish guitar accompaniment.

SESSION VS. DUET

If you're going to be an accompanist in an Irish music setting, you'll find yourself playing either in a session, which is a group setting that is often comprised of fiddle, button accordion (squeeze box), tin whistle, tenor banjo, and bodhrán; or in a duet, in which you play with only a melodist, such as a fiddler. This lesson applies to both settings, but primarily to a session.

Because so much is going on in a session musically, your main job on the acoustic guitar is essentially to avoid overplaying or stepping on the other musicians' toes. To help guide you, here's a list of Dos and Don'ts:

DO

▸ The guitar is strictly a rhythm instrument in this setting, so lock into the bodhrán beat. Don't exactly mirror what he's playing; instead, find a simple counterpoint and stick to it.

▸ Stick to the low end of your guitar's register, occasionally flirting with its mids. Most of the other instruments are melody instruments, so they will handle the high end.

▸ Many jigs and reels are played in sets of three or four. Ask for the form of the set, and if you find that you don't know one of the tunes, watch and listen to the other players or drop out altogether until you learn or recognize it.

DON'T

▸ Don't play the melody—it will end up sounding like bluegrass.

▸ Don't overplay. Plenty of other instruments will be present, so leave room for them.

▸ Don't "swing" your rhythm or speed it up. Although jigs, which are played in 6/8 time, invite a swing feel, lock in with the bodhrán and drive along in even 8th notes.

▸ No solos! Check your inner Eddie Van Halen at the pub door.

Drop D Tuning

Before we dive into the rhythms, make sure that your guitar is tuned to Drop D: D–A–D–G–B–E. Although DADGAD tuning is also quite common in Irish guitar accompaniment, Drop D offers the opportunity to learn these rhythm techniques while using familiar chord shapes. Here are some of the essential chord shapes in the key of D, in Drop D tuning:

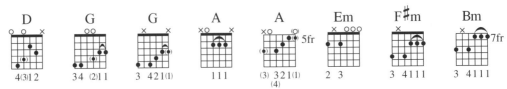

"Black and Decker, Black and Decker"

The universal strum pattern for a reel is a driving 8th-note rhythm, plied in strict down-up strokes. But Irish players don't count it in the traditional "One-and, two-and …" manner. Instead, the measure is divided in two, and the pulse is counted "1-2-3-4, 1-2-3-4," or using the mnemonic "Black-and-Deck-er, Black-and-Deck-er." Try it with the following open D5 chord, with a slight palm mute—another key Irish guitar technique—throughout.

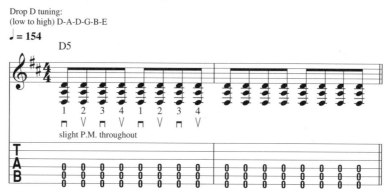

That steady down-up, 1-2-3-4 motion will remain a constant as you accompany reels, but the rhythmic interest is increased via the use of accents. However, in Irish music, using accents doesn't mean that you simply play them louder while continuing to strum full chords in between. Instead, the chords between the accents should be somewhat muted—almost like a scratch strum. Plus, you should focus on hitting primarily the lower strings. This "percussive" approach is an example of when locking in with the bodhrán beat becomes important, as the beat will largely determine where you place the accents.

Below is a simple but popular three-chord phrase. Strum through it initially with even 8th notes, and then add the accents. You may want to isolate one bar of the accents and work on the rhythm without the chord changes.

TRACK 80
0:00 **EXAMPLE 1**

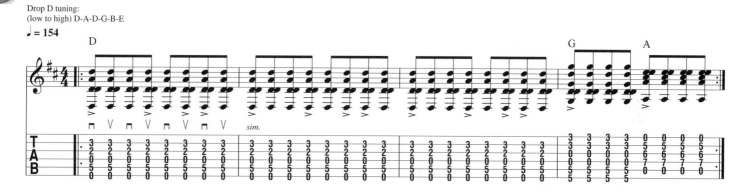

Irish tunes generally have A and B (and sometimes C) sections and the song form may be ABAB or AABB. As a result, rhythm guitarists must be able to substitute chords and perhaps add some rhythmic variety like syncopation to keep the song fresh. Example 1 was basically the A section of a tune called "Crowley's." This next example is essentially the B section. The original chords appear in parentheses above the chords that you'll actually play. Note the substitution of Em for G and Bm for D—the relative minors—as well as the addition of the B♭m passing chord and the anticipatory change to A on the "and" of beat 2 in measure 4.

TRACK 80
0:15 **EXAMPLE 2**

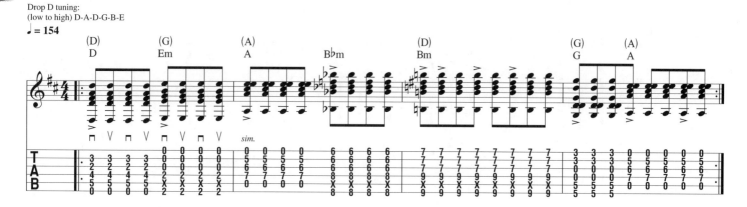

LESSON #82: IRISH GUITAR ACCOMPANIMENT: JIGS

In this lesson, we'll apply the essential concepts of Irish guitar playing and more to the popular Irish jig form. All of the examples use Drop D tuning.

"Rashers and Sausages"

Lunchtime? No, the phrase "rashers and sausages" is used to teach beginning Irish guitar students the basic strum pattern in an Irish jig. The jig is in 6/8 time and, therefore, typically has six strums per measure, which are counted "1-2-3, 1-2-3." However, unlike the reel where you used strict alternating (i.e., down-up) strumming, the jig throws a curveball: every group of three beats is strummed "down-up-down." Consequently, you have to play two consecutive down-strums in the middle of each measure.

Let's try out that rhythm on an open D5 chord. Begin slowly, focusing on keeping your time and attack consistent, particularly on the consecutive down-strums, and then gradually speed up.

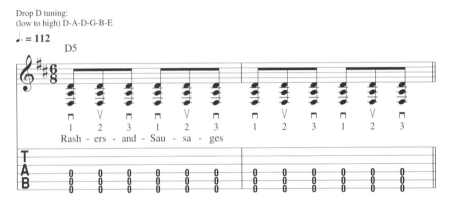

Time to Get Jiggy

Let's take a look at the A section of "Gallagher's Frolics," which contains a basic jig harmony that utilizes just three chords, or what's called a "three-chord trick."

TRACK 81 0:00 **EXAMPLE 1**

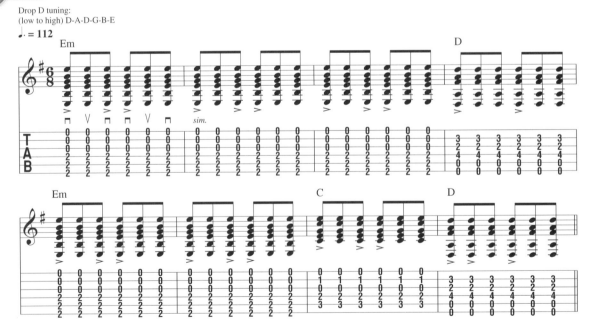

"Gallagher's Frolics" is played in AABB format, so you might play something simple like Example 1 the first time through and then create a more harmonically complex progression on the second pass. This next example moves chords around a bit, colors them with major 7ths and "add" notes, and adds an Am7 substitution.

EXAMPLE 2

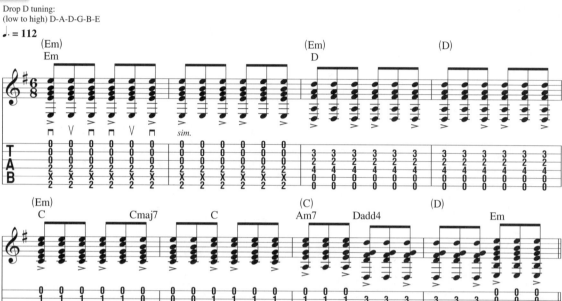

And here is the reharmonized B section, embellished with chord suspensions (measure 3), and given some voice leading in the bass (measures 5–6). Plus, measure 7 contains a relative minor substitution (Am for C), and the D chord comes in a beat early for a touch of syncopation. The original three-chord trick changes appear in parentheses above the actual chords, so you can more readily see the changes.

EXAMPLE 3

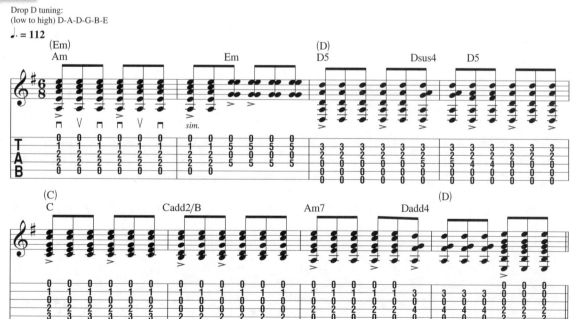

This merely scratches the surface of what is played in sessions across the world every night. Plus, many more Irish song forms are still out there to be discovered. While there's no substitute for learning from traditional Irish musicians in real sessions, I do highly recommend John Doyle's *Irish Rhythm Guitar* instructional DVD which, along with advice from a very good Irish musician friend, informed this lesson. *Sláinte!*

LESSON #83: SOLO CELTIC GUITAR

Irish and Celtic music comprises some of the most beautiful melodies of any cultural style and is particularly well-suited to solo acoustic guitar arrangements. These melodies come in several forms, including ballads, airs, jigs, hornpipes, and reels, often based on specific dance steps. In this lesson, we'll explore three of these various Celtic song forms as arranged for solo acoustic guitar.

Tune-Up Time

Although Celtic guitar and DADGAD tuning may sometimes seem synonymous, the truth is that you can use any number of tunings when arranging these traditional melodies for solo guitar. In this lesson, we're going to use Drop D tuning (D–A–D–G–B–E), as well as DADGAD.

Hornpipe

Legend has it that the hornpipe was named for a dance that mimicked the movements of a sailor aboard a sailing vessel. Whether or not this is true, one of the most popular hornpipe melodies is "The Sailor's Hornpipe." This lilting and fairly straight 8th-note melody in Drop D tuning is backed by a steady quarter-note bass line. Play the downstemmed bass notes with your thumb and the upstemmed melody notes with your fingers.

TRACK 82
`0:00` **EXAMPLE 1**

The rhythm in "The Sailor's Hornpipe" is an exception, not the rule. Most hornpipes are played in a dotted-8th/16th-note rhythm, as depicted in the following arrangement of "The Harvest Home," played in DADGAD tuning. Watch out for the triplets in measure 4—you'll want to use an index-finger barre across the 2nd fret for the first half of that measure.

TRACK 82
`0:15` **EXAMPLE 2**

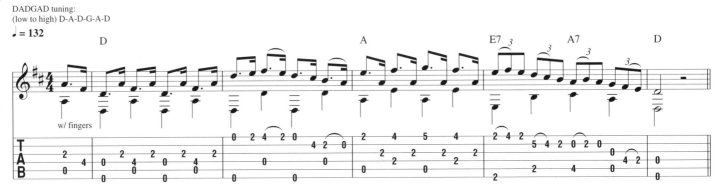

Reel

The reel is played in a driving two-beat feel and is the most popular dance step for country and square dancing. The following example is an arrangement of "St. Anne's Reel," played in Drop D tuning. It utilizes an arranging device known as "harp-style" melody lines, in which separate strings are used for successive notes to create a ringing, legato sound.

TRACK 82 0:27 **EXAMPLE 3**

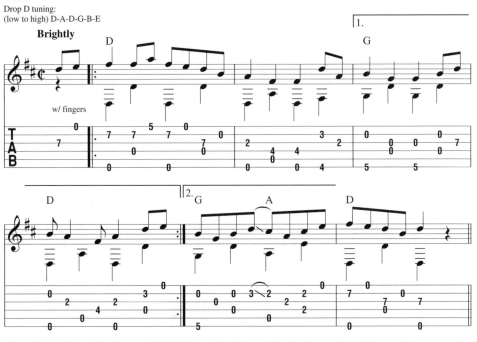

If you're new to the harp-style approach, it may feel counterintuitive at first, as notes lower in pitch often fall on *higher* strings, but with focused practice it will soon fall into place.

Jig

The jig is an Irish folk dance in 6/8 time generally played at a lively tempo, with the pulse felt in a two-beat feel, on each dotted quarter note. The most popular Irish jig is "The Irish Washerwoman." The dance itself has a rather humorous history: it contains much stomping and grimacing, and when danced by a woman, it's been said that she represents an angry Irish washerwoman whose husband has been "delayed" at the local pub. When danced by a man, it's said to symbolize the story of Paddy's Leather Breeches, which shrunk because of a careless Irish washerwoman!

The following arrangement of "The Irish Washerwoman" is played in Drop D tuning and features bass notes on the strong beats (1 and 4); that is, on each dotted quarter note. When two consecutive notes appear on the same string, like the G notes on beats 2–3 and 5–6 of measure 1, use different fingers to pluck them.

TRACK 82 0:42 **EXAMPLE 4**

LESSON #84: BRAZILIAN JAZZ

Harmonically, Brazilian jazz is essentially the same as its North American cousins: swing, bebop, cool jazz, and fusion. Its harmonic basis consists of seventh chords and their extensions, all within the venerable ii–V chord progression. What sets Brazilian jazz apart from traditional North American jazz, however, is its *rhythm*. In this lesson, we'll explore three essential rhythmic feels of this South American tradition.

Bossa Nova

The bossa nova gets its free-spirited feel from the combination of a tight, even rhythm section and a freely phrased melody. Here, we'll focus on the rhythmic aspects. The basic bossa-nova comping rhythm is a one-measure figure that alternates between bass notes on beats 1 and 3 and chord voicings filling the gaps, as in this Dm9–G13–Cmaj7 example.

TRACK 83 0:00   **EXAMPLE 1**

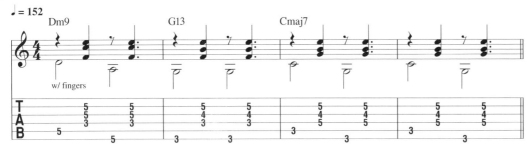

This next example adds a chord stab on the upbeat of beat 4, which not only adds a little motion to the comping pattern, but also sets up rhythmic and harmonic anticipation, or a "kick," to the coming chord change.

TRACK 83 0:10   **EXAMPLE 2**

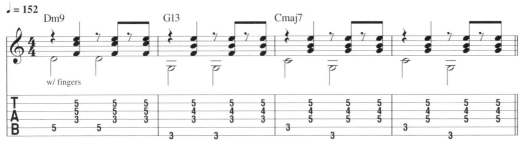

In the following eight-bar bossa-nova example, note how the kick is tied to the downbeat of the following measure—a very common rhythmic tool in Brazilian jazz.

TRACK 83 0:20   **EXAMPLE 3**

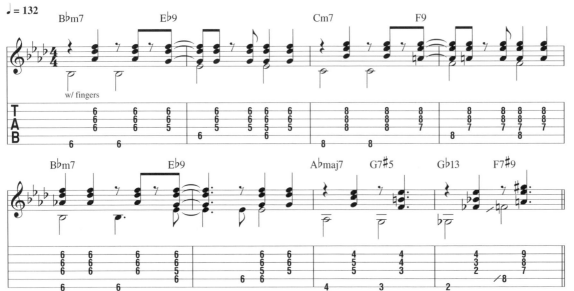

Samba

The samba is the oldest of Brazilian grooves; in fact, the bossa nova is derived from it! The samba is typically faster than the bossa nova and has a two-beat feel, so you'll often see it written in 2/2 or 2/4 time. Another big difference between the samba and bossa nova is that, in a samba rhythm, the bass notes are usually played in unison with the chords, though like the bossa nova, alternation of the two voices is acceptable.

To begin, let's first take a look at the samba clave, which is a repetitive rhythm pattern that is central to the song (all other rhythm patterns in the song relate to it). This first one is called a forward samba clave:

TRACK 83
0:38 **EXAMPLE 4**

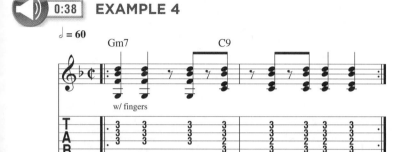

As you may have guessed, a reverse samba clave also exists, which simply reverses the order of the two measures that comprised the forward samba clave.

TRACK 83
0:50 **EXAMPLE 5**

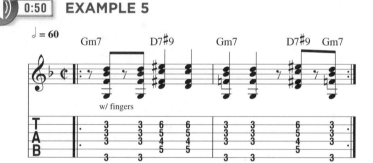

Once you're comfortable with those two claves, try to apply them to the chord changes in Example 3.

Baião

The baião rhythm comes from northern Brazil and has a pattern common to many other styles, but here it is played with the Brazilian feel and interpretation. The guitar typically plays two attacks per measure in a baião—on beat 1 and the "and" of beat 2—while the bass plays a distinctive root–5th–root pattern. Here, we've combined and arranged the two voices for guitar.

TRACK 83
1:03 **EXAMPLE 6**

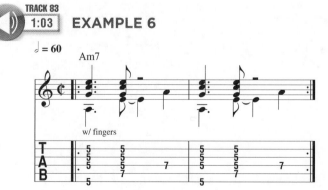

These examples merely scratch the surface of this broad-ranging jazz format. As is true when learning most musical styles, listening to the masters is the best education. Seek out the recordings of Antonio Carlos Jobim, Luiz Bonfá, João Gilberto, and Baden Powell, to name just a few, and soon your "Girl From Ipanema" will make you sound like *you're* from Ipanema!

Flamenco music comes to us from the south of Spain—specifically, the region of Andalucía, where Gypsies who were traveling from India settled sometime around the 14th century. Initially comprising song and dance, guitar wasn't added as an accompaniment instrument in flamenco music until the mid-1800s. Since that time, the flamenco style has become one of the most beautiful art forms ever plied on our nylon-string friend. In this lesson, we'll explore requisite strumming techniques of this popular Spanish sound.

Rasgueado

The most characteristic of all flamenco guitar techniques, rasgueado, which is Spanish for "strumming," ranges from a simple one-finger strum to the much more sophisticated—and challenging—five-stroke variety. We'll start with the simplest one, but before we do, let's take a look at the chords that you'll be strumming.

Much flamenco music is based on the harmonized Phrygian mode (1–♭2–♭3–4–5–♭6–♭7), but with a major tonic. So, in the key of E, you would have the following chords: E–F–G–Am–B°–C–Dm. From that set of chords comes one of the most popular progressions in flamenco music: iv–III–II–I, which in the key of E is Am–G–F–E.

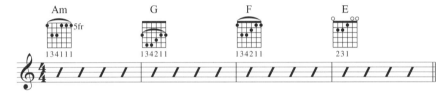

Now let's play that progression with rasgueado. The simplest version of rasgueado is the one-finger strum, which is performed with your index finger. With your fingers curled in a loose fist and positioned above the low E string, and your thumb in playing position resting on the low E, strum the chords in alternating down-up fashion by extending your index finger for the downstroke, and then flexing it back up to perform the upstroke, brushing it with your nail in both directions.

TRACK 84
0:00 **EXAMPLE 1**

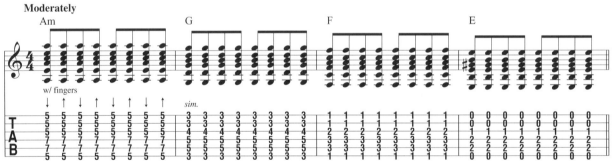

> ### PREPARE TO NAIL IT
> If you're at all serious about playing flamenco guitar, you're going to need some serious fingernails on your picking hand. Strong and somewhat long fingernails not only help to create bold and bright rasgueado strumming, but also consistent attack when playing in the picado style. You may even want to use a clear polish—or even acrylic nails and/or wraps—for reinforcement and protection.

Triplet Rasgueado

The next type of flamenco strum is called the triplet rasgueado, which comprises—as you probably guessed—three strokes. You can attack the triplet rasgueado a couple of ways: 1) with an index-finger downstroke followed by successive up- and downstrokes with the thumb, or 2) with a thumb-based upstroke followed by successive downstrokes with your index finger and thumb. If you watch an experienced flamenco guitarist perform this technique at tempo, his hand appears to move in a circular motion.

EXAMPLE 2

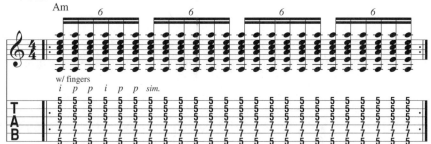

Flamenco's Signature Rasgueado

And now we come to the five-stroke rasgueado, which truly is the signature strum and sound of flamenco guitar. When performing this rasgueado, you'll successively downstrum all of the strings with each of your fingers, beginning with your pinky and ending with an index-finger upstrum. To get started, makwe a loose fist with your picking hand and center it over the strings. Then extend your pinky, strumming all six strings as you do. Next, extend your ring finger, then your middle finger, and then your index finger, wrapping up the rasgueado with an index-finger upstrum.

EXAMPLE 3

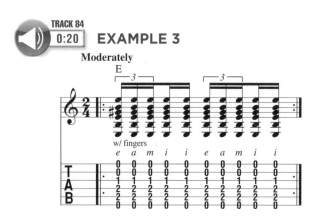

Below is a I–iv progression with an F note embellishment on both the E and Am chords, which drives home the Phrygian sound.

EXAMPLE 4

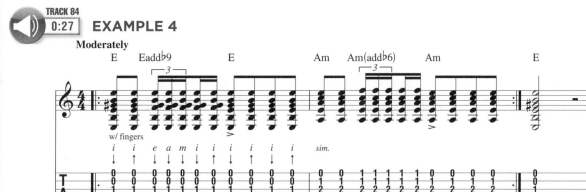

Finally, here's a classic I–iv–III–II–I flamenco progression that uses the five-stroke rasgueado throughout:

EXAMPLE 5

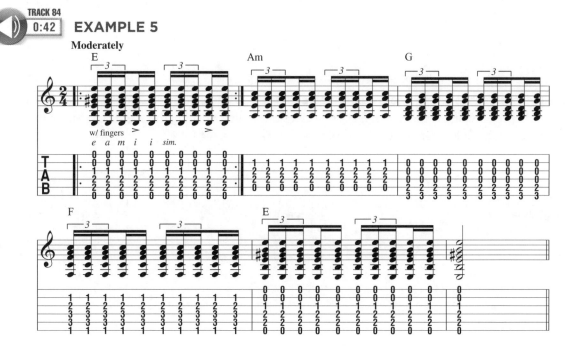

In this lesson, we'll explore four essential flamenco guitar techniques: arpeggios, golpe, tremolo picking, and picado.

Arpeggios

In addition to rasgueado technique, one of the most popular ways to play chords in flamenco music is via arpeggios. The first arpeggio technique that we'll tackle is a more free-flowing approach, like the one shown below, featuring an Am–E7 progression. Note that you'll attack this example differently than you would in a traditional fingerstyle approach. For example, play the first four notes of the opening Am arpeggio with successive downstrokes of your thumb, and then catch the B note on the top string with your ring finger, kicking off a reverse roll (*a–m–i*) before striking the high C note with your ring finger. Use a similar approach throughout the example.

TRACK 85 0:00 **EXAMPLE 1**

Golpe

Flamenco is a highly rhythmic music and one way to reinforce that on the guitar is via the percussive technique called the golpe, which is simply a tap on the soundboard or pickguard of your acoustic guitar. The golpe is usually performed with either your ring or middle finger and can be performed in its own rhythmic space or simultaneously with another plucked note. In this first example, the golpe takes up its own rhythmic space.

TRACK 85 0:13 **EXAMPLE 2**

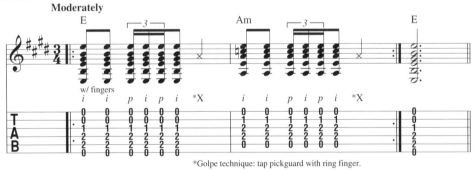

*Golpe technique: tap pickguard with ring finger.

Here, the golpe is played simultaneously with a plucked note during an arpeggiated passage. Nailing that golpe while plucking a note with another finger is a rather challenging technique at first, so take it slowly, even isolating the event, and then expand it to one or two notes on either side of the golpe before eventually playing the entire passage.

TRACK 85 0:26 **EXAMPLE 3**

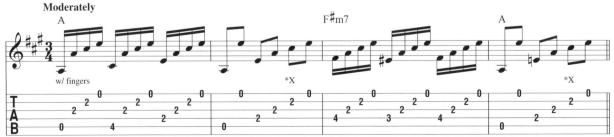

*Golpe technique: tap pickguard with ring finger.

Tremolo Picking

Another popular flamenco guitar technique is tremolo picking. Classical guitarists also use tremolo picking; however, while classical guitarists use a three-finger attack, flamenco guitarists use a four-finger pattern: index–ring–middle–index (*i–a–m–i*)

TRACK 85
0:37   **EXAMPLE 4**

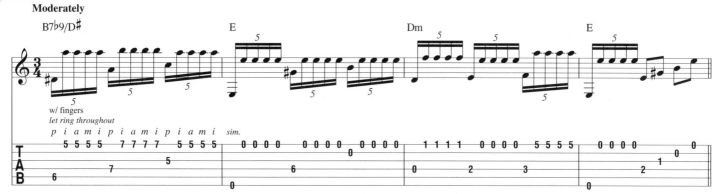

Picado

So far, we've focused on the rhythm guitar aspects of flamenco guitar. Now we'll take a look at the single-note technique called picado. Like classical guitarists, flamenco players use alternating strokes of their index and middle fingers.

Your fingers should be aligned perpendicular to the strings, with your thumb resting on the low E string (except when it's being played) for stability. Further, you should use the apoyando, or "rest stroke," whereby after each attack you rest that finger on the lower adjacent string to anchor your fingers. Let's try it on an E Spanish Phrygian scale:

TRACK 85
0:50   **EXAMPLE 5**

Although the Spanish Phrygian scale, the fifth mode of the harmonic minor scale, generally is the scale of choice for flamenco music, guitarists will often incorporate chromatic tones as in this next line.

TRACK 85
1:00   **EXAMPLE 6**

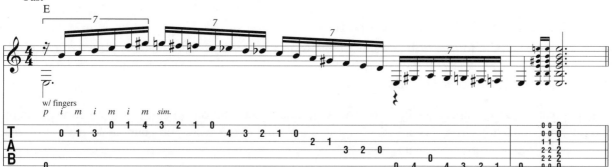

When learning any new style or technique, it's always in your best interest—if not requisite—to devote a lot of time to *listening* to its masters, especially flamenco guitar. Be sure to check out the works of Paco de Lucía, Ramón Montoya, and Niño Ricardo, among others, taking in the stylistic subtleties, feel, and rhythm as much as listening to the techniques themselves.

LESSON #87: SWING RHYTHM GUITAR

"It don't mean a thing, if it ain't got that swing." Rarely have truer words been spoken. Although Duke Ellington cut that famous track in 1932, cats like Eddie Lang and Lonnie Johnson were already swinging hard for nearly a decade. But when Freddie Green (with Count Basie) and Charlie Christian (with Benny Goodman) hit the scene in the mid to late thirties, swing guitar was officially in, well… full swing. In this lesson, we're going to take a look at essential swing guitar rhythm techniques, from Freddie Green's pioneering approach to "rhythm changes," essential substitutions, and more.

Four to the Bar

Swing music is typically played in a big band setting, where a horn section takes the melody and the guitar is relegated to the rhythm section. To suit this expectation, Count Basie Orchestra guitarist Freddie Green pioneered a rhythm approach, often called "four to the bar" or "four on the floor," in which he strummed steady quarter-note chord stabs with accents on beats 2 and 4.

Further, Green navigated the fast tempos of swing music with shell voicings, which are stripped-down chord shapes that contain only the root, 3rd, and 7th of each seventh chord, or the root, 3rd, and 6th of each sixth chord. Below are essential chord shapes for major, minor, and dominant seventh chords and sixth chords, with roots on both the sixth and fifth strings.

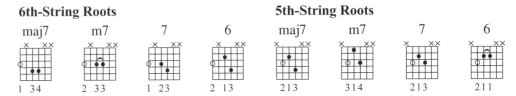

Let's plug some of those shapes into the ubiquitous I–VI–ii–V progression known as "rhythm changes," so-named for the chord structure of Gershwin's swing standard "I Got Rhythm." Two versions are presented below; the first version is pretty straightforward, while the second version substitutes C6 for Cmaj7 and places the bass note of every chord on the sixth string to fatten the bass and provide a bit of voice leading. In the resultant Dm7/A chord, the root (D) is replaced with the 5th (A).

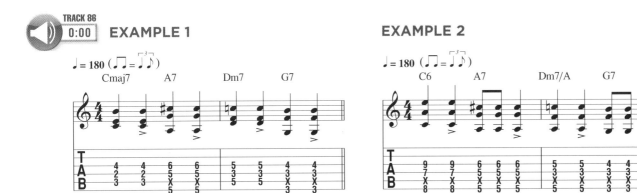

Substitution and Reharmonization

"I Got Rhythm" is in a 32-bar AABA form, which is standard for swing songs. As you can imagine, playing the same chord pattern for 16 consecutive bars can get old—fast. To remedy this sonic boredom, swing guitarists would often substitute alternative chords, effectively reharmonizing the progression.

One of the most popular ways to reharmonize a progression is via tritone substitution, whereby each functioning dominant chord is replaced with a dominant seventh chord that is located a tritone (#4/b5) away. For example, instead of playing A7 in the Cmaj7–A7–Dm7–G7 progression, you could play Eb7. Also, if you replace the G7 with its tritone sub, Db7, you get the following very cool chromatic descent.

**EXAMPLE 3**

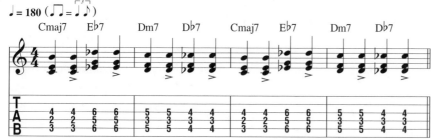

The B section of "I Got Rhythm" cycles through dominant chords that are separated by an interval of a 4th, where each preceding seventh chord serves as a functioning dominant (e.g., E7 is the functioning dominant of A7). In the key of C, you have this eight-bar section:

**EXAMPLE 4**

Instead of sitting on each seventh chord for two bars, you might consider substituting a ii chord for a couple of beats, just to break up the monotony and keep the progression bouncing along.

**EXAMPLE 5**

Color Those Chords

In the true spirit of jazz, you'll occasionally want to dress up those functioning dominant chords to include extensions (9ths, 11ths, 13ths) and altered tones (♭9th, #9th, ♭5th/#11th, #5th/♭13th). Doing so will typically require that you add a fourth note to those handy three-note shell voicings, but the result is well worth the effort.

Let's reharmonize those B-section seventh chords with the aforementioned tools.

**EXAMPLE 6**

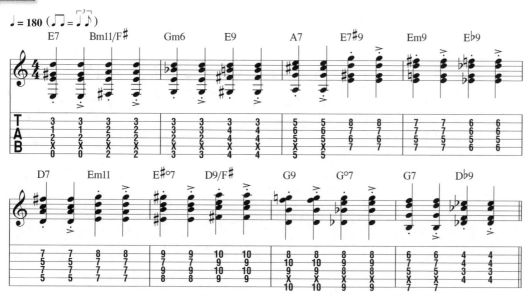

Note all the voice leading that occurs in this reharmonization. In fact, the resultant bass line in the first two measures is borrowed directly from George Gershwin!

INTRODUCTION TO SWING SOLOING

Although guitarists of the early swing era typically provided accompaniment only, guitarists in modern acoustic jazz ensembles often get a turn at a little improv. And, because the blues is at the root of so many swing styles, we're going to present this introduction to swing soloing with essential blues tools such as sixth- and seventh-chord arpeggios, neighbor tones, common tones, passing tones, and more.

Chord Tones

One way to almost guarantee a great-sounding solo is to make sure that you're hitting the chord tones. Although this approach is not as simple as just playing arpeggios, a thorough knowledge of arpeggio shapes is essential. In blues-based swing music, you will frequently encounter sixth chords and dominant seventh chords. Here are some helpful arpeggio shapes for both of those qualities, for the I, IV, and V chords of a G blues:

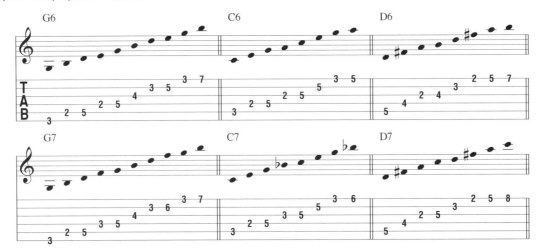

Let's take a look at a few swing licks that incorporate these arpeggios.

TRACK 87
0:00 **EXAMPLE 1**

EXAMPLE 2

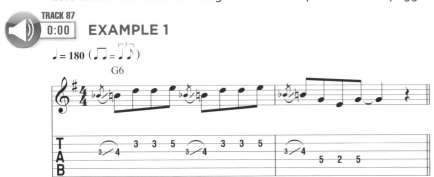

Neighbor Tones

While a safe avenue, playing chord tones exclusively will soon leave your listeners bored. One of the easiest—and jazziest—ways to embellish those arpeggios is to add neighbor tones, which are typically notes that fall either a half step below (lower neighbor tone) or above (upper neighbor tone) a given chord or scale tone. Below are a couple of phrases that use neighbor tones. Note that both licks use the 6th *and* 7th chord tones—yet another way to expand your color palette.

TRACK 87
0:11 **EXAMPLE 3**

EXAMPLE 4

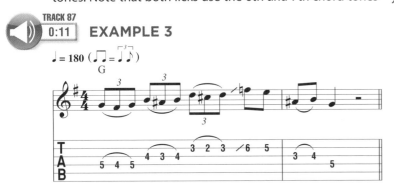

Melodic Motifs

Another fabulous soloing tool in any style, but especially in blues and swing, is the use of themes, or melodic motifs. In this next example, set over I–IV chord changes, we create a melody over the I (G) chord and then transpose the exact motif to the IV (C) chord.

TRACK 87
0:22 **EXAMPLE 5**

Common Tones

In the previous example, we transposed an arpeggio-based phrase from the I chord to the IV chord. But there's another way to achieve a similar effect—common tones, whereby you change only those notes that must be changed to fit the new chord.

The phrase in measure 1 of the following example is based on a G6 arpeggio (G–B–D–E). In measure 2, we change only *one* note—B becomes B♭—to create a Gm6 arpeggio (G–B♭–D–E), which fits perfectly over the C7 chord (C–E–G–B♭). See how three of the four tones are common to both chords? Further, the D note in the Gm6 arpeggio is the 9th of C7, so it works equally well.

TRACK 87
0:29 **EXAMPLE 6**

Chromatic Passing Tones

Finally, you also can use chromatic passing tones, or notes that belong neither to the chords or the underlying scale, to further jazz up your lines.

In this final example, which covers a V–I chord change, or the last four bars of a swing blues, you'll notice several chromatic lines. In the first measure following the pickup, a C♯ note serves as a passing tone during the descent from the root (D) to the ♭7th (C), followed by a B–B♭–A chromatic line. In measure 2, the D–C♯–C line is reiterated an octave lower. In measure 3, the B–B♭–A phrase is repeated, only this time it serves as a 3rd–♭3rd–2nd line over the I (G7) chord, leading to the root and the closing G13 voicing.

TRACK 87
0:35 **EXAMPLE 7**

These licks may be fairly basic and introductory, but the concepts are applicable to all levels of blues and swing improvisation. When you're ready to break from blues-based swing harmony, try to apply some of these licks and approaches to the "rhythm changes" progression.

LESSON #89: SLACK KEY GUITAR

When you think of Hawaiian music, typically two things come to mind: ukuleles and hula dancing. But the acoustic guitar has also played a prominent role in the music of "paradise," beginning in the late 19th century when Mexican cowboys first brought the instrument to the islands and taught the native Hawaiians the basics of playing. Left to develop a style of their own, guitarists turned to traditional Hawaiian dance and music, and the result became known as "slack key" guitar. In this lesson, we'll explore the tunings and techniques that have made this beautiful and relaxing music a treasured art form.

The Tunings

What's called slack key tuning in Hawaii is known as open or altered tunings on the mainland. In its simplest description, a slack key tuning is any guitar tuning in which one or more strings on the guitar are loosened, or "slackened," often resulting in a major chord, though major sevenths and sixths are used as well.

The most common slack key tuning is called taro patch, or as you know it, Open G: D–G–D–G–B–D. Other important slack key tunings include the family of major seventh tunings called wahine and the sixth chord tuning known as Mauna Loa. The adjacent table shows several of the most common slack key tunings.

Taro Patch (Open G)	D–G–D–G–B–D
Open D	D–A–D–F♯–A–D
Open C	C–G–C–G–C–E
G Wahine	D–G–D–F♯–B–D
D Wahine	D–A–D–F♯–A–C♯
Mauna Loa	C–G–E–G–A–E
Old Mauna Loa	C–G–C–G–A–D

Because taro patch (Open G) is by far the most popular slack key tuning, you'll want to have a handful of grips for various G, C, and D chords at your disposal. Here are a few essential ones:

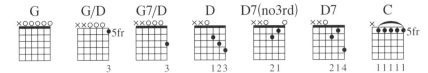

The Techniques

As you can see from the tunings above, getting the Hawaiian sound surely isn't just about tuning. Slack key guitar consists of a set of essential techniques, too, including alternating bass lines (à la Travis picking), with the chords and melody plucked on the top three or four strings, and ornamentations such as hammer-ons, pull-offs, and slides, among others.

Our first example is a standard slack key Hawaiian phrase in taro patch tuning. It incorporates the style's trademark steady bass, as well as legato slides and a tasty pull-off.

TRACK 88
0:00 **EXAMPLE 1**

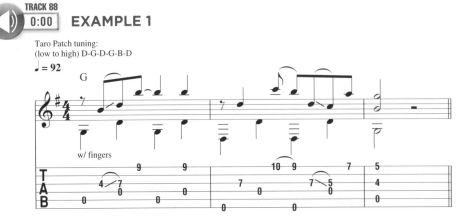

This next example is a two-bar vamp that really captures the "cowboy" roots of Hawaiian music. It is in the G wahine tuning and features a couple of key techniques: hammer-ons from nowhere and 16th-note rolls.

TRACK 88
0:11 **EXAMPLE 2**

G Wahine tuning:
(low to high) D-G-D-F♯-B-D

Below is another example with cowboy roots, but in B♭ wahine tuning (F–B♭–C–F–A–D)—a surprising exception to the rule of slack tunings, as the two lowest strings are actually *raised* a half step! Be sure not to rush those hammer-ons; keep it smooth and let all the notes ring throughout.

TRACK 88
0:26 **EXAMPLE 3**

B♭ Wahine tuning:
(low to high) F-B♭-C-F-A-D

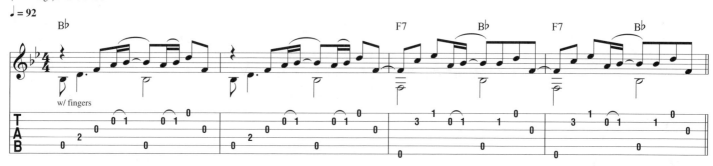

For the final example, we'll go back to taro patch tuning. This chord riff features a rather tricky 16th-note triplet roll—a common technique in slack key guitar. The ascending rolls on the top three strings are played with your index, middle, and ring fingers, on the third, second, and first strings, respectively. Start slowly, focusing only on the triplet move until you can get them up to tempo, and then add the alternating bass line and staccato chord stabs.

TRACK 88
0:42 **EXAMPLE 4**

Taro Patch tuning:
(low to high) D-G-D-G-B-D

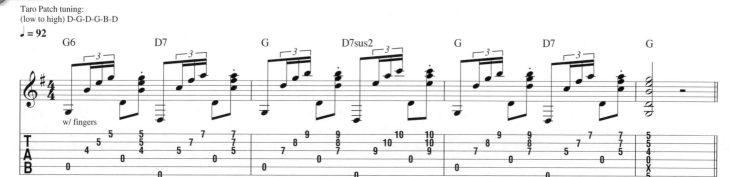

This lesson merely scratches the surface of slack key guitar. In addition to listening to plenty of traditional Hawaiian music, be sure to check out the music of slack key guitar greats like Leonard Kwan, Gabby Pahinui, Peter Moon, and Keola Beamer. You may also want to check out Beamer's slack key instructional books and videos.

LESSON #90: OLD WORLD SOUNDS

The acoustic guitar may be the most popular portable stringed musical instrument on the planet, but it's just one of many. A whole world of interesting stringed-instrument sounds exist out there, many of which—with a little manipulation—can be copped on our six-string friend. In this lesson, we'll explore ways to mimic instruments such as the cuatro, sitar, kora, and others with a steel-string acoustic guitar.

East vs. West

We've all been raised on the tenets of Western music; that is, music originating in Europe and the Americas (North and South). In the Western tradition, the emphasis is on strict melody occurring over harmony, and the music is typically pre-composed. In the Eastern tradition (e.g., India, Middle East, Eastern Asia), however, more emphasis is placed on improvised and ornamented melody occurring over drones, often in odd time signatures.

The Lute Family

When you hear the word "lute," you might think of a court jester strumming his pear-shaped medieval instrument before his king. But in today's musicological terms, "lute" has come to refer to all plucked instruments with strings and a fingerboard, including the Puerto Rican cuatro, the Russian balalaika, the Indian sitar, the Chinese pipa, and many others.

INDIAN SITAR

Most guitarists are familiar with the sound of the Indian sitar, as Beatles guitarist George Harrison helped bring it to popular music in his work with Ravi Shankar. The sitar typically features six or seven strings—three for drones, and the rest for melodies—plus 11 or more sympathetic strings that resonate along with the main strings. We can capture the sitar's "halo effect" of ringing overtones and drones by using drone strings in open tunings. Our sitar-like example is in a D–A–D–G–B–D tuning (Double Drop D tuning) and features not only open droning strings, but also the slides and grace-note ornaments that are key to much of Indian music.

TRACK 89 0:00 EXAMPLE 1

Double Drop D tuning:
(low to high) D-A-D-G-B-D

CHINESE PIPA

The Chinese pipa is a pear-shaped, four-string lute instrument tuned A–D–E–A. Its thin body and scalloped frets make the pipa conducive to pre-bends, delicate picking, and fast, undulating vibrato. Much like some modern-style acoustic guitarists, pipa players use the whole instrument, generating percussive sounds and other effects, pulling the strings in wide bends, and fanning the strings with the back of their fingers for a light and smooth tremolo sound. In the following example, which only grazes the tip of the iceberg for pipa-like technique and sounds, you'll use a pick to strum very close to the bridge (sul ponticello) to produce a bright tone. The ringing open-A and open-D strings offer a droning, suspended backdrop against the main melody, while the vibrato on the repeated 10th-fret A note is emblematic of Chinese music and the pipa. The natural harmonics lend further Asian authenticity to the sound.

EXAMPLE 2

The Harp Family

Instruments belonging to the harp family consist of plucked strings that are stretched between two points and fixed in pitch. Similarly, if the instrument has a soundboard or resonating box beneath the strings, it belongs to the zither family. In this lesson, we'll take a look at one of each.

KORA

Unique to the African sub-Saharan region, the kora features a resonating gourd body, a neck-like column, and at least 21 strings (arranged in two sets) radiating from it. The instrument is played in complex, polyphonic grooves that feature ostinato riffs. The kora is played by plucking the strings with the thumb and index finger of each hand. A key component of kora players' technique is a distinctive style of glissando in which notes are clustered together in tight intervals. One way to mimic this technique is via the use of pull-offs—a guitar technique with which you're probably already proficient.

EXAMPLE 3

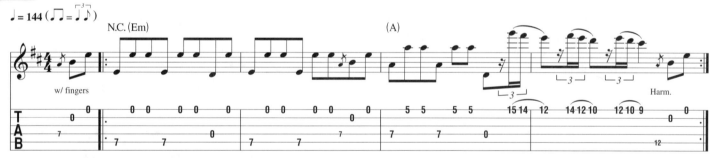

PERSIAN SANTUR

Many types of hammered dulcimers (zither family) can be found throughout the world, but all are said to be variations on the Persian santur, a 2,000-year-old instrument that is still an essential sound in the classical music of Iran. The santur usually has four unison strings for each note, which produce a rich, transparent sound. The courses are hammered with a pair of light mallets called mezrabs. To capture this sound on an acoustic guitar, we're going to use open-string drones and a "hammer" (e.g., a chopstick or a knitting needle) to strike the strings. Hold your hammer near its end in such a manner that it's allowed to bounce off the strings near the soundhole. Use your free fret-hand fingers to dampen non-played strings as much as possible.

EXAMPLE 4

The outside-the-box ideas in this lesson merely scratch the surface of the myriad world sounds that you can create on a standard acoustic guitar. For a more complete and expertly presented take on this topic, check out *Guitar Explorer* and *World Guitar*, both authored by Greg Herriges and published by Hal Leonard Corporation, and which informed this lesson.

LESSON #91: DJANGO'S GYPSY JAZZ STYLE

Although jazz is generally considered an American idiom, one of its greatest and most influential practitioners was a Belgium-born Gypsy named Django Reinhardt. That he became one of the most important jazz guitarists in history is even more impressive when you consider that, when he was just 19, his fret-hand's ring and pinky fingers were crippled in a fire—*and* he did all of this in the thirties on an acoustic guitar, when the guitar typically was relegated to a rhythm role. In this lesson, we'll explore Django's unique and influential approach to Gypsy jazz soloing.

Arpeggios

Like any great jazz soloist, many of Django's lines were based on arpeggios—only Django was among the first to do it. He also typically added chromatic passing tones that would target the chord tones.

The first example depicts a typical line based on a Gm7 arpeggio (G–Bb–D–F), with the b9th (Ab) serving as a passing tone to the root. Be sure to use sweep picking on that initial Gm arpeggio, just as Django did.

Another signature sound of Django's Gypsy jazz soloing was the diminished arpeggio. The next two examples demonstrate two approaches to the popular V–i progression often heard in Gypsy jazz, where a F#°7 arpeggio is substituted for the D7 chord.

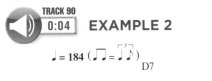

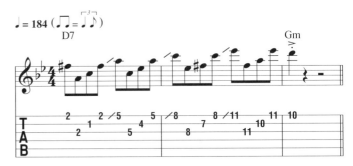

Open to Chromaticism

Django was a master of using open strings, both as a space-filler and as a pedal tone. This next lick, which employs the open high-E string as a pedal tone against A minor scale tones, is similar to one he used in "Minor Swing."

Django also used open-string pedal tones in cross-picking fashion, as in this G Mixolydian-based lick:

TRACK 90
0:22 **EXAMPLE 5**

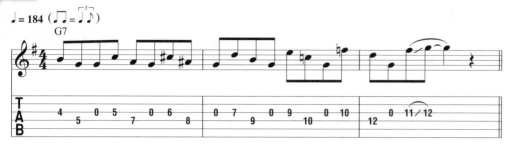

We touched on Django's fondness for chromatic passing tones, but below are a couple of his favorite heavily chromatic moves. The first one features a series of trills that descend chromatically and is useful when you encounter two bars of a static chord.

TRACK 90
0:30 **EXAMPLE 6**

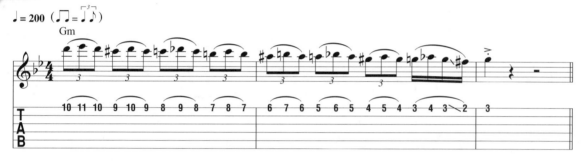

This second chromatic lick is an ascending run that Django loved to use. When he got to the high E string, he would slide his fret-hand's index finger right up the string.

TRACK 90
0:36 **EXAMPLE 7**

Don't Forget the Melody!

As much as Django is revered for his unbelievable technical proficiency and fiery lines, the guitarist also possessed wonderful melodic sense and could play charming, light-hearted chord tone-based melodies with the best of them.

TRACK 90
0:41 **EXAMPLE 8**

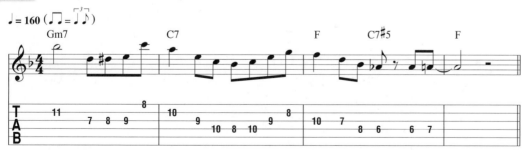

As you explore Django's playing and the Gypsy jazz style, be sure to check out other masters of the genre, like Bireli Lagrene and John Jorgenson.

LESSON #92: JOHNNY CASH

As if the Carter family of Virginia wasn't already influential enough, Maybelle's daughter June Carter pretty much singlehandedly rescued a country singer/guitarist from his drug- and alcohol-fueled downward spiral to self-annihilation in the mid-sixties. His name was Johnny Cash, also known as the "Man in Black." The couple got married in 1968, and over the next 35 years, Cash himself would go on to realize his enormous talent and become one of the most important artists of the 20th century. In this lesson, we'll explore the key elements of Cash's "boom-chucka" guitar style.

Boom-Chucka

If Johnny Cash has a signature guitar technique, it's the "boom-chucka" rhythm strum. Although his mother-in-law, Maybelle Carter, may have invented it, Cash made it famous. This ubiquitous acoustic rhythm approach is heard in "Folsom Prison Blues," "Walk the Line," "Ring of Fire," and "Man in Black," to name just a few. The boom-chucka rhythm involves playing a chord tone—almost always the root—as a bass note on beats 1 and 3 and a pair of 8th-note strums on the upper strings on beats 2 and 4, similar to how drummers use the bass and snare, respectively. Here's an acoustic rhythm guitar part that you would typically hear from Cash:

 TRACK 91 0:00 **EXAMPLE 1**

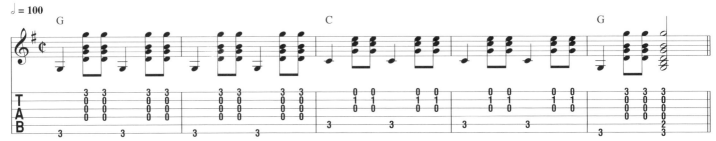

Like Maybelle Carter before him, Cash would sometimes alternate the bass notes in his strumming, playing the root on beat 1 and either the 5th or (less often) the 3rd on beat 3.

 TRACK 91 0:09 **EXAMPLE 2**

Boom-Chick

Now, if you listen to any of Cash's aforementioned hit songs, you'll also hear longtime Cash lead guitarist Luther Perkins knockin' out a single-note rhythm part called the boom-chick, tendered with a bright-toned electric guitar and a touch of slap-back echo. To emulate these parts, you'll want to palm-mute the strings by lightly resting the heel of your picking hand across the strings, just above the bridge of your guitar. To produce the "boom," Perkins typically played the root note on beat 1 and the 5th on beat 3, and then answered with either the upper root (octave) or the 3rd on beats 2 and 4 to produce the "chick."

 TRACK 91 0:18 **EXAMPLE 3**

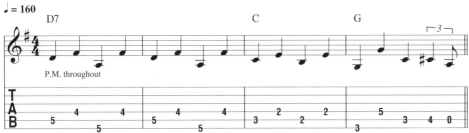

Shifting Meters

In the intro to one of Cash's biggest hits, "Ring of Fire," the meter shifts from 4/4 to 2/4 several times during the intro and verse. Now, I imagine that if you asked Johnny Cash why he would shift meters in the middle of a verse, he might reply, "Because I *can*, son." But truth is the famous tune was written by June Carter Cash and Merle Kilgore. Still, it's a brilliant piece of time play.

If you're not familiar with shifting meters, you can attack them two ways. The first way is to tap your foot and count "1–2–3–4" for each measure of 4/4 time, and "1–2" for each occurrence of 2/4. While this seems logical, the fast tempo of 200 quarter-note beats per minute makes it a bit impractical, as you may soon wear out. Instead, you might want to try the second alternative, which is to count in "cut time," wherein a half note gets the pulse. In that case, consider beats 1 and 3 as the downbeats (count: "1–2"), with beats 2 and 4 marking the upbeats, so when you get to a measure of 2/4, you'll actually only count "one."

TRACK 91
0:28 **EXAMPLE 4**

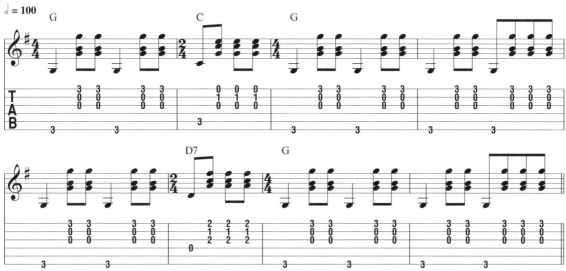

Bass Lines

Again, like his mother-in-law Maybelle before him, Cash would often incorporate bass line melodies into his acoustic accompaniment. Typically, these bass lines walked either up or down to the next chord change. Here's an example in the style of "I Walk the Line":

TRACK 91
0:41 **EXAMPLE 5**

JAMES TAYLOR

He may be the poster boy for the "sensitive singer/songwriter," but while that label often is used in mocking tones, James Taylor is the real deal. Taylor's songwriting resonated with a Vietnam war-era America that was seeking solace and healing, and his tremendous command of his instrument helped to ensure a long and successful career to come. In this lesson, we'll explore the key attributes and techniques of Taylor's guitar style.

Taylor-Made Fingerings

A good portion of Taylor's smooth sound comes from his strong and precise fingerpicking technique. Although the chord voicings that he typically employs are deceptively simple, the grips that he uses to play them are rather unique.

The two must-know fingerings from Taylor's arsenal are the open D major and open A major chords. In both shapes, he uses his fret-hand's index finger on the 3rd, or the top fretted note of the chord.

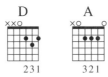

Taylor has chosen these unusual fingerings because he finds them more conducive to chordal embellishments like hammering onto the 4th or pulling off to the 2nd (see Example 1 to hear it in action). Of course, standard fingerings of these two chords also allow for those types of embellishments, but in Taylor's vast experience, these work best for him. Give it a shot—you may prefer them, too!

Another atypical fingering is shown below. Here, Taylor plays the bass line of an Aadd4–Aadd4/F♯–Aadd4/B progression with his fret-hand's ring finger. In isolation, this approach might not make much sense, but when coming from or going to certain chord changes (see Example 2), the benefits become more apparent.

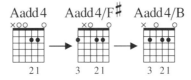

The Signature Lick

What do "Fire and Rain," "Sweet Baby James," "Carolina on My Mind," and several other Taylor tracks have in common? This lick:

TRACK 92
0:00   **EXAMPLE 1**

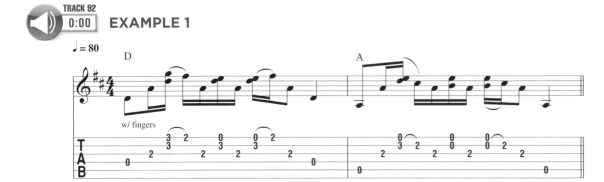

Example 1 is where Taylor's custom fingerings for the open D and open A chords may come in handy. It looks and sounds pretty easy, but some serious syncopation and suspension is occurring in this example via those hammer-ons and pull-offs. To perform this example up to Taylor's standard, your fret hand must play the ornaments as strongly as your pick hand attacks the strings, or it will sound unbalanced. Let the notes ring as long as possible.

Bass-ics

Another hallmark of Taylor's playing is incorporating bass lines into his chord progressions. Earlier, we showed you the chord grids for Aadd4, Aadd4/F♯, and Aadd4/B chords. Now we'll incorporate those shapes into a riff that is similar to the one he plays in "Little Wheel."

EXAMPLE 2

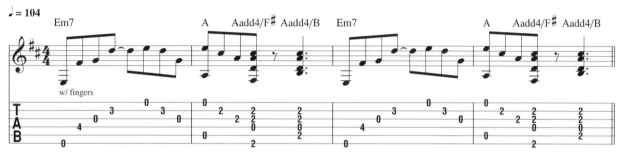

Below is a more commonly encountered progression with a built-in bass line, and an instance where Taylor's fingering for the D chord is the better choice. Using his grip, the change from D/C♯ to Bm11 requires that you only lift your pinky finger off the fifth string and shift your index from the first string to the fifth, leaving your middle and ring fingers on the A and D notes, respectively.

EXAMPLE 3

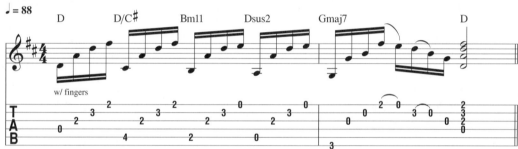

A Touch of Jazz

Occasionally, Taylor will flavor his ballads with a dash or two of soft jazz. We're not talking bebop or taking it "outside," but rather gentle color with a drop of unpredictability. Similar to "Don't Let Me Be Lonely Tonight" and loosely based on a ii–V–I–vi progression, the example below features jazzy extended chords supplying the color, and the D♯°7 and F♯°7 chords the unpredictability.

EXAMPLE 4

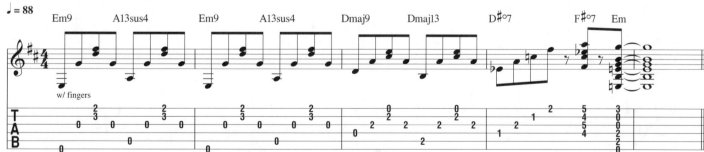

Although few artists or songwriters have earned the "timeless" label, James Taylor is one of them. And while his songwriting has stolen the spotlight, no one can deny that his masterly guitar skills have played a critical role in his success. We say it with most lessons, but it's truer in this case than most: take your time while mastering each aspect of these techniques so that your playing might be as fluent and transparent as Taylor's.

LESSON #94: LEO KOTTKE

Athens, Georgia native Leo Kottke is one of the most influential acoustic guitarists of all time. His aggressive attack, typically in open tunings, down as many as two full steps and often on a 12-string guitar, helped to create a signature sound that has become somewhat commonplace in today's acoustic guitar world. In this lesson, we'll explore some of the technical tools that Kottke often employs.

Six- and 12-String Guitar

As his benchmark 1969 release *6 and 12 String Guitar* so aptly shows, Kottke is a master of both instruments. Because the 12-string guitar is not a very common instrument, all of the examples in this lesson are presented for six-string guitar. If you do have a 12-string, the notation and tab remains the same, but you'll get a much more Kottke-esque tone and experience—particularly if you are able to tune it to the low tunings described in each example.

Syncopation

Like many fingerstyle acoustic guitarists, Kottke often uses an alternating bass line, but one of the signature aspects of his style is syncopation, which can be created via a slight accent. In this first example, the bass notes of each chord alternate between the root and the 5th or the root and the 3rd—a very common technique. But what makes this one "Leo," is the slight accent on every fourth 8th note, which in this case is the open-G string. The accent provides a slight syncopation feel and helps propel the line forward.

TRACK 93 `0:00` **EXAMPLE 1**

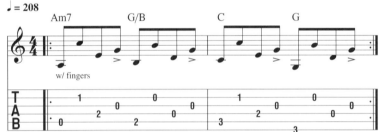

This next example utilizes various triad shapes, with dyad stabs on continually changing beats in each measure—another Kottke-esque syncopation staple.

TRACK 93 `0:07` **EXAMPLE 2**

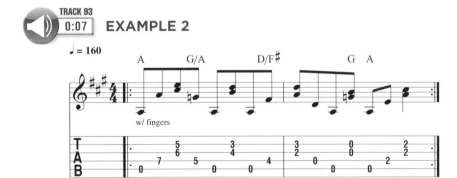

Keeping with the moving triad shapes and shifting rhythm of the previous example, the next one incorporates a classic fingerstyle fretting technique: hammer-ons and pull-offs between chord voicings—another of Leo's favorite devices. Note that this example is in Drop D tuning (D–A–D–G–B–E).

EXAMPLE 3

Unison Bass

A signature sound that is heard in much of Kottke's music is a driving feel, like a locomotive barreling down the fretboard. Bass notes on a down-tuned 12-string contribute mightily to that sound, but playing two, or even three, unison bass notes really drives it home. The following riff, played in Open G tuning, down 1-1/2 steps (B–E–B–E–G♯–B), features octave D notes that are played on three strings in the first measure to set up a great chugging effect before rumbling down the Mixolydian mode to the V (A) chord, which triggers the repeat.

EXAMPLE 4

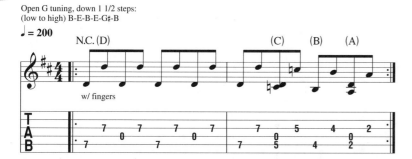

The next example, fashioned in the style of his song "Jack Fig," combines the unison-bass concept with the aforementioned syncopated chord stabs to create a thoroughly Kottke-style riff.

EXAMPLE 5

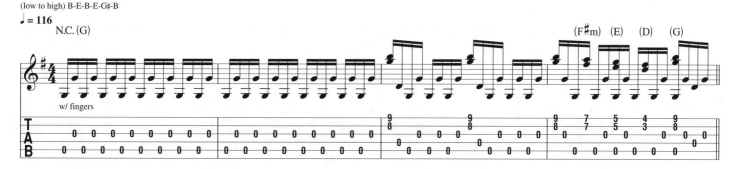

Learning to play in the style of Leo Kottke is a challenging goal, especially given the physicality of his technique. Because so much of his style is based on syncopation and subtle accents, often at fast tempos, be sure to start slowly and master the techniques at "normal" speed, and then gradually work up to his blazing tempos.

LESSON #95: THE BEATLES

In less than 10 years, the Beatles redefined nearly every aspect of pop music. Although they are most often associated with jangly electric Vox guitar tones, their acoustic guitar style drove many of their songs—particularly their older material. In this lesson, we're going to explore the unplugged sounds and techniques of the Fab Four.

Propulsive Strumming

Despite the complexity of many of their arrangements, a simple, strummed acoustic part provided the backbone for many of the Beatles' greatest hits. Depending on the type of song, John, Paul, and George would vary their approach accordingly. For example, in a ballad the acoustic guitar would be employed to lay down a harmonic bed of quarter- and 8th-note strums.

EXAMPLE 1

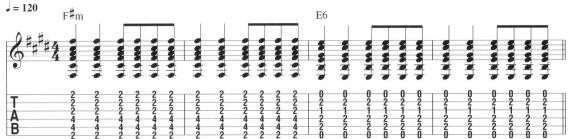

As simple as that seems, the key is execution. Strive for a smooth sound with even volume throughout.

Another common sound that is heard in their early catalog is the skiffle feel, which is a fast, bluegrass-like style. The skiffle is defined by a heavily accented backbeat; that is, you strum harder on beats 2 and 4.

EXAMPLE 2

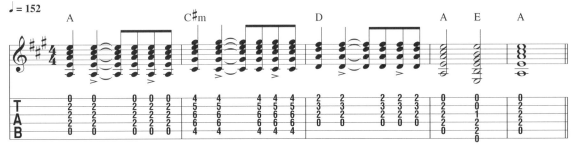

Embellishments and Bass Lines

The Beatles dressed up many strum patterns by mixing in chord embellishments and short bass lines to create melodies within the accompaniment.

This example uses grace-note hammer-ons and a bass line in a rowdy 6/8 feel. Dig into the chords for that classic jangly Beatles sound.

EXAMPLE 3

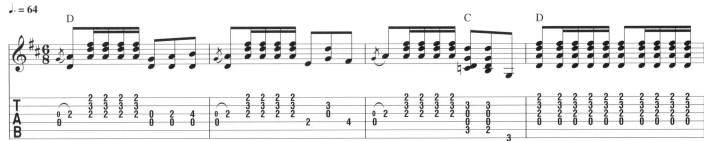

The next example, which features a basic strum pattern that includes a descending bass line, is one that is heard time and time again in pop music, and was another favorite of the Fab Four.

EXAMPLE 4

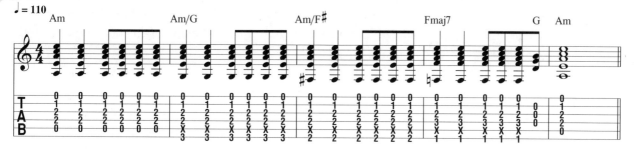

Fingerstyle Approach

Much of the Beatles' acoustic catalog comes courtesy of John Lennon and Paul McCartney. Though Paul was primarily the bass player, he wrote and recorded a surprising amount of acoustic guitar material.

PAUL McCARTNEY TECHNIQUE

When it came to fingerstyle guitar, McCartney preferred a thumb and index finger approach, often using that index finger to play "mini strums" of dyads and triads. He's also pretty much responsible for bringing the 10th interval to popular use in pop music. Here's an example:

EXAMPLE 5

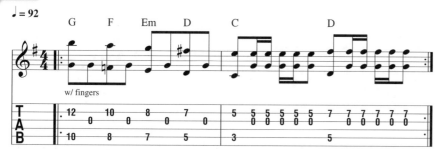

JOHN LENNON TECHNIQUE

John Lennon used a more traditional Travis-style approach, alternating bass notes and filling gaps on treble strings. One aspect that made Lennon's approach interesting is that he generally stuck to a 5–4–6–4 thumb pattern, regardless of the chord changes.

EXAMPLE 6

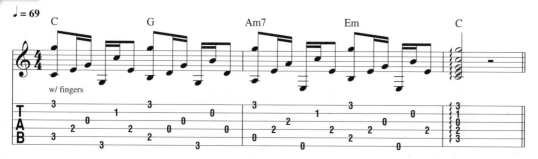

The Beatles' catalog is chock-full of incredible acoustic guitar parts—enough to keep a guitarist interested in learning their style very busy for a very long time. For essential listening, check out "Yesterday," "Blackbird," "Norwegian Wood," "Dear Prudence," "Julia," "While My Guitar Gently Weeps," "Here Comes the Sun," "Can't Buy Me Love," "And I Love Her," "Across the Universe," and "You've Got to Hide Your Love Away."

LESSON #96: JIMMY PAGE

Three words: "Stairway to Heaven." That song in itself might be enough to justify talking about the influence that Led Zeppelin guitarist Jimmy Page has had on the world of acoustic guitar in rock music. But Page's contributions to acoustic rock go so far beyond that song that it's almost immeasurable. Songs like "Stairway," "Black Mountain Side," "Bron-Y-Aur Stomp," "Going to California," and "Over the Hills and Far Away" show off Pagey's mastery of contrary motion, open and altered tunings, and Celtic sounds, all of which we'll explore in this lesson.

Axe of the Gods

Early in his career, Page used a Harmony acoustic guitar, but later his axe of choice was a 1971 Martin D-28 equipped with Ernie Ball Earth-woods strings and a Barcus-Berry pickup that was taped to the guitar. But according to Page, one of the main keys to his acoustic tone was the Altair Tube limiter. "I found out about the unit from a chap named Dick Rosmeni," Page told *Guitar World Acoustic* magazine. "It turned out to be so good and reliable we were still using it on our last studio album, *In Through the Out Door*."

Movable Open Chords

A technique that Page favored, and which has since become a staple of acoustic hard rock, is moving those cowboy chords that we all learn in the first month of playing guitar *out* of open position to create chiming suspended, add, and extended chords filled with droning open strings. One of the most popular instances of this approach in the Led Zeppelin catalog is heard in "Ramble On," from *Led Zeppelin II*. Here is a riff in that style:

TRACK 95 0:00 **EXAMPLE 1**

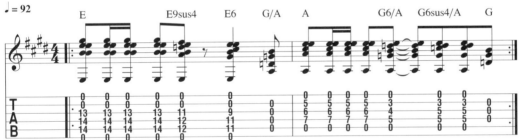

Altered and Open Tunings

Jimmy Page loved to play in altered and open tunings, likely a result of his love of blues and Celtic folk music. One of his favorites was DADGAD tuning, also known as "Celtic tuning." His most famous deployment of DADGAD tuning is heard in Led Zeppelin's "Kashmir," but he also used it acoustically on "Black Mountain Side" (*Led Zeppelin I*), which is based rather blatantly on the Bert Jansch acoustic classic "Blackwaterside." (Jansch's original was recorded in Drop D tuning.) In "Black Mountain Side," Pagey combines his love of acoustic blues with his penchant for Celtic folk to form a riff that sees bluesy ♭3rds and ♭7ths taking on a prominent role. Here's a riff in the style of the Jansch… er, Page tune.

TRACK 95 0:15 **EXAMPLE 2**

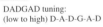
DADGAD tuning:
(low to high) D–A–D–G–A–D

For the bluesy "Friends" on *Led Zeppelin III*, Page "made up" a C6 tuning (low to high: C–A–C–G–C–E), which is also found on "Bron-Y-Aur" from *Physical Grafitti*. Next is a fast-shuffle chord riff in C6 tuning crafted in the style of the former tune.

EXAMPLE 3

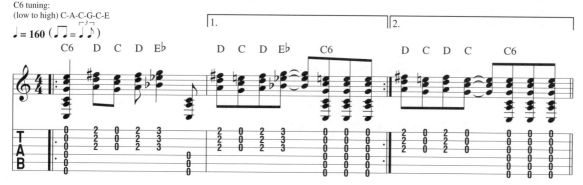

Here is a chordal riff that features some of the same Open G chord shapes that Page used in "That's the Way" from *Led Zeppelin III*.

EXAMPLE 4

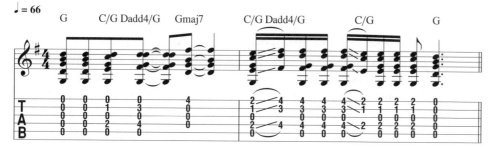

Contrary Motion

Page also understood a thing or two about counterpoint—specifically, contrary motion. Defined as two melodic lines moving in opposite directions, contrary motion is most famously heard in the opening salvo to Led Zeppelin's epic "Stairway to Heaven" (*Led Zeppelin IV*). In the following riff, you'll see the highest note, or melody note, descend in pitch with each chord change while the lowest note, or bass note, ascends with each change.

EXAMPLE 5

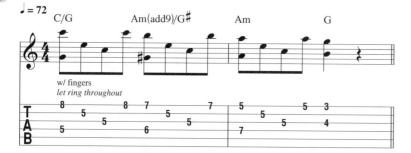

Celtic Influence

You already heard a touch of Page's affinity for Celtic sounds in the "Black Mountain Side" example. In fact, Page later reworked the hammer-on/pull-off portion to serve as the intro to "Over the Hills and Far Away." Here is a similar riff that is arranged in a Celtic-style 6/8 time signature:

EXAMPLE 6

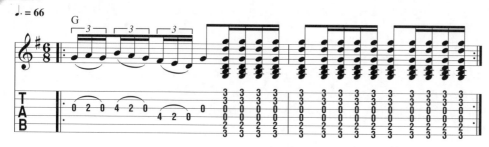

LESSON #97: JONI MITCHELL

Canadian songstress Joni Mitchell may often get lumped in with the folk singer-songwriter movement of the late sixties and early seventies, but she also has left an indelible mark on acoustic guitar playing. But analyzing or categorizing her guitar style is a somewhat exhaustive exercise, because in Joni's world only one rule exists: if it sounds good, it is good. Nonetheless, in this lesson we'll take a look at some of the key elements of her approach to the acoustic guitar.

Forks in the Tuning Road

One of Mitchell's calling cards is her use of a seemingly endless number of tunings. She has been quoted as saying that she's used over 50 tunings during the course of her career, from standard tuning to Open G and Open D to tunings like B–F♯–B–E–A–E, which she used for "The Magdalene Laundries" and says was inspired by the pitch of birdsongs and the environment's frequency on the day that she came up with it.

> ### TUNING BY NUMBERS
>
> To help keep track of her myriad tunings, Mitchell devised her own number system based on standard tuning being 5-5-5-4-5, wherein the low string is E and the fifth string is tuned to the 5th fret of the sixth string, and so forth. Using such a system helps to quickly decipher a tuning like D–G–C–F–A–D, which is just standard dropped down one whole step. The tuning looks complicated in letter form, but when written as D–5–5–5–4–5, it becomes clearer.
>
> While this system has its advantages for categorizing unusual tunings, it can at times be an unnecessary encumbrance. For example, D–5–7–5–4–3 seems a bit intimidating in "Joni" tuning, but if you spell it out, it becomes quickly recognizable as Open G tuning: D–G–D–G–B–D.
>
> The lesson here is that, if you like to work frequently in open and altered tunings, Mitchell's system may be helpful—just make sure it doesn't unnecessarily cloud the issue.

We'll begin with a look at Mitchell's use of open tunings. This first example, similar to her song "Chelsea Morning," is in Open D tuning (D–A–D–F♯–A–D), or what Joni would call D75435 tuning. One of her pet techniques is to play familiar chord shapes in open or altered tunings to get colorful and sometimes unusual chord sounds. Here, a barre at the 5th fret generates a G major chord, but then her use of the "cowboy-shape E chord" fingering produces Dmaj7 and G6/9 chords.

TRACK 96 `0:00` **EXAMPLE 1**

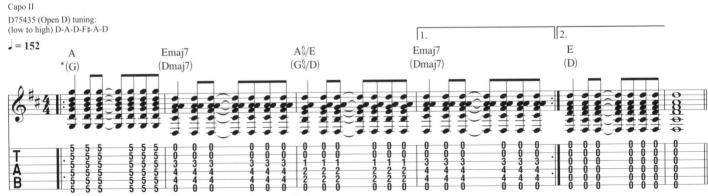

*Symbols in parentheses represent chord names respective to capoed guitar. Symbols above reflect actual sounding chords. Capoed fret is "0" in tab.

The next example, similar to "Big Yellow Taxi," uses the same Open D tuning as in the previous example, but ornaments the major barre chords with a 6th and some percussive, muted scratches. The basic open-E chord shape is further altered to create G/D and D7 chords. Mitchell uses a motif similar to this one in her song "You Turn Me On, I'm a Radio."

TRACK 96
0:18 **EXAMPLE 2**

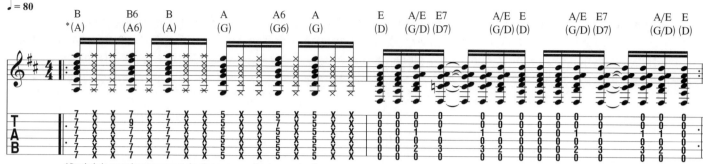

Capo II

D75435 (Open D) tuning:
(low to high) D–A–D–F♯–A–D

♩ = 80

*Symbols in parentheses represent chord names respective to capoed guitar.
Symbols above reflect actual sounding chords. Capoed fret is "0" in tab.

Joni's Weird Tunings

Now let's take a look at some of what Mitchell calls "Joni's weird tunings." This first one, C77374 (C–G–D–F–C–E), was used in her gorgeous song "Ladies of the Canyon." Next up is a fingerpicked riff in that style.

TRACK 96
0:35 **EXAMPLE 3**

Capo II

C77374 tuning:
(low to high) C–G–D–F–C–D

♩ = 108

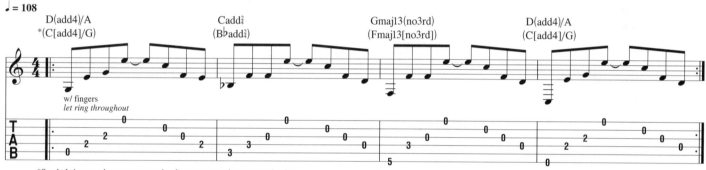

*Symbols in parentheses represent chord names respective to capoed guitar.
Symbols above reflect actual sounding chords. Capoed fret is "0" in tab.

Below is an example styled after "The Magdalene Laundries," which Mitchell played in B75557 tuning (B–F♯–B–E–A–E). You also can see here how Mitchell didn't worry much about "precise" strumming; instead, she attacked the strings rather freely, much like Neil Young and other folk rockers do.

TRACK 96
0:57 **EXAMPLE 4**

B75557 tuning:
(low to high) B–F♯–B–E–A–E

♩ = 60

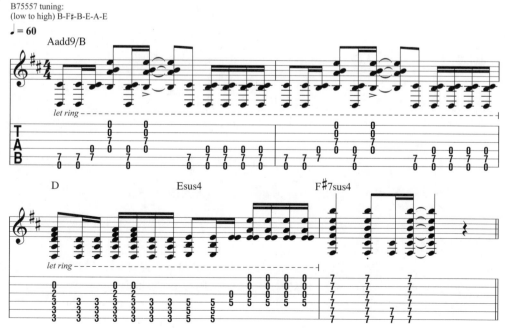

LESSON #98: ADRIAN LEGG

English fingerstylist Adrian Legg has some of the most adept and fluid fingerpicking on either side of the Atlantic. And while he does keep some crafty tricks up his sleeve, for the most part, Legg's deft technique is simply the result of perfecting basic fingerpicking techniques. In this lesson, we'll explore how Legg combines a standard fingerstyle approach with altered tunings and unorthodox moves like partial capos to create his gorgeous sounds.

Banjo Rolls

One of Legg's calling cards is his fluid banjo-roll technique, whether forward, backward, or a combination of the two. So what's the secret—or *secrets*—behind his flawless attack? Practice, practice, and *patterns*. To develop his own fingerstyle chops, Legg would practice the following three patterns repeatedly: *p-i-m-i*, *m-i-p-i*, and *i-m-i-p*. Mastering all three patterns enables you to get used to the downbeat occurring in different locations within the roll.

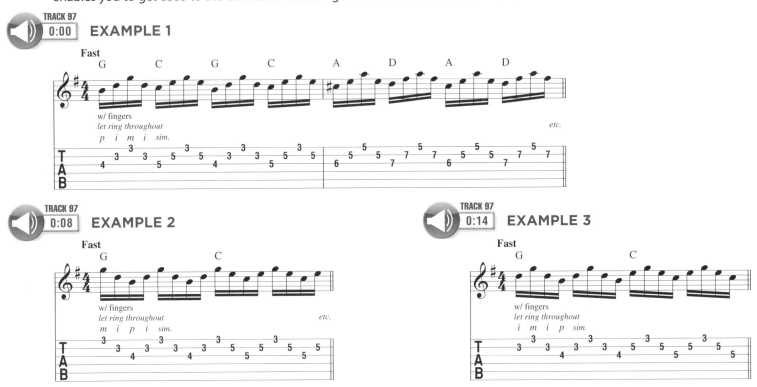

Then you take those rolls, add a bass note, and you get this Legg-style riff:

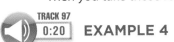

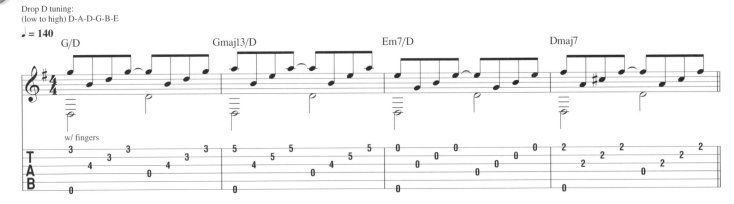

Altered Tunings and Partial Capos

Legg often plies his art in altered tunings, from simple Drop D to DADGAD to Open C tuning (C–G–C–G–C–E), and more. The first example in this section depicts a Legg-style cascading descent in Open C tuning. The next lick also features a fair amount of legato technique, which is another key element of Legg's approach and helps to give the phrase a smooth, fluid sound.

EXAMPLE 5

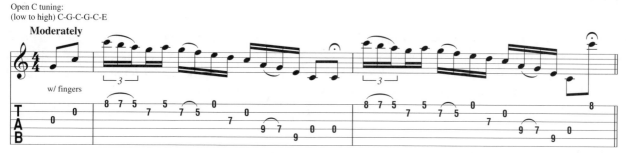

Also like many fingerstylists, Legg makes frequent use of a capo. Unlike most of his peers, however, Legg typically uses partial capos, covering some strings while leaving the remaining ones open. In this next example, Legg creates a harp-like sound with a capo across strings 6–3 at the 10th fret. Here he frets only the top two (i.e., non-capoed) strings, while the bottom four (capoed) strings serve as drones.

EXAMPLE 6

Conversely, Legg will also use the open top strings as drones while fretting notes *in front* of a partial capo.

EXAMPLE 7

Legg takes that approach even further, occasionally using *two* capos at once. For instance, to create Open C tuning without touching the tuning pegs, he may employ a full capo across the 3rd fret in standard tuning, and then add a partial capo across strings 4–2 at the 5th fret. Don't be afraid to experiment with your own partial capo creations.

Uncle Adrian's Secret Weapons

As his fans are well aware, Legg's beautiful acoustic sound actually comes out of a custom *electric* guitar that was built by British luthier Bill Puplett. The chambered guitar is equipped with a custom DiMarzio Waffair Theene magnetic pickup, as well as Graph Tech saddle pickups, to produce his acoustic sound. One of Legg's coolest "secret weapons" is his use of banjo tuners with mechanical stops, which enable the guitarist not only to retune his guitar very quickly and precisely, but also to use the tuning pegs to instantly and accurately change a string's pitch mid-song by preset half or whole steps to create innovative melodic contours.

It all began with a rooftop party in Charlottesville, Virginia, back in 1991. Since that humble yet successful beginning, the Dave Matthews Band has become one of the most popular and successful touring acts in history—a well-deserved distinction in light of the intensity of their live shows. In this lesson, we're going to examine some of the quirky acoustic guitar stylings that have made leader Dave Matthews one of the most influential artists of the past 20 years.

Tripping Chord Voicings

The Dave Matthews Band features instrumentation like few others: the standard guitar, bass, and drums, plus the more unconventional (in a pop/rock context) violin and saxophone. As a result, Matthews's approach to chord voicings tends to be more minimalist, often focusing on just the root and the 3rd, allowing the sax and violin to fill in color tones. Below are some shapes that Matthews often uses, shown diatonic to the key of D (note the droning open D string throughout). You might want to keep your ring finger planted on the third string while your middle finger frets the sixth string for the minor voicings and your index finger grabs the major ones.

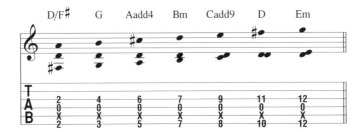

As you may know, the chord shapes are just one part of the rhythm guitar equation; the other is rhythm, and Matthews certainly knows how to leverage that aspect to great advantage.

The next example is composed entirely of 8th-note strums. What's the big deal, you ask? Note how almost all the chord changes take place on the upbeat, giving the riff that signature DMB funky, syncopated feel.

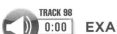
TRACK 98
0:00 **EXAMPLE 1**

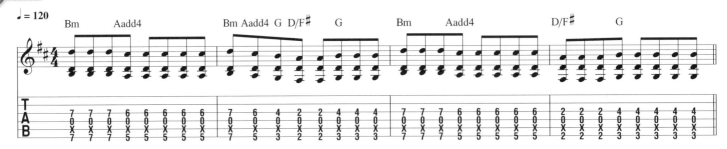

Crashing Drones

The chord voicings in the previous section featured a droning open D note. That approach is not surprising, as Matthews is a big fan of droning notes. He's been quoted as saying that he "tries to find the right drones to build bridges on," which is exactly what we do in this section. The next example features a static, droning E5 power chord with a simple bass line establishing the riff's harmony.

EXAMPLE 2

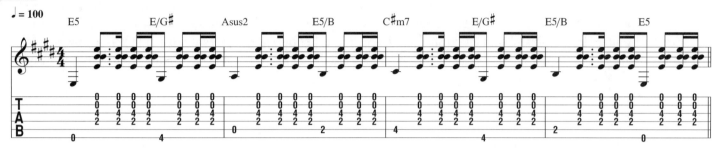

Of course, drones don't always need to consist of open strings or a static chord. The next riff is an example of what Matthews calls "circular modal motion," whereby the entire riff is composed of perfect 5th intervals, also called quintal harmony. The result is a droning, hypnotic pattern in 3/4 time.

EXAMPLE 3

Slides, Scratches, and Octaves Marching

Considering the highly rhythmic nature of his compositions, Dave Matthews' fondness of muted scratch technique should come as no surprise. Add his penchant for staccato attacks, slides, and octaves, and you have the fixin's for some mighty tasty riffery. This final example pulls all those elements into one funky package.

EXAMPLE 4

What's the take-away message of this lesson? That Dave Matthews has crafted a singular acoustic guitar style by straying miles from the ordinary, while staying grounded in the almighty groove. Although some very useful tools are presented here, remember the old but true cliché: it's all about the *song!*

LESSON #100: TOMMY EMMANUEL

Australian guitarist Tommy Emmanuel received his first guitar at age 4, and when at age 7 he heard American guitar legend Chet Atkins, he found his calling, working tirelessly to learn Atkins' fingerpicking style. Some 18 years later and already one of Australia's top guitarists, Emmanuel came to the U.S. and finally met and played with his idol, who then took the Aussie picker under his wing. And then in 1999, Emmanuel's hard work and study culminated in him being honored by Atkins as a "Certified Guitar Player"—a rare distinction shared by only four other people in the world. The title was a crowning moment for Emmanuel, one that the self-proclaimed "humble, uneducated, country kid" from Down Under takes very seriously. In this lesson, we'll explore a few of the signature techniques of Mr. Tommy Emmanuel, C.G.P.

Certified Fingerpicker

When you think of Tommy Emmanuel and acoustic guitar playing, the first thing that comes to mind is his otherworldly fingerstyle technique. At times sounding like three instruments playing at once, Emmanuel obviously took to heart all the tips and advice that he received from Chet Atkins. Of course, like Chet and anyone else who ever plucked the ol' string box, Emmanuel built his impressive technique on the basic constructs of a steady, solid bass line, crisp and well-placed chord stabs, and melody that weaves throughout the arrangement.

The first example in this lesson combines a quarter-note bass line—occasionally using dyads—with chord partials to form a fairly simple, yet essential, fingerstyle pattern with a dash of syncopation. Although Emmanuel uses a thumbpick, your thumb will do just fine.

TRACK 99 0:00 **EXAMPLE 1**

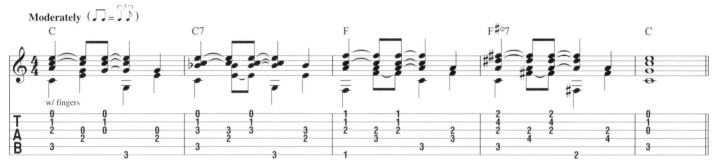

This next example takes the previous pattern one step further and breaks those chord stabs into arpeggios. Notice how the thumb actually finishes the arpeggios on the fourth string.

TRACK 99 0:14 **EXAMPLE 2**

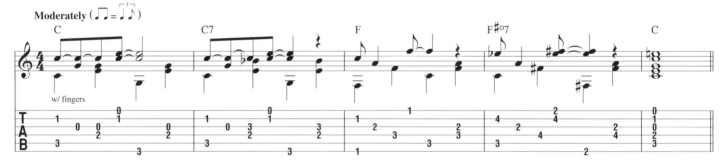

Once you're comfortable with those two patterns, try to use them over other chord progressions, adding ornamentations (hammer-ons and pull-offs) to expand the melody.

Breau-mance

Although Chet Atkins is Emmanuel's primary influence, the Aussie plucker has also studied and mastered Lenny Breau's beautiful use of harmonics. The following example demonstrates how Emmanuel uses natural harmonics to generate a lovely, melodic riff in the style of "Antonella's Birthday" from his album *The Mystery*.

EXAMPLE 3

Capo II
G6 tuning:
(low to high) D-G-D-G-B-E

$\quad = 140$

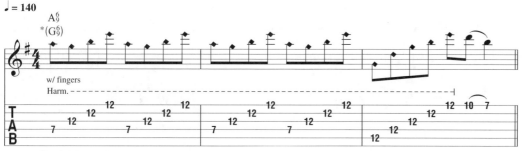

*Symbols in parentheses represent chord names respective to capoed guitar.
Symbols above reflect actual sounding chords. Capoed fret is "0" in tab.

In the next example, inspired by the title track to his 1987 release *Up From Down Under,* we see how Emmanuel applies Breau's harp-style harmonic approach, combining fretted notes and artificial harmonics to create scalar lines. Using a thumbpick here as Emmanuel does will help to generate clearer artificial harmonics.

EXAMPLE 4

Certified Lead Guitarist

Emmanuel may best be known for his fingerstyle plucking, but he's also an accomplished lead guitarist who can generate some rip-roarin' single-note flurries. This first phrase is a slightly elaborate one that creates a "rippling" effect similar to the artificial harmonics in Example 4 by alternating fretted and open notes—a technique that Emmanuel picked up from Breau, as well as Atkins and country pickin' legend Jerry Reed.

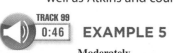

EXAMPLE 5

The next phrase illustrates how Emmanuel can intelligently shred the G hybrid blues scale (G–A–Bb–B–C–Db–D–E–F) over a G9 chord—on acoustic guitar!

EXAMPLE 6

$\quad = 120$

Get Better at Guitar

...with these Great Guitar Instruction Books from Hal Leonard!

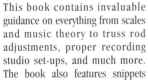

101 GUITAR TIPS

INCLUDES TAB

STUFF ALL THE PROS KNOW AND USE

by Adam St. James

This book contains invaluable guidance on everything from scales and music theory to truss rod adjustments, proper recording studio set-ups, and much more. The book also features snippets of advice from some of the most celebrated guitarists and producers in the music business, including B.B. King, Steve Vai, Joe Satriani, Warren Haynes, Laurence Juber, Pete Anderson, Tom Dowd and others, culled from the author's hundreds of interviews.

00695737 Book/CD Pack..$16.95

AMAZING PHRASING

INCLUDES TAB

50 WAYS TO IMPROVE YOUR IMPROVISATIONAL SKILLS

by Tom Kolb

This book/CD pack explores all the main components necessary for crafting well-balanced rhythmic and melodic phrases. It also explains how these phrases are put together to form cohesive solos. Many styles are covered – rock, blues, jazz, fusion, country, Latin, funk and more – and all of the concepts are backed up with musical examples. The companion CD contains 89 demos for listening, and most tracks feature full-band backing.

00695583 Book/CD Pack..$19.95

BLUES YOU CAN USE – 2ND EDITION

by John Ganapes

This comprehensive source for learning blues guitar is designed to develop both your lead and rhythm playing. Includes: 21 complete solos • blues chords, progressions and riffs • turnarounds • movable scales and soloing techniques • string bending • utilizing the entire fingerboard • and more. This second edition now includes audio and video access online!

00142420 Book/Online Media..................................$19.99

FRETBOARD MASTERY

INCLUDES TAB

by Troy Stetina

Untangle the mysterious regions of the guitar fretboard and unlock your potential. *Fretboard Mastery* familiarizes you with all the shapes you need to know by applying them in real musical examples, thereby reinforcing and reaffirming your newfound knowledge. The result is a much higher level of comprehension and retention.

00695331 Book/CD Pack..$19.99

FRETBOARD ROADMAPS – 2ND EDITION

ESSENTIAL GUITAR PATTERNS THAT ALL THE PROS KNOW AND USE

by Fred Sokolow

The updated edition of this bestseller features more songs, updated lessons, and a full audio CD! Learn to play lead and rhythm anywhere on the fretboard, in any key; play a variety of lead guitar styles; play chords and progressions anywhere on the fretboard; expand your chord vocabulary; and learn to think musically – the way the pros do.

00695941 Book/CD Pack..$14.95

GUITAR AEROBICS

INCLUDES TAB

A 52-WEEK, ONE-LICK-PER-DAY WORKOUT PROGRAM FOR DEVELOPING, IMPROVING & MAINTAINING GUITAR TECHNIQUE

by Troy Nelson

From the former editor of *Guitar One* magazine, here is a daily dose of vitamins to keep your chops fine tuned! Musical styles include rock, blues, jazz, metal, country, and funk. Techniques taught include alternate picking, arpeggios, sweep picking, string skipping, legato, string bending, and rhythm guitar. These exercises will increase speed, and improve dexterity and pick- and fret-hand accuracy. The accompanying CD includes all 365 workout licks plus play-along grooves in every style at eight different metronome settings.

00695946 Book/CD Pack..$19.99

GUITAR CLUES

INCLUDES TAB

OPERATION PENTATONIC

by Greg Koch

Join renowned guitar master Greg Koch as he clues you in to a wide variety of fun and valuable pentatonic scale applications. Whether you're new to improvising or have been doing it for a while, this book/CD pack will provide loads of delicious licks and tricks that you can use right away, from volume swells and chicken pickin' to intervallic and chordal ideas. The CD includes 65 demo and play-along tracks.

00695827 Book/CD Pack..$19.95

INTRODUCTION TO GUITAR TONE & EFFECTS

by David M. Brewster

This book/CD pack teaches the basics of guitar tones and effects, with audio examples on CD. Readers will learn about: overdrive, distortion and fuzz • using equalizers • modulation effects • reverb and delay • multi-effect processors • and more.

00695766 Book/CD Pack..$14.99

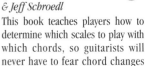

PICTURE CHORD ENCYCLOPEDIA

This comprehensive guitar chord resource for all playing styles and levels features five voicings of 44 chord qualities for all twelve keys – 2,640 chords in all! For each, there is a clearly illustrated chord frame, as well as *an actual photo* of the chord being played! Includes info on basic fingering principles, open chords and barre chords, partial chords and broken-set forms, and more.

00695224..$19.95

SCALE CHORD RELATIONSHIPS

INCLUDES TAB

by Michael Mueller & Jeff Schroedl

This book teaches players how to determine which scales to play with which chords, so guitarists will never have to fear chord changes again! This book/audio pack explains how to: recognize keys • analyze chord progressions • use the modes • play over nondiatonic harmony • use harmonic and melodic minor scales • use symmetrical scales such as chromatic, whole-tone and diminished scales • incorporate exotic scales such as Hungarian major and Gypsy minor • and much more!

00695563 Book/Online Audio $14.99

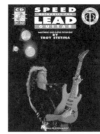

SPEED MECHANICS FOR LEAD GUITAR

INCLUDES TAB

Take your playing to the stratosphere with the most advanced lead book by this proven heavy metal author. *Speed Mechanics* is the ultimate technique book for developing the kind of speed and precision in today's explosive playing styles. Learn the fastest ways to achieve speed and control, secrets to make your practice time really count, and how to open your ears and make your musical ideas more solid and tangible. Packed with over 200 vicious exercises including Troy's scorching version of "Flight of the Bumblebee." Music and examples demonstrated on CD. 89-minute audio.

00699323 Book/CD Pack..$19.95

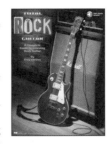
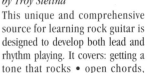

TOTAL ROCK GUITAR

INCLUDES TAB

A COMPLETE GUIDE TO LEARNING ROCK GUITAR

by Troy Stetina

This unique and comprehensive source for learning rock guitar is designed to develop both lead and rhythm playing. It covers: getting a tone that rocks • open chords, power chords and barre chords • riffs, scales and licks • string bending, strumming, palm muting, harmonics and alternate picking • all rock styles • and much more. The examples are in standard notation with chord grids and tab, and the CD includes full-band backing for all 22 songs.

00695246 Book/CD Pack..$19.99

1115

FINGERPICKING GUITAR BOOKS

Hone your fingerpicking skills with these great songbooks featuring solo guitar arrangements in standard notation and tablature. The arrangements in these books are carefully written for intermediate-level guitarists. Each song combines melody and harmony in one superb guitar fingerpicking arrangement. Each book also includes an introduction to basic fingerstyle guitar.

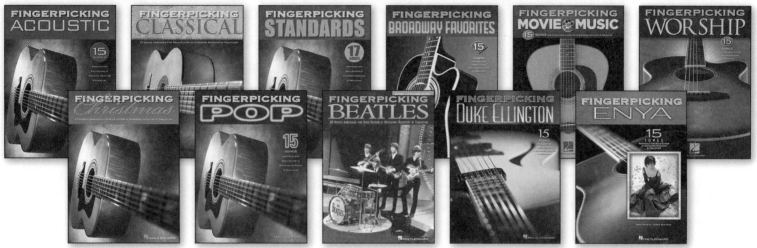

FINGERPICKING ACOUSTIC
00699614...$10.99

FINGERPICKING ACOUSTIC ROCK
00699764...$9.99

FINGERPICKING BACH
00699793..$8.95

FINGERPICKING BALLADS
00699717..$9.99

FINGERPICKING BEATLES
00699049..$19.99

FINGERPICKING BEETHOVEN
00702390..$7.99

FINGERPICKING BLUES
00701277 ....$7.99

FINGERPICKING BROADWAY FAVORITES
00699843..$9.99

FINGERPICKING BROADWAY HITS
00699838..$7.99

FINGERPICKING CELTIC FOLK
00701148..$7.99

FINGERPICKING CHILDREN'S SONGS
00699712..$9.99

FINGERPICKING CHRISTIAN
00701076 ....$7.99

FINGERPICKING CHRISTMAS
00699599..$9.99

FINGERPICKING CHRISTMAS CLASSICS
00701695..$7.99

FINGERPICKING CLASSICAL
00699620..$8.95

FINGERPICKING COUNTRY
00699687..$9.99

FINGERPICKING DISNEY
00699711..$10.99

FINGERPICKING DUKE ELLINGTON
00699845..$9.99

FINGERPICKING ENYA
00701161..$9.99

FINGERPICKING GOSPEL
00701059..$7.99

FINGERPICKING GUITAR BIBLE
00691040 ....$19.99

FINGERPICKING HYMNS
00699688..$8.95

FINGERPICKING IRISH SONGS
00701965..$7.99

FINGERPICKING JAZZ FAVORITES
00699844 ....$7.99

FINGERPICKING JAZZ STANDARDS
00699840..$7.99

FINGERPICKING LATIN FAVORITES
00699842..$9.99

FINGERPICKING LATIN STANDARDS
00699837..$7.99

FINGERPICKING ANDREW LLOYD WEBBER
00699839..$9.99

FINGERPICKING LOVE SONGS
00699841..$9.99

FINGERPICKING LOVE STANDARDS
00699836 ....$9.99

FINGERPICKING LULLABYES
00701276..$9.99

FINGERPICKING MOVIE MUSIC
00699919..$9.99

FINGERPICKING MOZART
00699794..$8.95

FINGERPICKING POP
00699615..$9.99

FINGERPICKING PRAISE
00699714..$8.95

FINGERPICKING ROCK
00699716..$10.99

FINGERPICKING STANDARDS
00699613..$9.99

FINGERPICKING WEDDING
00699637..$9.99

FINGERPICKING WORSHIP
00700554..$7.99

FINGERPICKING NEIL YOUNG – GREATEST HITS
00700134..$12.99

FINGERPICKING YULETIDE
00699654..$9.99

HAL•LEONARD®
CORPORATION

7777 W. BLUEMOUND RD. P.O. BOX 13819 MILWAUKEE, WI 53213

Visit Hal Leonard online at **www.halleonard.com**

Prices, contents and availability subject to change without notice.

0915

HAL·LEONARD GUITAR PLAY-ALONG

AUDIO ACCESS INCLUDED

INCLUDES TAB

This series will help you play your favorite songs quickly and easily. Just follow the tab and listen to the CD or online audio to hear how the guitar should sound, and then play along using the separate backing tracks. Playback tools are provided for slowing down the tempo without changing pitch and looping challenging parts. The melody and lyrics are included in the book so that you can sing or simply follow along.

1. ROCK
00699570 Book/CD $16.99

2. ACOUSTIC
00699569 Book/CD $16.95

3. HARD ROCK
00699573 Book/CD $16.95

4. POP/ROCK
00699571 Book/CD $16.99

5. MODERN ROCK
00699574 Book/CD $16.99

6. '90s ROCK
00699572 Book/CD $16.99

7. BLUES
00699575 Book/CD $16.95

8. ROCK
00699585 Book/CD $14.99

10. ACOUSTIC
00699586 Book/CD $16.95

11. EARLY ROCK
0699579 Book/CD $14.95

12. POP/ROCK
00699587 Book/CD $14.95

13. FOLK ROCK
00699581 Book/CD $15.99

14. BLUES ROCK
00699582 Book/CD $16.95

15. R&B
00699583 Book/CD $14.95

16. JAZZ
00699584 Book/CD $15.95

17. COUNTRY
00699588 Book/CD $15.95

18. ACOUSTIC ROCK
00699577 Book/CD $15.95

19. SOUL
00699578 Book/CD $14.99

20. ROCKABILLY
00699580 Book/CD $14.95

21. YULETIDE
00699602 Book/CD $14.95

22. CHRISTMAS
00699600 Book/CD $15.95

23. SURF
00699635 Book/CD $14.95

24. ERIC CLAPTON
00699649 Book/CD $17.99

25. LENNON & McCARTNEY
00699642 Book/CD $16.99

26. ELVIS PRESLEY
00699643 Book/CD $14.95

27. DAVID LEE ROTH
00699645 Book/CD $16.95

28. GREG KOCH
00699646 Book/CD $14.95

29. BOB SEGER
00699647 Book/CD $15.99

30. KISS
00699644 Book/CD $16.99

31. CHRISTMAS HITS
00699652 Book/CD $14.95

32. THE OFFSPRING
00699653 Book/CD $14.95

33. ACOUSTIC CLASSICS
00699656 Book/CD $16.95

34. CLASSIC ROCK
00699658 Book/CD $16.95

35. HAIR METAL
00699660 Book/CD $16.95

36. SOUTHERN ROCK
00699661 Book/CD $16.95

37. ACOUSTIC METAL
00699662 Book/CD $22.99

38. BLUES
00699663 Book/CD $16.95

39. '80s METAL
00699664 Book/CD $16.99

40. INCUBUS
00699668 Book/CD $17.95

41. ERIC CLAPTON
00699669 Book/CD $16.95

42. 2000s ROCK
00699670 Book/CD $16.99

43. LYNYRD SKYNYRD
00699681 Book/CD $17.95

44. JAZZ
00699689 Book/CD $14.99

45. TV THEMES
00699718 Book/CD $14.95

46. MAINSTREAM ROCK
00699722 Book/CD $16.95

47. HENDRIX SMASH HITS
00699723 Book/CD $19.95

48. AEROSMITH CLASSICS
00699724 Book/CD $17.99

49. STEVIE RAY VAUGHAN
00699725 Book/CD $17.99

50. VAN HALEN 1978-1984
00110269 Book/CD $17.99

51. ALTERNATIVE '90s
00699727 Book/CD $14.99

52. FUNK
00699728 Book/CD $14.95

53. DISCO
00699729 Book/CD $14.99

54. HEAVY METAL
00699730 Book/CD $14.95

55. POP METAL
00699731 Book/CD $14.95

56. FOO FIGHTERS
00699749 Book/CD $15.99

57. SYSTEM OF A DOWN
00699751 Book/CD $14.95

58. BLINK-182
00699772 Book/CD $14.95

59. CHET ATKINS
00702347 Book/CD $16.99

60. 3 DOORS DOWN
00699774 Book/CD $14.95

61. SLIPKNOT
00699775 Book/CD $16.99

62. CHRISTMAS CAROLS
00699798 Book/CD $12.95

63. CREEDENCE CLEARWATER REVIVAL
00699802 Book/CD $16.99

64. OZZY OSBOURNE
00699803 Book/CD $16.99

66. THE ROLLING STONES
00699807 Book/CD $16.95

67. BLACK SABBATH
00699808 Book/CD $16.99

68. PINK FLOYD – DARK SIDE OF THE MOON
00699809 Book/CD $16.99

69. ACOUSTIC FAVORITES
00699810 Book/CD $14.95

70. OZZY OSBOURNE
00699805 Book/CD $16.99

71. CHRISTIAN ROCK
00699824 Book/CD $14.95

72. ACOUSTIC '90s
00699827 Book/CD $14.95

73. BLUESY ROCK
00699829 Book/CD $16.99

75. TOM PETTY
00699882 Book/CD $16.99

76. COUNTRY HITS
00699884 Book/CD $14.95

77. BLUEGRASS
00699910 Book/CD $14.99

78. NIRVANA
00700132 Book/CD $16.99

79. NEIL YOUNG
00700133 Book/CD $24.99

80. ACOUSTIC ANTHOLOGY
00700175 Book/CD $19.95

81. ROCK ANTHOLOGY
00700176 Book/CD $22.99

82. EASY ROCK SONGS
00700177 Book/CD $12.99

83. THREE CHORD SONGS
00700178 Book/CD $16.99

84. STEELY DAN
00700200 Book/CD $16.99

85. THE POLICE
00700269 Book/CD $16.99

86. BOSTON
00700465 Book/CD $16.99

87. ACOUSTIC WOMEN
00700763 Book/CD $14.99

88. GRUNGE
00700467 Book/CD $16.99

89. REGGAE
00700468 Book/CD $15.99

90. CLASSICAL POP
00700469 Book/CD $14.99

91. BLUES INSTRUMENTALS
00700505 Book/CD $14.99

92. EARLY ROCK INSTRUMENTALS
00700506 Book/CD $14.99

93. ROCK INSTRUMENTALS
00700507 Book/CD $16.99

94. SLOW BLUES
00700508 Book/CD $16.99

95. BLUES CLASSICS
00700509 Book/CD $14.99

96. THIRD DAY
00700560 Book/CD $14.95

97. ROCK BAND
00700703 Book/CD $14.99

98. ROCK BAND
00700704 Book/CD $14.95

99. ZZ TOP
00700762 Book/CD $16.99

100. B.B. KING
00700466 Book/CD $16.99

101. SONGS FOR BEGINNERS
00701917 Book/CD $14.99

102. CLASSIC PUNK
00700769 Book/CD $14.99

103. SWITCHFOOT
00700773 Book/CD $16.99

104. DUANE ALLMAN
00700846 Book/CD $16.99

105. LATIN
00700939 Book/CD $16.99

106. WEEZER
00700958 Book/CD $14.99

107. CREAM
00701069 Book/CD $16.99

108. THE WHO
00701053 Book/CD $16.99

109. STEVE MILLER
00701054 Book/CD $14.99

110. SLIDE GUITAR HITS
00701055 Book/CD $16.99

111. JOHN MELLENCAMP
00701056 Book/CD $14.99

112. QUEEN
00701052 Book/CD $16.99

113. JIM CROCE
00701058 Book/CD $15.99

114. BON JOVI
00701060 Book/CD $14.99

115. JOHNNY CASH
00701070 Book/CD $16.99

116. THE VENTURES
00701124 Book/CD $14.99

117. BRAD PAISLEY
00701224 Book/CD $16.99

118. ERIC JOHNSON
00701353 Book/CD $16.99

119. AC/DC CLASSICS
00701356 Book/CD $17.99

120. PROGRESSIVE ROCK
00701457 Book/CD $14.99

121. U2
00701508 Book/CD $16.99

122. CROSBY, STILLS & NASH
00701610 Book/CD $16.99

123. LENNON & MCCARTNEY ACOUSTIC
00701614 Book/CD $16.99

124. MODERN WORSHIP
00701629 Book/CD $14.99

125. JEFF BECK
00701687 Book/CD $16.99

126. BOB MARLEY
00701701 Book/CD $16.99

127. 1970s ROCK
00701739 Book/CD $14.99

128. 1960s ROCK
00701740 Book/CD $14.99

129. MEGADETH
00701741 Book/CD $16.99

131. 1990s ROCK
00701743 Book/CD $14.99

132. COUNTRY ROCK
00701757 Book/CD $15.99

133. TAYLOR SWIFT
00701894 Book/CD $16.99

134. AVENGED SEVENFOLD
00701906 Book/CD $16.99

136. GUITAR THEMES
00701922 Book/CD $14.99

137. IRISH TUNES
00701966 Book/CD $15.99

138. BLUEGRASS CLASSICS
00701967 Book/CD $14.99

139. GARY MOORE
00702370 Book/CD $16.99

140. MORE STEVIE RAY VAUGHAN
00702396 Book/CD $17.99

141. ACOUSTIC HITS
00702401 Book/CD $16.99

143. SLASH
00702425 Book/Audio $19.99

144. DJANGO REINHARDT
00702531 Book/CD $16.99

145. DEF LEPPARD
00702532 Book/CD $16.99

146. ROBERT JOHNSON
00702533 Book/CD $16.99

147. SIMON & GARFUNKEL
14041591 Book/CD $16.99

148. BOB DYLAN
14041592 Book/CD $16.99

149. AC/DC HITS
14041593 Book/CD $17.99

150. ZAKK WYLDE
02501717 Book/CD $16.99

152. JOE BONAMASSA
02501751 Book/Audio $19.99

153. RED HOT CHILI PEPPERS
00702990 Book/CD $19.99

155. ERIC CLAPTON – FROM THE ALBUM *UNPLUGGED*
00703085 Book/CD $16.99

156. SLAYER
00703770 Book/CD $17.99

157. FLEETWOOD MAC
00101382 Book/CD $16.99

158. ULTIMATE CHRISTMAS
00101889 Book/CD $14.99

160. T-BONE WALKER
00102641 Book/CD $16.99

161. THE EAGLES – ACOUSTIC
00102659 Book/CD $17.99

162. THE EAGLES HITS
00102667 Book/CD $17.99

163. PANTERA
00103036 Book/CD $17.99

164. VAN HALEN 1986-1995
00110270 Book/CD $17.99

166. MODERN BLUES
00700764 Book/CD $16.99

167. DREAM THEATER
00111938 Book/2-CD $24.99

168. KISS
00113421 Book/CD $16.99

169. TAYLOR SWIFT
00115982 Book/CD $16.99

170. THREE DAYS GRACE
00117337 Book/CD $16.99

171. JAMES BROWN
00117420 Book/CD $16.99

173. TRANS-SIBERIAN ORCHESTRA
00119907 Book/CD $19.99

174. SCORPIONS
00122119 Book/CD $16.99

175. MICHAEL SCHENKER
00122127 Book/CD $16.99

176. BLUES BREAKERS WITH JOHN MAYALL & ERIC CLAPTON
00122132 Book/CD $19.99

177. ALBERT KING
00123271 Book/CD $16.99

178. JASON MRAZ
00124165 Book/CD $17.99

179. RAMONES
00127073 Book/CD $16.99

180. BRUNO MARS
00129706 Book/CD $16.99

181. JACK JOHNSON
00129854 Book/CD $16.99

182. SOUNDGARDEN
00138161 Book/Audio $17.99

184. KENNY WAYNE SHEPHERD
00138258 Book/Audio $17.99

187. JOHN DENVER
00140839 Book/Audio $17.99

CLASSICAL GUITAR

PUBLICATIONS FROM HAL LEONARD

   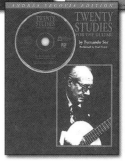 

THE BEATLES FOR CLASSICAL GUITAR

Includes 20 solos from big Beatles hits arranged for classical guitar, complete with left-hand and right-hand fingering. Songs include: All My Loving • And I Love Her • Can't Buy Me Love • Fool on the Hill • From a Window • Hey Jude • If I Fell • Let It Be • Michelle • Norwegian Wood • Obla Di • Ticket to Ride • Yesterday • and more. Features arrangements and an introduction by Joe Washington, as well as his helpful hints on classical technique and detailed notes on how to play each song. The book also covers parts and specifications of the classical guitar, tuning, and Joe's "Strata System" – an easy-reading system applied to chord diagrams.

_____ 00699237 Classical Guitar.....................$19.99

CZERNY FOR GUITAR

INCLUDES TAB

12 SCALE STUDIES FOR CLASSICAL GUITAR
by David Patterson

Adapted from Carl Czerny's *School of Velocity, Op. 299* for piano, this lesson book explores 12 keys with 12 different approaches or "treatments." You will explore a variety of articulations, ranges and technical perspectives as you learn each key. These arrangements will not only improve your ability to play scales fluently, but will also develop your ears, knowledge of the fingerboard, reading abilities, strength and endurance. In standard notation and tablature.

_____ 00701248 ....$9.99

MATTEO CARCASSI – 25 MELODIC AND PROGRESSIVE STUDIES, OP. 60

arr. Paul Henry

One of Carcassi's (1792-1853) most famous collections of classical guitar music – indispensable for the modern guitarist's musical and technical development. Performed by Paul Henry. 49-minute audio accompaniment.

_____ 00696506 Book/CD Pack......................$17.95

CLASSICAL & FINGERSTYLE GUITAR TECHNIQUES

INCLUDES TAB

by David Oakes • Musicians Institute

This Master Class with MI instructor David Oakes is aimed at any electric or acoustic guitarist who wants a quick, thorough grounding in the essentials of classical and fingerstyle technique. Topics covered include: arpeggios and scales, free stroke and rest stroke, P-i scale technique, three-to-a-string patterns, natural and artificial harmonics, tremolo and rasgueado, and more. The book includes 12 intensive lessons for right and left hand in standard notation & tab, and the CD features 92 solo acoustic tracks.

_____ 00695171 Book/CD Pack......................$17.99

CLASSICAL GUITAR CHRISTMAS COLLECTION

INCLUDES TAB

Includes classical guitar arrangements in standard notation and tablature for more than two dozen beloved carols: Angels We Have Heard on High • Auld Lang Syne • Ave Maria • Away in a Manger • Canon in D • The First Noel • God Rest Ye Merry, Gentlemen • Hark! the Herald Angels Sing • I Saw Three Ships • Jesu, Joy of Man's Desiring • Joy to the World • O Christmas Tree • O Holy Night • Silent Night • What Child Is This? • and more.

_____ 00699493 Guitar Solo $9.95

CLASSICAL GUITAR WEDDING

INCLUDES TAB

Perfect for players hired to perform for someone's big day, this songbook features 16 classical wedding favorites arranged for solo guitar in standard notation and tablature. Includes: Air on the G String • Ave Maria • Bridal Chorus • Canon in D • Jesu, Joy of Man's Desiring • Minuet • Sheep May Safely Graze • Wedding March • and more.

_____ 00699563 Solo Guitar with Tab $10.95

CLASSICAL MASTERPIECES FOR GUITAR

INCLUDES TAB

27 works by Bach, Beethoven, Handel, Mendelssohn, Mozart and more transcribed with standard notation and tablature. Now anyone can enjoy classical material regardless of their guitar background. Also features stay-open binding.

_____ 00699312 ....$12.95

MASTERWORKS FOR GUITAR

INCLUDES TAB

Over 60 Favorites from Four Centuries
World's Great Classical Music

Dozens of classical masterpieces: Allemande • Bourree • Canon in D • Jesu, Joy of Man's Desiring • Lagrima • Malaguena • Mazurka • Piano Sonata No. 14 in C# Minor (Moonlight) Op. 27 No. 2 First Movement Theme • Ode to Joy • Prelude No. I (Well-Tempered Clavier).

_____ 00699503 ....$16.95

A MODERN APPROACH TO CLASSICAL GUITAR

by Charles Duncan

This multi-volume method was developed to allow students to study the art of classical guitar within a new, more contemporary framework. For private, class or self-instruction. Book One incorporates chord frames and symbols, as well as a recording to assist in tuning and to provide accompaniments for at-home practice. Book One also introduces beginning fingerboard technique and music theory. Book Two and Three build upon the techniques learned in Book One.

_____ 00695114 Book 1 – Book Only...............$6.99
_____ 00695113 Book 1 – Book/CD Pack $10.99
_____ 00695116 Book 2 – Book Only...............$6.99
_____ 00695115 Book 2 – Book/CD Pack $10.99
_____ 00699202 Book 3 – Book Only...............$7.95
_____ 00695117 Book 3 – Book/CD Pack $10.95
_____ 00695119 Composite Book/CD Pack.....$29.99

ANDRES SEGOVIA – 20 STUDIES FOR GUITAR

Sor/Segovia

20 studies for the classical guitar written by Beethoven's contemporary, Fernando Sor, revised, edited and fingered by the great classical guitarist Andres Segovia. These essential repertoire pieces continue to be used by teachers and students to build solid classical technique. Features a 50-minute demonstration CD.

_____ 00695012 Book/CD Pack.....................$19.99
_____ 00006363 Book Only $7.99

THE FRANCISCO COLLECTION TÁRREGA

INCLUDES TAB

edited and performed by Paul Henry

Considered the father of modern classical guitar, Francisco Tárrega revolutionized guitar technique and composed a wealth of music that will be a cornerstone of classical guitar repertoire for centuries to come. This unique book/CD pack features 14 of his most outstanding pieces in standard notation and tab, edited and performed on CD by virtuoso Paul Henry. Includes: Adelita • Capricho Árabe • Estudio Brillante • Grand Jota • Lágrima • Malagueña • María • Recuerdos de la Alhambra • Tango • and more, plus bios of Tárrega and Henry.

_____ 00698993 Book/CD Pack.....................$19.99

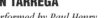

HAL•LEONARD®
CORPORATION

7777 W. BLUEMOUND RD. P.O. BOX 13819 MILWAUKEE, WI 53213

Visit Hal Leonard Online at **www.halleonard.com**